TOBIAS WOLFF

A Study of the Short Fiction

Also Available in Twayne's Studies in Short Fiction Series

Twayne's Studies in Short Fiction

Gordon Weaver, General Editor
Oklahoma State University

Tobias Wolff.   Photograph © Jerry Bauer.

TOBIAS WOLFF

A Study of the Short Fiction

James Hannah
Texas A & M University

TWAYNE PUBLISHERS
An Imprint of Simon & Schuster Macmillan
New York
PRENTICE HALL INTERNATIONAL
London   Mexico City   New Delhi   Singapore   Sydney   Toronto

Twayne's Studies in Short Fiction Series, No. 64

Copyright © 1996 by Twayne Publishers

Twayne Publishers
An Imprint of Simon & Schuster Macmillan
1633 Broadway
New York, New York 10019

Library of Congress Cataloging-in-Publication Data

Hannah, James.
    Tobias Wolff : a study of the short fiction / James Hannah.
       p.   cm.—(Twayne's studies in short fiction ; no. 64)
    Includes bibliographical references (p.   ) and index.
    ISBN 0-8057-0864-2 (cloth)
    1. Wolff, Tobias, 1945– —Criticism and interpretation.   2. Short
story.   I. Title. II. Series.
    PS3573.O558Z63   1996
    823'.54—dc20   95-32317
                                              CIP

10 9 8 7 6 5 4 3 2 1

Printed in the United States of America

For Cecelia
and
In Memory of Fred Ekfelt

Contents

Preface

> So this picture tells me a tale when I look at it, but not always the same tale. At different times it has been a comedy, a tragedy, and a miraculous narrative in which the lost are found, the dead brought back to life. And the story goes on. The Lord only knows where it will end.
>
> Tobias Wolff, "Long Found Friends"

Tobias Wolff is speaking of a friend's photograph—a fellow Vietnam veteran, a recovered alcoholic—but he could as easily be describing the essential nature of his short fiction. For his friend's struggle against constant and often contradictory obstacles is the battle waged by many of Wolff's central characters. Often there is comedy, often tragedy, but what fascinates and amazes Wolff—what engages his attention and inspires his work—is the mystery inherent in the fight for even a chance at a moment's meaning. As he says, for him the narrative is "miraculous." Sometimes, as in "The Missing Person," the lost are found. But in "Sister," the lost come to accept their hopelessness. The narrator of "In the Garden of the North American Martyrs" is stirred to life and delivers a scorching jeremiad against her culture's oppression and cruelty. In "The Rich Brother," an Abel checks his reach for the deadly stone. In "Face to Face" a woman wakens to life, while a man falls back into entropy.

Certainly Wolff's attitudes and concerns are partially fashioned by his Catholicism. Some of his most powerful stories are refashioned parables, and they seem to illustrate John F. Desmond's definition of contemporary Catholic fiction as work that "continues to affirm the fundamental mystery and sacramental character of our existence and the reality of the supernatural. Likewise, it affirms our radical incompleteness and the genuine possibility of redemption."[1] But the essential nature of short stories is also the apprehension of the mysterious at the core of human existence—the illumination of conflict and dilemma with or without resultant epiphanies of understanding. Nadine Gordimer asserts this when she compares novels with short stories:

The novelist may juggle about with chronology and throw narrative overboard; all the time his characters have the reader by the hand, there is a consistency of relationship throughout the experience that cannot and does not convey the quality of human life, where contact is more like the flash of fireflies, in and out, now here, now there, in darkness. Short-story writers see by the light of the flash; theirs is the art of the only thing one can be sure of—the present moment. . . . The short story is a fragmented and restless form, a matter of hit or miss, and it is perhaps for this reason that it suits modern consciousness—which seems best expressed as flashes of fearful insight alternating with near-hypnotic states of indifference.[2]

Wolff's discussion of Anton Chekhov's work—fiction which Wolff frequently admits has greatly influenced his own—echoes Gordimer's sentiments: "Love, happiness, right behavior, kindness, peace of mind—all these enter Chekhov's stories as luminous possibilities bestowing a momentary dignity on those who long for them, until, unredeemed by action, they glimmer away."[3]

A realist in the modern tradition, Wolff writes fiction that is middle-grounded, as Chekov taught. Like Chekhov and the modernists who followed—Joyce, Anderson, Hemingway, Carver—Wolff eschews plot-driven stories complete with traditional beginnings, middles, and ends. Instead he offers little if any introductory explication (commencing in media res) and often truncates his stories before they achieve traditional closure. Such works often depend on the reader to supply information while focusing on character rather than plot or event.

And while his fiction is influenced by his religious propensities, the very nature of short fiction speaks to revelation, the chance of redemption, the precarious moment of balance between hope and despair, the attempt to illuminate the mysteries at the dark heart of human existence. Sometimes Wolff produces startling parables of triumph; sometimes the situation is unmoved from tragedy.[4] "Our Story Begins," Wolff's only short story on the art of writing, concludes with the young writer describing his occupation: "Charlie imagined himself kneeling in the prow of that boat, lamp in hand, intent on the light shining just before him. All distraction gone. Too watchful to be afraid. Tongue wetting his lips and eyes wide open, ready to call out in this shifting fog where at any moment anything might be revealed."[5]

Though this book is a critical explication of Wolff's short fiction and not a literary biography, it is useful to briefly examine the influence of his life experience on his fiction. Tobias Wolff is the son of Arthur

Wolff, the central figure in his brother Geoffrey's memoir, *The Duke of Deception* (1979), which discusses the antics of a consummate confidence man who easily adopted numerous personas. Separated from his brother and father at an early age, Wolff was reared by his mother and stepfather, and his childhood is the subject of his first memoir, *This Boy's Life* (1989). Wolff captures the essence of a lonely boy, who, like his father, adopts disguises to survive. At the memoir's end, the boy has forged his way into a prestigious preparatory school by counterfeiting letters of recommendation that sing the praises of the idealized, fictional student that Wolff is far from being. In his subsequent fiction, Wolff's characters often lie, trying to fabricate a more exciting, meaningful existence from the threadbare details of their rather paltry lives. "Self-invention" is "very American," says Wolff. "The world is not enough."[6] It is interesting to consider not only the characters who reinvent themselves in Wolff's fiction but the overarching concept of fiction itself, which allows for the possibility of meaning in ways that ordinary living does not. Much of Wolff's short fiction is illuminated by this memoir and his second, *In Pharoah's Army: Memories of the Lost War* (1994).

Where his first memoir gives insight into Wolff's foundation as a fiction writer, his second provides insight into particular stories. Picking up a few years after the conclusion of *This Boy's Life*, the book discusses Wolff's failure at prep school—the setting of the short stories "Smokers" and "Smorgasbord"[7]—and his service in the army during the Vietnam War. Though Wolff dealt with his wartime experience initially in a novel, *Ugly Rumours*, published in England in 1975, over the years he has come to distance himself from what he considers a flawed work.[8] After writing the novel, Wolff returned to Vietnam in his fiction by an indirect route, treating the lives of soldiers stateside who have either yet to leave for the war or have returned from it. Examples are "Wingfield," "Soldier's Joy," "The Other Miller," and the novella *The Barracks Thief*. Only recently, in 1993, with the uncollected story "Memorial," has Wolff considered Vietnam more directly. This memoir, along with Wolff's novel, novella, and short stories about soldiers, elucidates the process by which factual event is transmorgified into fictional situation.

Few other contemporary writers' lives have been so thoroughly documented through biography and autobiography as has Tobias Wolff's. The central influences on his short fiction—his parentage, childhood, schooling, Vietnam service, and academic career (evidenced in such stories as "An Episode in the Life of Professor Brooke" and "In the Garden of the North American Martyrs")—are clearly reflected both in his collected stories and in his published but uncollected work.[9]

Though some of Wolff's stories are traditional and rely on plot and some are parables that blur into surrealism, he is in the main a practitioner of the modern short-story form, which eschews plot devices and exposition is favor of middle-grounded stories that dwell on character development and avoid definite closure. He belongs squarely within the generation of American short-story writers made up of Raymond Carver, Ann Beattie, André Dubus, Jayne Ann Phillips, and the like. His mentors are the giants of modern fiction: John Cheever, Ernest Hemingway, Sherwood Anderson, and James Joyce. Yet the single greatest influence must be the originator of the modern story, Anton Chekhov. Like Wolff, Chekhov overcame what might have been a devastating childhood; his father was a confidence man of sorts who abandoned the young boy. Chekhov triumphs over his life through the honest humanity of his fiction. Victory of this same dimension Wolff sees in the lives and fiction of two of his writer friends: the late Raymond Carver, who transformed his battle with alcohol into some of the finest fiction of this century, and André Dubus, whose recovery from a terrible automobile accident greatly depended on his dedication to honest expression. When Wolff writes that "Chekhov was not a cynic; he believed in [life's] possibilities" (*Doctor's*, xvi), he is speaking about himself and what he respects in the lives and works of others.

Finally, a word about the organization of this book. I have not arranged the stories around thematic concerns. Such a scheme, I believe, would destroy the author's careful arrangement of the individual stories that composes a collection and creates its unique tone. And, as any reader knows, thematic arrangements inevitably place stories under several often disparate headings, distorting the original intent and hindering the examination of a story's multiplicity of themes. I have treated the collections in order of their date of publication, and, within the collections, explicated the stories in order of their appearance.

This is a work of critical interpretation. I have attempted to defeat any tendency toward far-fetched readings. But as I mention in the introduction to part 2, a single voice of opinion emerges most fruitfully from the conversation of many.

Notes to Preface

1. John F. Desmond, "Catholicism in Contemporary American Fiction," *America,* 14 May 1994, 7.

2. Nadine Gordimer, "The Flash of Fireflies," in *Short Story Theories,* ed. Charles E. May (Athens: Ohio University Press, 1976), 180–81.

3. Tobias Wolff, introduction, in *A Doctor's Visit: Short Stories of Anton Chekhov* (New York: Bantam, 1988), xv; hereafter cited in the preface as *Doctor's.*

4. Jean W. Ross, "CA Interview," *Contemporary Authors,* no. 117 (Detroit: Gale Research, 1986), 496.

5. *Back in the World* (New York: Bantam, 1985), 177.

6. Bonnie Lyons and Bill Oliver, "An Interview with Tobias Wolff," *Contemporary Literature* 31, no. 1 (Spring 1990): 7.

7. "Smorgasbord," *Esquire,* Summer 1987, 236ff. This story is not discussed in this book.

8. James Hannah, "This Boy's War," *Nation,* 21 November 1994, 618–20.

9. At the time of printing, Wolff was expecting to publish a third story collection in late 1996.

Acknowledgments

I would like to acknowledge the valuable assistance of the staff of the interlibrary loan service at the Sterling C. Evans Library on the Texas A & M campus and of Annette Lillard, my excellent research assistant. Special thanks to my editor at Twayne, India Koopman, whose hard work made this a far better book.

The following essays and interviews are reprinted in this volume:

"Interview with Tobias Wolff," from *A Piece of Work: Five Writers Discuss Their Revisions,* edited by Jay Woodruff, by permission of The University of Iowa Press. Copyright 1993 by Tobias Wolff.

"An Interview with Tobias Wolff," conducted by Bonnie Lyons and Bill Oliver, *Contemporary Literature,* Vol. 21, No. 1 (Spring 1990). © 1990. Reprinted with permission of The University of Wisconsin Press.

"CA Interview," from *Contemporary Authors,* Vol. 117, by Hal May, editor, conducted by Jean W. Ross. Copyright © 1986 by Gale Research, Inc. Reprinted by permission of the publisher.

"Particular Truths [excerpts]," by Brina Caplan. Reprinted with permission from *The Nation* magazine, 6 February 1982. © The Nation Company, Inc.

Richard Orodenker, from *The North American Review* 267 (June 1982): 60. Reprinted with permission.

Anatole Broyard, "Books of the Times," *The New York Times,* 25 November 1981. Copyright © 1981 by The New York Times Company. Reprinted by permission.

Russell Banks, "Aging Clay and the Prodigal Son," *The New York Times Book Review,* 9 December 1985. Copyright © 1985 by The New York Times Company. Reprinted by permission.

Mona Simpson, "The Morality of Everyday Life," *The New Republic,* 9 December 1985. Reprinted by permission of The New Republic. © 1985 The New Republic, Inc.

Michiko Kakutani, "Books of the Times," *The New York Times,* 2

October 1985. Copyright © 1985 by The New York Times Company. Reprinted by permission.

Jonathan Penner, "Tobias Wolff and the Taste for Experience," *The Washington Post Book World*, 3 November 1985. ©1985, Washington Post Writers Group. Reprinted with permission.

Richard Eder, *Los Angeles Times Book Review*, 17 November 1985. Copyright 1985, Richard Eder. Los Angeles Times. Reprinted with permission.

Part 1

THE SHORT FICTION

In the Garden of the North American Martyrs

Introduction

> It seems to me that the final symptom of despair is silence,
> and that storytelling is one of the sustaining arts; it's one of
> the affirming arts. It's one of the most intimate things that
> people do together. . . . A writer may have a certain pessimism
> in his outlook, but the very act of being a writer seems to me
> to be an optimistic act.
>
> Tobias Wolff, from an interview with Jean W. Ross

In 1981, such an "optimistic act" as Tobias Wolff describes above took
place with the publication of his collection of a dozen stories intrigu-
ingly entitled *In the Garden of the North American Martyrs*, from a line
in Roger Weingarten's book of poems *Ethan Benjamin Bolt*—a line,
Wolff writes, that "just lashed out at me."[1] This addition to what was
then considered to be the renaissance of the American short story was
met with ample and favorable critical response. Richard Orodenker,
writing in the *North American Review*, states: "Through these gracefully
evoked tales, Wolff touches the heart of the human condition and
speaks in a voice that is sincere, original yet familiar—a voice that
sounds as if it must last."[2] In the *New York Times*, Anatole Broyard
comments that "in several of the 12 stories . . . [Wolff] tries to do
something difficult, subtle and technically ambitious."[3]

Later Wolff would attack the notion that there was ever a need
for a renaissance in the short story—a genre he considered far from
moribund. He would also lambaste postmodern experimentalism in
short fiction, as he has several times over his career. As early as 1983
he had written: "Literature is in danger of becoming . . . stylized and
self-absorbed. There is a vast and growing body of fiction that takes
as its subject the process of inventing fiction. . . . [M]ost of it has
become so ritualized and predictable that it is, in effect, simply another
form of silence: white noise."[4] In 1994, he reiterated this view: "In

the sixties we began to see a different kind of story here, resolutely unrealistic, scholastic, self-conscious—*postmodern*—concerned with exploring its own fictional nature and indifferent if not hostile to the short story's traditional interests in character and dramatic development and social context."[5]

Wolff interprets the so-called renaissance of the short story in the early 1980s as writing "in reaction" (*Vintage*, xiii) to the "white noise" of the earlier experimental fiction by such practitioners as John Barth, Donald Barthelme, and Robert Coover. By embracing the tenets of realistic modernism in the short story (which began with Anton Chekhov), Wolff joined his contemporaries André Dubus, Raymond Carver, Joyce Carol Oates, Jayne Anne Phillips, and their like. For Wolff, short fiction should focus on the human concerns of characters within a believable, realistic setting. Such stories are about "people who led lives neither admirable nor depraved, but so convincing in their portrayal that the reader had to acknowledge kinship" (*Vintage*, xiii).

Realistic characters in credible situations are what enable readers to make meaningful connections, says Wolff. Writers of short stories should therefore eschew surreal worlds and displays of technical arrogance that may intimidate the average reader and disrupt the necessary, meaningful connection between that reader and the story. "That sense of kinship [between the reader and the character on a page] is what makes stories important to us," Wolff writes. "The pleasure we take in cleverness and technical virtuosity soon exhausts itself in the absence of any recognizable human landscape. We need to feel ourselves acted upon by a story, outraged, exposed, in danger of heartbreak and change" (*Vintage*, xiii).

Indeed many of the stories in Wolff's first collection are modern short stories—that is, realistic stories that are "middle-grounded," with little background exposition, practically no plot, and often no sense of closure—all middle with no beginning or ending. The majority of the stories— "Next Door," "An Episode in the Life of Professor Brooke," "Smokers," "Face to Face," "Passengers," "Wingfield," "Poaching"—fit this definition with variations. Some are more traditional in being driven by plot; some achieve a greater degree of closure than others. Yet Wolff seems to be up to more than realism in several of the stories. "Hunters in the Snow" is surreal in its atmosphere and its conclusion. "Maiden Voyage" and "Worldly Goods" are emblematic tales of sorts. "In the Garden of the North American Martyrs" and

"The Liar" concern themselves with the subjects of redemption, grace, and transformation, moments of transcendence as religious as paintings from the cinquecento. Wolff's realism is sometimes akin to that of Flannery O'Connor's parables; sometimes it comes closer to André Dubus's fascination with the core mysteries of the human condition.

In the Garden of the North American Martyrs introduced an engaging writer who, though grounded in the modern realistic tradition, showed from the beginning that his fiction would not be easy to pigeonhole—even by the author himself. When Wolff writes about the essays of André Dubus, he could be describing the complexity of voices in his own first collection: "His is an unapologetically sacramental vision of life in which ordinary things participate in the miraculous, the miraculous in ordinary things."[6]

"Next Door"

A brief story, "Next Door" seems at first full of disparate events—the domestic quarrel next door, the seeming domestic tranquility of the narrator and his wife, the movie on television, the movie being imagined by the narrator. And yet these disparities produce verisimilitude—life as an assortment of unrelated events whose cement is the lives of the people experiencing them—as well as irony.

The reader, through dramatic irony, contrasts the frightening, violent lives next door with the apparent serenity in the dark bedroom. The reader begins by thinking the outlandish behavior next door antisocial and adopting the point of view and values of the narrator and his wife, but the focus shifts quickly to the disturbing situation in the narrator's own house and mind. The couple in the bedroom is frightened by the life next door and feel their security threatened. The wife fears reprisal against their cat if they call the police. She later "pulls the covers up to her neck"[7] in a symbolic withdrawal from a world other than the one she shares with her husband—a world in some ways more passionate and lively. Their white picket fence—against which the angry man urinates—"couldn't keep anyone out" (*Garden*, 4). They participate in the tumult next door—as perhaps many others live life—as voyeurs, witnesses to potential calamity, always desirous of self-effacement and the carefully regulated emotional response.

In fact, the reader questions their real reasons for disliking the troublesome neighbors, though at first fully understanding their reaction. The narrator finds them physically repugnant. "She has never eaten anything but donuts and milk shakes" (*Garden*, 5). In a xenophobic and perhaps racist reaction, the narrator finds the husband "dark and hairy" (*Garden*, 5). The wife he discounts because she screams at the baby (the narrator and his wife, both young, are childless). And the narrator's wife finds the savage beating of the dog followed by the neighbors' passionate embrace more than she can stand. She and her husband sleep in twin beds; she discourages his sexual advances, and the way they talk about sex is cloying in its indirectness. In sum, they are unnerved by the raucous lives next door. They feel threatened, and through dramatic irony the reader sees that their lives are in many ways as disturbing as those of their next-door neighbors.

Wolff's use of the late movie on television expands and deepens the story, revealing that the narrator is at least partially aware of the troubling ironies in his own life. In the movie, *El Dorado*, a group of people, led by a blind man, leave their hometown, their established lives, and search for a city of gold—for answers, redemption, happiness. The narrator decides not to watch the conclusion of the movie, which he predicts. In the film, hardship eliminates many, and greed leads to the ultimate demise of those remaining, as they murder one another within feet of their destination. The blind man staggers through El Dorado alone, and, unseeing, misses it entirely. But in the narrator's imagined ending, the men and women don't turn on each other. El Dorado becomes a meadow filled with flowers where the people cover themselves with blossoms.

The theme of Wolff's story becomes apparent when the two movies are examined. The movie on TV is about human frailties and concludes in death and despair, the blind man stumbling unawares through El Dorado. Notice, however, that this pessimistic ending is not necessarily the real one. It is supplied by the narrator, who guesses at the conclusion after he is in bed, the TV set off. As an anodyne to this imagined, indeed expected, ending, the narrator creates his own movie. In it there are deaths and misfortunes, but the people are "explorers" (*Garden*, 8) who seek the new and exotic. They depend on one another. Their eating of the dog in the film is its saddest event. At the end there is no El Dorado but a more spiritual place, an Elysian Field of comfort and rest. Here everyone is genderless, and the movie concludes with their arms upraised in celebration.

Outside his window the real world is chaotic and unsettling. Inside all is not right between him and his wife. From the window the couple look down on the world, condemning it without seeming to participate.

The world outside appears headed toward the TV movie's pessimistic conclusion. The narrator tries his hand at directing his own movie. Yet viewing is still the passivity of voyeurism. Where the blind man in the movie never realizes his goal, the narrator has become partially sighted. But whether imagining a better ending will lead from passivity to action is difficult to tell. Intellectual dissatisfaction may become the seed of change, but it may well be that the narrator and his wife will continue to be onlookers and no more. Both movies conclude—in despair or hope—but the lives in Wolff's story continue.

"Hunters in the Snow"

"Hunters in the Snow" is a disturbing story about the vagaries and cruelties of superficial friendships, about masculine camaraderie that appears sympathetic and fulfilling but that is in the end destructive and as barren as the frozen landscape in which the story takes place.

Landscape in "Hunters in the Snow" serves to heighten the story of the three men. Outside Spokane, their hometown, the surroundings are empty and barren. The three men appear isolated from the world. During the hunt, they move across a deserted landscape focusing the reader's attention on their interactions. The title itself, like the title of a painting, promises a minimalist portrayal of three men in pursuit of game in a world of whiteness that is lifeless and inhospitable.

Soon after the story opens, in the truck cab and during the deer hunt, the curious friendship the men share begins to reveal itself. Tub, the protagonist, has become the butt of Kenny and Frank's cruel jokes. Earlier they threatened to run him over with the truck and laughed when he sought a doorway for safety; they make a teasing reference to a baby-sitter—an in-joke they share between themselves but not with Tub. Later, Frank and Kenny refuse to make Tub's crossing of fences easier; they leave him behind and, at lunch, make fun of his weight.

It becomes obvious that the dynamics of this triangular friendship have altered lately, shifting the camaraderie away from Frank and Tub to Frank and Kenny, though it is important to note that the basis for their even knowing one another—much less the basis for any sort of friendship—is left unclear by Wolff. Tub knows the same people Kenny and Frank know. But the reader never learns if they live near one another, work alongside one another, or what. This lack of back-

ground is like the snowscape, an empty environment into which they
cast their bickering.

It is the shooting of an old, useless dog by Kenny that shifts the
dynamics of the relationship again. Tub feels sympathetic toward the
dog and afraid of Kenny. Mistakenly thinking that his own life is
threatened, Tub shoots Kenny. Minutes later, Tub, full of a newfound
power to alter his position in the triangular relationship, physically
forces Frank to take notice of him again. Perhaps, as in any other
such triumvirate, the control moves back and forth as individuals seize
initiatives that promise power if such, they feel, has been taken away.

Now the reader begins to understand the ironies that Wolff has
created. Tub, like some macho gunslinger in a western, has reasserted
himself by shooting the man who drew on him. Grabbing Frank's
collar, Tub shakes into him the realization that he is now a force to
be reckoned with. Ironically, Kenny was asked by the dog's owner to
put the elderly and suffering animal out of its misery; he did not kill
it out of cruelty, as Tub assumes. With Tub having asserted himself and
beginning again to become important in the dynamics of the triangular
relationship, the story's deepest irony is made manifest. The balance
of power now shifts as the seriously wounded Kenny is ignored in the
bed of the pickup. In fact, the story at this point becomes surreal, and
it is difficult to believe Wolff intends the reader to think he is following
a realistic premise at all. The two buddies, Tub and Frank, cruelly
overlook the bleeding victim who now inhabits Tub's former position
on the periphery of the friendship.

While opening up to each other, they become dismissive of Kenny.
To warm themselves from the blast of cold air coming in through the
broken windshield, they stop at a tavern. Frank chides Kenny for not
keeping the blankets tucked up around him. Frank talks to the
wounded man as if he were a troublesome child. Inside, and out of
the cold, Frank tells Tub all about his affair with the 15-year-old baby-
sitter. Tub, glad to be included again, listens and commiserates. At a
second stop on the way to the hospital, Tub confesses to Frank that
his eating problem is not glandular but simply gluttony. Then, in an
almost ritual act of friendship, Frank has Tub eat four orders of pan-
cakes. Returning to the pickup, in yet another unconscionable act of
cruelty, Tub and Frank remove Kenny's blankets, deciding the two
reacquainted friends will get more use from them than the wounded
man.

"Hunters in the Snow" concludes with the story's final and, for

Kenny, fatal irony. So involved as they are with their renewed friendship, Tub and Frank have lost the complicated directions (and, though only a few miles from the first stop, decide not to retrieve them). As it turns out, they are headed away from the hospital and any hope the wounded Kenny has to survive. "Hunters in the Snow," which begins realistically but ends in a surreal and tragicomic way, says nothing good about friendships engendered and sustained by superficial concerns. The shifting interpersonal dynamics of the three men—with one rising to imminence at the literal expense of the other—brings to mind the silly and often cruel tensions of high-school cliques, where one is either "in" or "out" depending on sophomoric whim. And the last line in the story, made in reference to the three heading away from the hospital and aid for Kenny, sums up the foundation of such fickle relations. "They had taken a different turn a long way back" (*Garden*, 26), Wolff writes. Surely this "turn" is one away from the sensitivity, love, and other positive characteristics of true friendship.

"An Episode in the Life of Professor Brooke"

In "An Episode in the Life of Professor Brooke," Wolff makes use of the world of academia and a regional conference of the Modern Language Association to examine the conservative life of his protagonist, Professor Brooke. Such an environment—intellectual, hermetically sealed off from much of the world, causing its inhabitants to spend time on esoteric and often egotistical pursuits—is perfect for Brooke, an intelligent, published scholar of middle age, full of confidence that his moral and intellectual perspectives are the correct and proper ones.

It is Riley, the Yeats scholar, Brooke's nemesis in the department, who at the start of their trip to the conference begins to cause Brooke some doubt in his beliefs. It is obvious that Brooke's supposed reasons for disliking Riley—his clothes, his rumored promiscuity with students, even his red hair—are not enough of an explanation. The reader comes to understand that Riley is a contrast to Brooke and offends him because he represents the possibilities of an alternate life Brooke has not only not chosen but has indeed come to detest in others. When on the drive to the conference Riley questions Brooke about the worst thing he has ever done, Brooke can think only of trivial actions he is sure Riley will laugh at. And yet Brooke is troubled by rather than prideful in his desire to be an honorable man. "When you tried to be good you ran the risk of seeming a prig, but what was the alternative? Brooke did not want to know. Yet at times he wondered if he had been too easily tamed" (*Garden*, 30).

Here, near the beginning, Wolff has given the reader the thematic concerns of the story. For already Brooke is questioning his stolid viewpoints. When Ruth, the nurse who becomes the focus of his attention, is introduced, he already does "want to know" and very soon decides, though implicitly, that he has indeed been "too easily tamed." Wolff makes much the same use of Riley as Thomas Mann does of the "red-haired" and "exotic" figure in "Death in Venice,"[8] whose incarnations of lascivious temptation lead the too-cerebral Aschenbach into mortal sensory delights. Riley, however, is far more human than evil, and Brooke far less prone to excess. But as with Aschenbach, the changes in Brooke are gradual, not sudden. Once at the conference, he is his usual arrogant self, upbraiding Abbot, a young scholar whose ideas he thinks are "wrongheaded."

But the meeting with Ruth over the canapes is the coincidence Brooke needs to alter his "too tamed" life, to become more daring and less certain of his own intent and his solid ideas about the world. For Ruth, it soon becomes clear, is not at all like Brooke or most people he knows in his academic surroundings. She is a passionate lover of literature, but in such a juvenile and naive manner that Brooke, operating still as the man with the "proper" perspective, is incredulous and must stifle his urge to confront her lack of sophistication.

Shortly after meeting Ruth, Brooke is confronted by Riley, who reminds him of a committee decision made a few weeks past in which Brooke rejected a woman for tenure. Brooke believes he did so out of just motives—she had failed to publish recently and was a poor teacher. But Riley condemns Brooke's views as too simple and reminds him of the woman's ill husband and her children. Angry and upset, Brooke leaves the hotel, and, outside, cannot rid himself of Riley's aggressive attack on his values. "He decided that he was right and Riley was wrong. But why did he feel so awful?" (*Garden*, 34). To avoid any future interrogation of the reasons for his actions, Brooke decides to leave without him that night.

But again Brooke meets Ruth, although he attempts to avoid her. Now seriously beginning to question his dull life and established values, Brooke, who is married, begins to respond sensually to Ruth. Intoxicated by her perfume, he agrees to accompany her to a poetry reading by a writer he detests, whose poetry is all popular poster declarations and romance. It is after this event that Ruth, seeing Brooke's intolerance for the poetry she loves, attacks *King Lear* as "junk" because it fails to be uplifting.

At the conclusion of the night's final meeting with Riley, who is accompanied by the now-drunken scholar Abbot, Brooke leaves with Ruth because Riley is being outrageously flirtatious. It is interesting to note that many of the events in the middle of the story are counterpointed by the presence of a group of scoutmasters having a convention at the same hotel. When Brooke meets Ruth at the reception, the scoutmasters are reciting the Pledge of Allegiance, and later they arm wrestle in the restaurant. When Brooke takes her out of the bar by the arm and away from the flirtatious Riley, the scoutmasters are singing a canoeing song about "clean and bright" paddles and wild geese in flight. Wolff intends irony by counterpointing Brooke's gradual abandonment of his conservative life for one more daring and different with the traditional values represented by the scoutmasters. And, at the same time, he calls into consideration these older men who cling to an uncomplicated value system of correct actions and virtues that more appropriately belong to a naive boyhood world lacking in ambiguity.

Though Brooke has slowly succumbed to Riley's view of his life, he does not attempt to rectify things by seducing Ruth. At first, he sees that her apartment mirrors her own shallow nature. But when she removes her wig, revealing her head, bald from chemotherapy, Brooke finds her exotic, like the "Frenchwomen whose heads had been shaved because they'd slept with Germans" (*Garden*, 39). Listening to her discuss poetry, he begins to understand her views. She needs poetry to be uplifting, she says, because it saved her life during the chemotherapy. Brooke then considers his own writing. "He was thinking that nothing he had ever thought or said could make a woman want to live again" (*Garden*, 41). As she reads her own poetry and then that of the writer they've just heard, and whom Brooke detests, "he began to enjoy it, and even allowed himself to believe what it was saying: that the world was beautiful and we were beautiful, and that we could be more beautiful if we just let ourselves go—if we shouted when we wanted to shout, ran naked when we wanted to run naked, embraced when we wanted to embrace" (*Garden*, 41).

Professor Brooke has undergone a tremendous change, an alteration that will force him to reconsider much of what he has come to believe as the truth about his life. At the beginning of the story, he was censorious of people unlike himself. When he first met Ruth he thought her unsophisticated and naive, a lover of trashy literature. But he soon saw the pleasant liberation her view of the world offered. At first he thought Riley immoral and a rogue, but by the end, and because of his own sexual adventure with Ruth, he no longer judges the man deficient. "From now on he would sit in the front of the church and let Riley, knowing what he did, watch him. He would kneel before Riley as we must all, he thought, kneel before one another" (*Garden*, 43).

Once a man who tied up episodes in his life the way a novelist concludes the end of a chapter, Brooke realizes he will never again be able to sum things up neatly. So recently a patronizing and smug man, Brooke has become that kneeling, humble man who bows before the amazing variety of life. Wolff, as he does in "Next Door," reveals to his protagonist the possibility of examining one's life in light of other lives more mysterious, more ambiguous, and therefore more compelling and frightening. In "Next Door," the narrator imagines his life as a movie with a happy ending. But imagining is still passive. Professor Brooke actually makes contact with another's life when he spends the night with Ruth. Once censorious and priggish, Brooke is transformed by having made a connection with another person. At the story's end, he emerges a more forgiving and understanding man, because through his actions he has become more human, more needful of others' sympathy himself.

"Smokers"

"Smokers" is the poignant story of a teenage boy's desire to abandon his middle-class past and turn his future into a boundless vista of social power and wealth reminiscent of that of Fitzgerald's Jay Gatz, who reinvents himself as the fabulous Jay Gatsby: "I'll tell you God's truth," Gatsby lies on first meeting Nick Carraway, "I am the son of some wealthy people in the Middle-West . . . brought up in America but educated at Oxford."[9] It is important to the theme of Wolff's story that the narrator is left unnamed. In his newspaper stories he refers to himself simply as "the boy." In one way he represents every boy who must somehow construct an adult personality from the often vague and disparate material of childhood. But perhaps more important, the unnamed narrator sees himself as yet unformed; his personality is shadowy and his own character eludes him. So unformed a personality does not warrant a name. Finally, perhaps his betrayal of fellow student

Eugene Miller at the conclusion of the story makes him wish to remain anonymous to the reader.

At first it is difficult to understand exactly what the narrator wishes to escape from in his past. Though he provides only the spottiest of information about it—as if he were embarrassed—his life to this point has not been one of poverty or disorder. Instead it appears perfectly normal and middle class. His father takes him hunting, his mother has his sister wear hand-me-downs, and his brother attends the University of Oregon on an athletic scholarship. It becomes clear then that what the boy is ashamed of is exactly these traits—the middle-class mediocrity of his past, the lack of prestige and power. Though his family is not wealthy enough to send him to Choate, he is intelligent enough to have won a full scholarship. As the story opens, it becomes clear that he has decided that no obstacle in the world will force him to remain weak and unformed.

Consider his reaction to Eugene Miller, who proves to be the unwitting nemesis of the narrator. According to the boy, Eugene must be avoided because he too is from the plebeian hinterlands of middle-class America and is also on scholarship. But unlike our narrator, who wishes very much to fit in seamlessly with the privileged boys around him, Eugene is quite natural and oblivious to such desires. Remaining true to himself throughout the story, Eugene dresses oddly in his feathered Alpine hat and is full of bluster and bombast. Though outrageous to the reader and the others at Choate, he easily establishes a comfortable niche for himself at the exclusive school.

As in the stories "Next Door" and "Hunters in the Snow," irony provides much of what is to be learned in "Smokers." Eugene becomes the roommate of Talbot Nevins, the quintessential Choate student with a powerful father. It is Talbot the narrator so wants to impress, but he remains isolated, outside the camaraderie Eugene takes for granted. What's more, the narrator's roommate is also an outsider, a Chilean boy who adores Adolf Hitler and whose mother's death causes him to leave in the middle of the semester, thus intensifying the narrator's sense of isolation. Eugene's bluster and directness win Talbot's attention, where the narrator's obsequious and ingratiating ways fail.

Halfway through the year, at Christmas vacation, the narrator's failure to win recognition and acceptance and so rid himself of his bourgeois past is made painfully clear. While Eugene is asked to visit Talbot's family house in posh Boston, the narrator is forced to visit relatives he's never met in prosaic Baltimore. So Eugene becomes privy to the world of Talbot's father, who drives Grand Prix sports cars and cavorts with movie stars.

Perhaps the most telling use of irony in "Smokers" is rather indirect, concerning the narrator's stories in the school newspaper. They all involve "the boy" as protagonist in sentimental, melodramatic fantasies. These reveal his discontent with his past and his growing frustrations at Choate because of his inability to make friends with boys like Talbot. His imaginary heritage becomes a revisionist version of what little we know of his past: "The boy's father came from a distinguished New York family. In his early twenties, he had traveled to Oregon to oversee his family's vast lumber holdings. His family turned on him when he married a beautiful young woman who happened to be part Indian. The Indian blood was noble, but the boy's father was disowned anyway. The boy's parents prospered in spite of this and raised a large, gifted family" (*Garden*, 54). In "the boy's" current adventures, his "only friends were a beautiful young dancer who worked as a waitress in a café near the school, and an old tramp. . . . The boy and girl were forever getting the tramp out of trouble for doing things like painting garbage cans beautiful colors" (*Garden*, 54).

Though Talbot probably never reads these stories that so clearly reveal the narrator's unhappiness, he does get the idea that the narrator is a writer. After learning Talbot is failing in English, the narrator volunteers to write his essays for him. But this too fails to win Talbot, and the narrator is devastated by the news that Talbot and Eugene will be roommates again the next semester. And to further inflame the wound, Talbot is the one waiting for Eugene to agree to their sharing a room. Humiliated, having failed time after time to gain entry to the privileged world at Choate that Eugene has so easily accessed, the narrator cuts his ties to Talbot.

Through a chain of coincidences, Eugene is unfairly blamed for smoking and immediately expelled from Choate. This leaves the narrator free to press himself on Talbot again. Dispirited just an hour before, he was perhaps beginning to disengage himself from his opportunistic and cynical quest. Now sympathetic to Eugene's predicament and unable to watch him leave, he considers clearing the matter up with the headmaster. For in this instance, it was Talbot who had been smoking and left behind the tell-tale odor of cigarettes. But to implicate Talbot would also be to implicate himself, since he took a puff from Talbot's cigarette. While he is willing to let Eugene, and even Talbot, suffer expulsion, the narrator is not willing to remove himself from the opportunities Choate represents.

It is finally Talbot, now without a roommate, who asks the narrator to share a room. And in a moment of triumph, "the boy" is arrogant and condescending and says he will have to give it some thought, at the same time telling himself that, because Eugene had been guilty of smoking before, no injustice had really been done.

Though a poignant story of a young boy's attempt to gain acceptance into a social class opened to him not through his familial position or wealth but through his superior intelligence, it is also a sinister story of the corruption of the boy's personality. Where Eugene is accepted by the boys at Choate because of his natural abilities and inherent strength of character—he never doubts who he is or what he has to offer to others—the narrator tries to alter himself to fit what he thinks are their expectations. He exploits his ability to write by completing Talbot's essays, and he denies his sympathy for Eugene and his desire to tell the truth by rationalizing that Eugene had been guilty of smoking at one time or another. So when Talbot does ask the narrator to room with him, the narrator arrogantly toys with Talbot, as if he must weigh the request. Naturally, he soon acquiesces.

At the story's end, the reader must feel there is little hope for the narrator, who has given himself over by finally perverting his sense of justice. And yet Wolff does not shut the door completely. Though the narrator may become a Talbot, he may also become a Eugene—a person with a true sense of self. All this rests very delicately on the assumption that the boy is intelligent and has, once before, seen clearly that he is a malcontent because he "knew that something was wrong but didn't know what it was" (*Garden*, 54). Unlike Talbot, he is *not* part of the world of the careless rich; he is more like Eugene. But he so passionately desires to be powerful that it is uncertain at best whether he will come to the view that truth to oneself is more valuable than anything from Talbot's world.

As he did in "Hunters in the Snow," Wolff critically examines the dynamics of a friendship based on the need for acceptance and belonging and devoid of honest commitments and assessments. As in "Episode" and "Next Door," Wolff presents another variation on the recurring theme of those who consider themselves somehow outside a more intriguing life that could offer mystery, fulfillment, or—in the case of "Smokers"—power and acceptance.

Part 1

"Face to Face"

"Face to Face" is a story about loss and loneliness and the ways in which two people deal with them. They are Virginia and Robert, each recently divorced, who have just begun to date each other. Wolff gets at the essence of the theme at the beginning of the story, when Virginia considers the impact of her divorce on her son, Ricky. Although he no longer asks about his father's return, his schoolwork suffers and his sketches have regressed to childish scrawls. His drawings divulge both the problem and his attempt to solve it, to seek some sort of personal equilibrium that reinstates his connection with people and the world. "All the pictures showed the same thing: a man and a woman with a little boy between them, holding hands and grinning off the page" (*Garden*, 61).

Ricky is ill-equipped to make sense of his loss. But perhaps the resilience of his age will help. For Virginia and Robert there is no such youthful energy. For them the loss, and the resulting loneliness and mistrust of others, has provoked grim reassessments of the value of their lives. Of the two, Robert is the more injured by his divorce. His cousin, Alice, talks about him as if he has "suffered some great wrong" (*Garden*, 62). And though the odor that clings to him "like the smell of a newly painted house" (*Garden*, 62) is explained later by his actually being a housepainter, the "acrid odor" is symbolically indicative of something spoiled, gone off a bit and faintly repugnant. It is difficult to determine if Robert's negative attitude toward women led to his failed marriage or if the divorce and ensuing loneliness brought about his attitude. Perhaps it is safe to say that his chauvinism was present and contributed to his divorce but has, as a result of his sense of failure with women, become more intense.

A shy and polite man, considerate of Ricky, Robert is suffering from his inability to become a functional human being again. He needs to reassert himself, to take some control over his life. He needs to seek out and develop a relationship with a woman, though he distrusts women and his ability to attract them. He has failed once and is not sure he can risk failure again.

Though the reader cannot tell cause from effect, it is apparent that Robert is sexually dysfunctional. At the fireworks display he is embarrassed by a couple under a blanket. On dates with Virginia, he can only squeeze her hand passionately. When he finally does kiss her, she is shocked to find "his eyes were wide and startled" (*Garden*, 65).

In Vancouver on a weekend trip together, he is so insecure and anxious that he must drink himself into some sort of confidence. And when he does perform sexually, it is an animalistic assault—as if getting it done and over with were the goal. The first night he forces Virginia's legs apart and hurts her. The second night he attempts sex while she's asleep.

Add to these insulting, degrading attacks the curious event in the movie theater. Virginia is uncomfortable accompanying Robert to an afternoon movie, as if it were unnatural. And the audience of older men implies those with burdensome time on their hands and hints at sexual ambivalence as well. In the theater, Robert attempts a juvenile groping at Virginia's thighs, a regression that recalls that of her son Ricky in his drawings. It is as if Robert's divorce and his resulting mistrust and dislike of women and of himself have destroyed his mature human sensibilities.

Having felt himself to be a victim of his wife, he is now a victimizer of women. Desirous of being the victor, he acts pompously in a restaurant. There, as he does later on the drive to Vancouver, he extricates stories of Virginia's former husband that make him look ridiculous so he, Robert, can by comparison think himself superior. When Virginia attempts to discuss Florence, Robert's former wife, she forces Robert back to the realization of his own vulnerability, his own role as victim. He avoids this as long as possible and, when finally forced, describes her as a whore to whom he can feel superior. He broadens his attack to include Virginia and all women who quickly excuse one another's behavior.

Robert is pitiable and finally unable to repair the damage done to him by his divorce. He becomes not only divorced from Florence but from contact with all women. And though Virginia urges him not to give up on himself and others just because their relationship failed, she realizes that "he had left her, gone back to his injury" (*Garden*, 72).

But where Robert fails to regain his equilibrium in the world and is unable to bridge the chasm of his own pain, Virginia comes through her loneliness and is triumphant. She, too, could have succumbed to injury and become a fragmented, dysfunctional person, but she does not. And even though her divorce also "took the life out of her, and she didn't think much about going out with men" (*Garden*, 62), she takes the chance, risks pain and humiliation, partly because she is thinking of her son but, most important, because she never lacks hope.

Unlike Robert, Virginia discloses her married life at the risk of Robert's ridicule. Though despondent at the beginning of the story, she is never dishonest in her assessments of her misery. And she, unlike Robert, who cannot acknowledge her pain without revealing his own, recognizes his unhappiness and feels great sympathy for him. She tries to reestablish his self-worth by telling him he's "a good man" (*Garden*, 66). When he comes into their hotel room silent and drunk their first night in Vancouver, Virginia worries about how she should react without upsetting him. After the next morning's sexual assault, she starts out wanting to murder him, but "after a while she decided she would settle for understanding him" (*Garden*, 67).

Even after his second assault, which she repulsed, she later attempts to assuage his confused anger. "Virginia could feel Robert's misery. She softened. In the morning she reached out to him and began rubbing his back. She had to do this" (*Garden*, 71). Throughout the story, Virginia is reaching out to comfort and console Robert.

Early on Wolff connects the title to one of the major aspects of the theme. "He bent toward Virginia and they were face to face. She looked at him and wondered what he saw when he looked at her, if he saw his life running out" (*Garden*, 66). Here are two people damaged by divorce and distrustful of future commitments. Though the seeds of Robert's attitude may always have been present and may have helped destroy his marriage and his happiness, he now certainly despises women. He is anxious and insecure about his abilities to perform socially or sexually in a relationship. He is apprehensive about risking any more damage to his psyche. And despite Virginia's pleading, he chooses, at the story's end, not to take the risk of contact but to withdraw into his pain.

Virginia, impaired by her divorce, is not mortally wounded in spirit. She is willing to give herself, to lavish her sympathy and compassion on Robert. And, in a way, this damaged man brings her around to living again. The face-to-face realization is that time is running out for her. His decision to hide from life in isolation is a sharp lesson. "He looked at her with sudden panic and she knew that he was deciding at that moment always to be alone. She started out of herself, became enormous in her pity for him" (*Garden*, 72). And it is this compassion for another that shatters the suffocating carapace of self-pity, the pernicious introversion that continues to paralyze Robert. And though pity is, in ways, a superior and condescending attitude, it does clarify and define levels of misfortune. On the quiet drive home, Virginia can pity Robert and also stare "greedily ahead" (*Garden*, 72), and the reader understands that the lives of Virginia and Ricky have a chance of being salvaged but that Robert's is almost certainly lost.

In "An Episode," Professor Brooke comes to understand and sympathize with Riley by acknowledging the same temptations and possibilities in himself. Here Virginia, in a reversal of this scenario, manages to save herself once she is confronted with Robert's self-destructiveness. Indeed, "An Episode" and "Face to Face" stand in direct contrast to "Next Door" and "Hunters in the Snow." In "Next Door" the narrator remains unengaged and passive, though he is dissatisfied with his life. In "Hunters in the Snow" the superficial human contact is grotesque and feeds on a cruel disregard for others. In these stories Wolff presents the consequences of inaction or wrong action. "An Episode" and "Face to Face" present an opposite course of evolvement. Professor Brooke connects with the lives of others. Virginia, though she tries and fails to help Robert, comes to reevaluate her own connections with others in the face of his painful and destructive loneliness. In both stories, Wolff offers the reader reminders of the need people have for honest, careful contact with each other.

"Passengers"

Near the end of "Passengers," Glen, the protagonist, hides in a basement closet. Moments before he had recalled hunting geese with his stepfather. "As the geese wheeled south and crossed in front of the sunrise they called back and forth to each other with a sound like laughter, and their wings were outlined in gold. Glen had felt so good that he had forgotten his gun. Maybe [being high] would be like that, like starting all over again" (*Garden*, 86). Now, in the basement, he smokes two joints of marijuana left in the car by Bonnie, a hippie hitchhiker. He hopes that somehow the drug will alleviate his newly located but vaguely defined unhappiness—an unhappiness the reader knows is generated by his subservience to Martin, his roommate and employer. But the marijuana brings no sense of euphoria, no sense of renewal and regeneration. In fact, his newly discerned sense of entrapment is underscored by the appearance of Martin in the basement to iron his shirts.

Literally trapped in the closet, Glen listens to Martin's supercilious and arrogant belittlement of everything on the radio. Wolff's imagery at the story's close puts Glen in a hell in which Martin's cacophonous singing cruelly makes fun of the blues and, by extension, those who are, like Glen, the subjects of the blues: the powerless, the dispossessed, the unhappy. In the final burst of hellish imagery, Glen is enclosed by " absolute darkness," the steam iron emitting a "bubbling sigh" and "Martin's aftershave the odor of sulphur" (*Garden*, 87). The closet is filling with a "pall of smoke," and Glen believes he may never escape the nightmarish confines of the small room.

"Passengers" is the story of Glen's gradual realization that his life is unhappy, that he is practically powerless in his enslavement to the cruel, despotic Martin, whose fascism perverts everything he touches. Though it is obvious to the reader early on, Glen is reluctant to admit his servitude, the obliteration of his personality. But the indications of his predicament are everywhere. He is afraid of breaking Martin's rules condemning hitchhikers. He uses Martin's automobile and credit card. He squeezes a tennis ball because Martin suggests it will improve his golf grip. His single Peter, Paul, and Mary tape is relegated to the glove box; it is Martin's "easy listening" music he plays instead.

Martin is the quintessential entrepreneur whose philosophy of business—connected entirely with managing one's life—is naturally at odds with Bonnie's 1960s condemnations of the "military-industrial complex." Martin is no such fringe dweller, but a full participant in capitalist consumerism. His nature is best displayed by his attitude toward the modern Israelis he uses as models for his business philosophy— a philosophy based primarily on the will to power over less strong personalities (like Glen's). He believes that the Jews of the Holocaust were much like some of his own employees who are no longer viable as such and need firing. The Holocaust pruned the Jewish community of dead weight and allows the modern Israelis to be willful and tough-minded, certain to attain their goals.

When Glen admits to having given Bonnie a lift, Martin explodes in anger. Glen passively waits for Martin to settle down, but before this, Martin interjects his attitude toward people who are powerless. "When you put yourself into someone else's power you're nothing, nobody. You just have to accept what happens" (*Garden*, 86). Though directed toward Bonnie, Martin's definition describes Glen's relationship with Martin. The ominous finality of the previous sentence seems born out by the end of the story when Glen, trapped in the closet, thinks he can never escape.

But it is Bonnie who serves to bring Glen's dilemma into focus, though it is perhaps wrong to say Glen has had no inkling of his victimization. For one thing, Glen is intelligent and thoughtful, so surely Martin's tyrannical presence has bothered him before. Also, Glen's emerging resentment of Martin and his discovery of how unhappy he is under Martin's control come very quickly, as if the seed had been swollen and ready to germinate.

In almost all ways, Bonnie is unlike Glen. Where Glen represents the young and focused entrepreneur, Bonnie is the cultural dropout, critical of everything her society represents, though her own existential philosophy permits a goodly amount of egoism. Wolff plays out their shared ride against the backdrop of Vietnam and the social unrest of the 1960s. And though the war is mentioned only obliquely, it signals the reverberations of a culture uneasy with itself, a society examining itself and unhappy with its findings—rethinking the relationships between citizens and their institutions, between citizens invigorated by the contemporary culture and those sapped and disillusioned by it. This historical backdrop is the perfect setting for Glen's reassessment of his life.

Though not free of the egotism of the times—maintained by those certain they knew how to cure all of the culture's ills—Bonnie does present Glen with sharp contrasts to his own unsatisfactory life. She has few possessions outside her dog, Sunshine, and her guitar. She is quick to condemn the business community, "the military-industrial complex," for its profiteering motives in the war. In fact, she is as intolerant of others' opinions and tastes as is Glen, who, using Martin's frame of reference, quickly categorizes her as one of those freeloaders who criticize other people but are not productive themselves.

But a conflict of values is not what "Passengers" is about. For as different as the two are, they share human qualities that transcend political perspectives and socioeconomic categories. Though Bonnie "walks the check" at Denny's, she leaves the waitress a tip. Though Glen finally gives her $20, he rushes off feeling guilty, knowing he should have offered her a place to stay and more sustained help than he provided.

They are argumentative and, at times, angry with each other. But when they lay aside the superficiality of political dogma and, for instance, discuss the significant people in their lives, they realize they share some mutual concerns. It is worth noting that their first genuine exchange takes place just after a moving van has passed them in the fog. The logo on the van reads, "WE MOVE FAMILIES NOT JUST FURNITURE." From the ensuing conversation about their relationships, the reader learns that Glen, when asked by anyone about his sex life, lies and says he is engaged. If he eventually has to update the status of his relationship, he says the engagement never worked out. And though Bonnie has had a lover, he recently left her; he wants children and thinks Bonnie might have damaged her genes from having dropped acid. Glen, who admits to himself that he was initially attracted to Bonnie, decides the man left her because she is old. But whatever the truth, it is obvious to the reader that both passengers have been damaged emotionally by others. And it is Glen's odd lie about being engaged—and his realization that it is a strange tack to take—that convinces the reader that his problems are more profound than Bonnie's.

Such discussions, such revelations about their lives, place them on a more intimate level that obscures their egotistical differences and underscores their shared humanity. But it is the near collision of the car that makes them most aware of their frailty. The reprieve from death, as Bonnie characterizes it, makes her want to change her ways: She will write the mother she hates, be nicer to her dog, stop shoplifting. Glen, only just beginning to reassess his life, gradually approaching his desire for the flock of geese that once brought a sense of rejuvenation and possibilities, admits that he, too, will change his ways "though he wasn't sure just what was wrong with his ways" (*Garden*, 82).

This sentence is the pivotal moment in "Passengers." For from this moment until the end, Glen becomes increasingly aware of his dissatisfaction and the need to somehow begin his life again. This emerging revelation leads directly to the story's conclusion, where he is trapped in the basement closet, with Martin as Cerberus.

When he delivers Bonnie to her friend's house, her request for his help, her statement that she does not "want to get caught up in all this again" (*Garden*, 83), is a foreshadowing of his own displeasure at having to face Martin. And though he denies help to Bonnie because of his continuing subservience to Martin (this is also a foreshadowing: his refusal to help Bonnie signals his own helplessness at the conclusion), there is the first true glint of his new self-assessment when he considers the chaos and displeasure that Bonnie, her dog, and her lifestyle would bring to Martin. "Martin would die. Glen savored the thought, but he couldn't, he just couldn't" (*Garden*, 84). And the reason that "he couldn't" is that his reevaluation of his life has not fully emerged. This is shown in his fear of both the passing police car and his connection with the hippie Bonnie, now busy chasing her dog down the street.

"Passengers" is the story of Glen's gradual realization of the unhappiness of his powerless life. The title of the story serves to describe Bonnie and Glen. They are passengers together, human travelers joined for only a few hours. What Glen comes to see in Bonnie is not so much an alternative to his life but the context of another's person's problems and unhappiness. He would like to help her, but he cannot. At the story's end he can not help himself. He is unable to re-create any sense of the renewal and possibility of change that his childhood view of the geese had once provided. He remains trapped by the hellish figure of Martin, whose will to power belittles and subverts other people's lives.

It seems doubtful that Glen can begin again. Yet he has seen himself clearly for the first time in years. He has emerged from the fog Wolff uses as a symbol throughout the story. Fog produces a sense of isolation, it hides shapes, blurs distinctions. Before he descends to the basement, Glen feels the fog "all around the house, thickening the air; his breath in his lungs made him feel slow and heavy" (*Garden*, 86). But objects suddenly emerge from the fog: the moving van with its message of family, the rushing log trucks that could have spelled his death in a crash. And now Glen's self-awareness has emerged from the blurring fog of years of shortsightedness, of concentration on work, to an awareness of both his slavish relationship to Martin and a desire to begin his life again.

Again, as is often the case in this collection, Wolff brings a character to a moment of self-assessment by holding up one life against another. Unlike Virginia in "Face to Face," Glen has not expressed a full measure of compassion for Bonnie and so remains less fully aware of his predicament—a life dominated by Martin and so constricted and unfulfilling. Though the story is not as positive as "An Episode" or "Face to Face," it does not present the pessimistic conclusions of "Next Door" and "Hunters in the Snow." It inhabits a middle ground along with "Smokers." The protagonists are aware of their dilemmas; they seem capable of saving themselves by mending their lives. But whether or not they will remains unclear. In stories like these, the reader's attitude plays an important role. Wolff has left the story open at the end. An optimist might imagine for the characters a future quite different from that imagined by a pessimist.

"Maiden Voyage"

In "Maiden Voyage" Wolff offers one of his most cynical and symbolic stories. A harsh look at love and marriage, the story examines the failed relationships of Howard and Nora, Ron and Stella, as they take a vacation cruise. Bill Tweed, the opportunistic and sinister social director of the cruise, pays crude lip service to love and cruel commentary on the scene. He is much like one of the avatars of sensuality in Thomas Mann's "Death in Venice," the leader of the troupe of street singers who is "of the comic type . . . half pimp, half actor, brutal and bold-faced, dangerous and entertaining. The actual words of his song were merely foolish, but in his presentation, with his grimaces and bodily movements, his way of winking suggestively and lasciviously licking the corners of his mouth, it had something indecent and vaguely offensive about it" (Mann, 1599). (Compare Wolff's use of a similar character in the person of Riley in "An Episode.")

The setting of the story furnishes a fascinating backdrop for the development of Wolff's view of the nature of relationships. Though the ship is making its maiden voyage, the two couples at the center of the story are no longer fresh and virginal; indeed, Nora and Howard, both in their 70s, are near the end of their long voyage, while Stella and Ron, newlyweds, are at the beginning of what looks to be a bleak future. And any purity Bill Tweed once had has long since turned to scornful manipulation. The name of the ship, the *William S. Friedman*, evokes the prosaic "everyman" aspect of this cruise—the thematic direction Wolff desires in this stark analysis. And, ironically, no one on board is a "freed man." Each is entangled in some permutation, perhaps even perversion, of love.

The setting of the ship contradicts the stereotype of the "Love Boat," where couples celebrate marriage, romance, and love under a full moon sparkling across the dark open sea. Wolff wishes to upset the stereotype with what he sees as the more likely truth, the more realistic possibilities. This play off the expected is exemplified even in the names of the shipboard chefs Tweed introduces as Monsieur and Madame Grimes—the last name jarring the ear after the French, forcing the shock of prosaic truth into the idealized, the romanticized. When Tweed and Stella have sex in the lifeboat—the stereotypical location for such romances—the reader has already reached judgments about the two characters that preclude words like *shipboard romance* and *love*.

Furthermore, Wolff stages this story rather than sets it realistically. The characters perform on a ship seemingly empty of other passengers. This isolation produces a dramatic and disquieting atmosphere. Interestingly, Wolff makes the reader imagine more complete surroundings and thereby underscores the dissonance between the expected romantic setting and the problematic nature of the real relationships on board the ship.

Howard, a mischievous and cantankerous old man, is for the most part unblinkingly honest; he pulls few punches. He recognizes his daughter's lack of intelligence, and his assessment of his wife Nora's appearance is direct: "Sick, she looked more than ever like Harry Truman, for whom Howard had not voted" (*Garden*, 90). On this voyage Howard's lack of love for Nora emerges, as does his recollected fear of being torpedoed by a German submarine years before as he sailed home from World War I. "Howard had a sense of things catching up with him" (*Garden*, 90).

When Stella and Howard dance, Stella talks about their mutually passionate natures and informs Howard that she and Ron, though newlyweds, have an open marriage. Nora is angered by their contact and guesses the nature of their conversation. She forces Howard to admit Stella's resemblance to Miriam Selby, obviously a woman for whom Howard once felt affection—indeed, must have loved. Though the affair is more than 50 years distant, it resurfaces (like the German submarine Howard fears) to threaten his and Nora's peace of mind. Howard hollowly assures Nora of his love, and she quickly calms down. Later, when he and Stella, alone, talk about love, Howard is unable to confess that his life with Nora has been a travesty. Instead, he says that marrying Nora was "the smartest thing I ever did" (*Garden*, 97); love, he says, does not last, cannot be trusted.

And yet the surfacing of Howard's repressed feelings about Miriam Selby and Nora are instigated by a woman who, if she represents the alternative for Howard—a life of unbridled passion—comes across as unsavory, perhaps sinister. She is decadent, having packaged her sensuality cheaply: "Stella had platinum hair going brown at the roots and long black fingernails" (*Garden*, 92). When they danced, "Howard could see the dank glimmer of gold in her back teeth" (*Garden*, 93). Her brief liaison with Tweed and lack of consideration for her newlywed husband, Ron, make her a carnal partner for Tweed, the equally opportunistic master of ceremonies on this perverse love boat. If, in a rather unexpected way at the end, Nora is costumed as Venus, Stella, in a "low-cut peasant girl's smock" (*Garden*, 98), is the venereal.

Bill Tweed is the most abstract, symbolic character in the story. Sinister, glib, and superficial, he is a sexual opportunist who talks endlessly of the virtues of love in the huckster's voice of product marketing. Even more than Stella, Tweed represents the degradation of romance. In the spotlight as master of ceremonies, sporting his Errol Flynn mustache, he is reminiscent of a cabaret emcee sarcastically mouthing clichéd phrases of love. For him the old are "senior sailors" (*Garden*, 90), children are the "poor man's riches" (*Garden*, 91), love is "the artillery of heaven" (*Garden*, 98).

Wolff's harsh focus is best illustrated in the final scene of the story, where the characters assume costumes that disclose their personalities. Ron, the cuckolded and ineffectual husband, is dressed as a Confederate officer, which accentuates his gallant but defeated attitude toward Stella. Stella herself wears a tiara of fake diamonds and the bawdy dress of a peasant girl. Though a champion of the sensual and the romantic, she is plainly cheap and decadent, using the pretense of love as Tweed uses it—to achieve sexual gratification. Howard is dressed elaborately in a buccaneer's costume with eye-patch and sword. He is described as "a sort of gentleman pirate" (*Garden*, 97). Though it seems an oxymoronic phrase, it does describe Howard well. If Stella is correct in her perception that Howard is a passionate man who should be free to love as many women as he desires, then he could be pirate-like in his flouting of conventions. Yet aboard the *Friedman* (freed man), Howard has not only been reminded of his past with Miriam Selby but has been forced to acknowledge his responsibilities to Nora. Attracted to the licentiousness of Stella and Tweed, he remains the gentleman attached to the duties of devotion.

Nora, dressed in a toga, is Venus, the goddess of love and desire. At first this may seem a cruel irony. But actually it turns Wolff's theme a little toward the positive. When asked by Tweed to come into the spotlight and deliver a testimonial to the audience on how two people can complete "a hundred years of love" (*Garden*, 99), Nora rises, suddenly powerful, and forces the unwilling Howard to accompany her. "Howard shrank back but Nora pulled him along. He let her lead him to the middle of the room, unsettled by her forcefulness" (*Garden*, 99). Though her practical and naive sentiments about nurturing such a lengthy relationship are savagely undercut by Howard's bleak assessment and Stella's leering grin, Nora surprises Howard and the reader with her strength and determination. She is fully aware of Howard's feelings toward her; she has become, over 50 years, the familiar, the trustworthy. Yet she is the only character in the story who takes action to save her relationship with another. Howard has realized his need for Nora, but at the conclusion must turn "slowly around to escape Stella's grin" (*Garden*, 100). Nora, however, is open with Howard: "Nora moved close to him, pressed her cheek to his" (*Garden*, 100).

"Maiden Voyage" is a cynically symbolic story about the nature of love. For the characters in the story, love is an easily mouthed cliché, serving as a mindless precursor to sex, or something long forgotten, abandoned in the distant past only to rise occasionally as a marker of regret. For the sensualists, Tweed and Stella, love is carnality devoid of obligations. For Nora and Howard, the question of love is more complex and problematic. It is quite easy for Howard to say that love does not last, cannot be trusted. Many couples marrying in the flush of passionate romance realize that over the years commitment requires some transmutation of that first passion into channels more durable than physicality. But most relationships at least *begin* with love of some sort. "Maiden Voyage" makes it evident that while Nora loves Howard, he has never loved her. And this she knows full well. In a way, for Howard to profess duty and devotion to her seems as vacuous a claim as Tweed's and Stella's declarations of love. Only the cuckolded Ron appears to be genuinely in love, and the story dismisses him as a fool.

Certainly the actions of Nora at the story's conclusion show her as decisively intervening to assert control over her marriage and the vacillating Howard. For her, duty outlasts love; indeed it can replace it altogether. What Nora claims is her rightful place in Howard's life, a place due her because of her long tenure. At the end of the story, as Nora forces her cheek against him as they dance, Howard must turn away from Stella's knowing grin.

Throughout the collection Wolff has written about the uneasy relationships between people. In "An Episode" and "Face to Face" the reader comes to believe that contact between couples can lead to sympathy and understanding. Even in "Next Door" there exists the inkling of change through awareness of the need for it. But in "Maiden Voyage" the lives of Nora and Howard are beyond alteration. For them love has not gradually come to mean an elderly couple's fond familiarity with each other. Obligation is what holds them together. And while such a bond may be stronger than the transient sexuality of Stella and Tweed, it is unfortunate that there is nothing more.

"Worldly Goods"

"Worldly Goods" is the story of the corruption of one man's virtue. Davis is a southerner (his name evoking Jefferson Davis, President of the Confederacy), whom Wolff equips with a sense of politeness and honor almost antebellum in their composition—and just as archaic. Such characteristics are sharply counterpointed by the northerners, in this story epitomized by cynical New Yorkers, antithetical to Davis's polite, self-effacing demeanor. In this setting, his attributes are magnified until they become almost ridiculous, and most certainly impractical, as he attempts to deal with people interested less in some abstract ethics of correct behavior than in self-protection and urban survival. He is much like the character Prince Myshkin in Dostoyevsky's *The Idiot*, whose truthful conduct and unartful social manners rouse more contempt and pity than admiration. The prince is told he is "so strange" that he is "not like other people." He operates in the world from "innate inexperience," an "unusual simplicity of heart and . . . lack of any sense of proportion."[10]

Wolff's story opens with Davis sensing a need for personal change. Typecast by people as conservative and predictable, he rebels by purchasing an old car that reminds him of his youth in Louisiana. The car becomes the central symbol in the story; to Davis it represents his youth, a time of lively innocence in a place understood and comfortable, but it is also symbolic of anachronistic sensibilities vulnerable to victimization. Wolff's symbolic use of the automobile and his presentation of the dichotomy of North and South is boldly obvious.

Further on in the story, Wolff creates a "them" versus "us" equation that places people like Davis and Clara—who is typified as weak and subject to her husband's physical bullying—at the mercy of "city-smart" survivors who not only detect the weak and ineffectual but who often prey on them. When her car collides with Davis's, Clara frets that she will be blamed because she is a woman. "You know how they always talk about women drivers . . . they'll claim it's my fault in the end" (*Garden*, 103). Though unspecified by her, she likely means those people who can negotiate city traffic, who rarely get into car accidents, and who can cope with such situations if they do. Wolff develops an affinity between Clara and Davis, and the reader supposes that Clara's eventual scheme to blame the accident on him probably results from her fear of her husband's brutality. The division of "they," the competent, cynical city-dwelling northerners, and "us," the impotent potential victims, is seen more clearly when Davis goes to Clara's home to convince her to drop her fraudulent claim. It is not just the fear of her husband that keeps him in his car across the street; it is the certainty that no matter how well-intentioned his visit, his reasons for it will be subverted:

> If he got out his car and went up to Clara's door, they would find a way of using his honesty against him as they had used his good manners against him. He pitied her and he pitied himself.
> Oh Clara, he thought, why can't we tell the truth? (*Garden*, 113)

Though certainly not a Christ figure amidst the decadence of wealth and power, as Myshkin is in *The Idiot*, Davis is, on a lesser plane, the polite and gallant southerner among egocentric New Yorkers. His is a sense of honor not only foreign to the modern city but potentially disastrous to the person upholding it. It is his consideration that initiates the plot of the story. He commiserates with Clara's distress; he takes partial blame for the accident to make her feel better. The reactions of the city dwellers around him are intriguing; they sense the presence of someone unusual. Davis's attitude is irregular and upsetting. It is admired as antique; pitied as chivalrous and romantic. It enrages many of the characters in the story, though they almost immediately apologize as one would after having spoken too harshly to a child.

The reaction of the insurance adjuster is a good example of this and is central to "Worldly Goods." He is fearful of the city around him and especially bigoted toward blacks. He is incredulous that Davis wishes to tell the truth in the accident report they must file. He espouses the notion that in the city it is every man for himself; to have no protection from people—which the falsified report would provide—is asking to be victimized. But the adjuster has had some earlier experiences with southerners and stereotypes Davis's behavior. "Down there you have all that tradition. Honor. Up here . . . all they know is grab. I tell you, it is hard to be a good man" (*Garden*, 107). The facile categorizing of Davis's virtue as foreign to the modern city is an easy way to deal with it. Here the story recalls Flannery O'Connor's "A Good Man Is Hard to Find," an examination of the position and nature of virtue in an increasingly violent and meaningless world.

Even at the moment of Davis's corruption—when the adjuster reveals he has not submitted the truthful account of the collision and conspires with Davis to concoct the false one he suggested earlier—

the adjuster admonishes Davis for the trouble his politeness has caused. "No more polite," he tells Davis. "This is time for impolite" (*Garden*, 111). And at the story's conclusion, when the adjuster telephones Davis to invite him to dinner as a friend, he quickly berates Davis's attitude and, just as quickly, apologizes, seemingly unable to fully comprehend and handle anyone whose attitude practically begs for victimization and, at the same time, demands at least grudging admiration.

Such reactions to Davis prevail throughout the story. The husband of the couple from Louisiana accuses Davis of ostentatiously displaying his virtues and of never being satisfied with things, only to immediately apologize. The second car repairman is frustrated by Davis's inability to quickly ascertain the nature of the proposed insurance scam. Davis becomes a simple victim for repairmen and the thieves who eventually steal the old automobile. For others, however, who recognize his vulnerability and begrudgingly sense some virtue absent in themselves, he is an object of pity, ridicule, and grudging respect.

At the end of the story, Wolff returns to the dual nature of the old automobile, the central symbol of "Worldly Goods." At first, when the car thieves drive down Davis's street, his dream of the car is the "memory" of it. In the dream he and a friend are again in Louisiana, speeding along a back road at night. They are drinking and singing, the recollected moment one of vivaciousness, of shared innocence. But out in the street, in the "actual" car, the thieves are the ones singing, and when they cause the engine to backfire, Davis is startled from his sleep, feeling the explosion in his heart. For the "actual" car is now a symbol of Davis's antiquated, if compromised, values. Throughout the story the car is described as a classic automobile worthy of admiration but impractical for daily use. The repairman warns Davis that even though it looks good after being repaired, it does not function very well; Davis needs to be wary of broken locks and failing brakes. Immediately after the purchase, Davis, convinced of its impracticality, decides he'll drive it until it falls apart.

With his vestigial southern honor besmirched, Davis will not become the outcast Prince Myshkin did. Instead, having lost his honor, he may have gained a more canny understanding of the city. In truth, the car and his archaic code of conduct, which the car represented, have been stolen. In the future he may become a city dweller, more like his friends from Louisiana who have adapted to the city, maybe even more like the claims adjuster; certainly he will not be himself again in the old sense of the word—a Clara, a victim of the cynical, the "street-smart." But such a loss reduces a person to some lower denominator. What is lost is much more precious than what is gained; the exchange of virtue for cynicism, though perhaps in this case necessary, is unfortunate.

The theme of "them" versus "us" as presented in "Worldly Goods" is a variation on a theme that runs through several stories in this collection. The lives of others appear mysterious and inexplicable. Often there is a desire on the part of a character to fashion his life along other lines, to adapt himself to his surroundings. In "Smokers," the unnamed boy desperately desires to be accepted at Choate, to become what he is not—a self-confident (though shallow and vain) person like Talbot, in other words one of "them." Davis, in contrast, is a reluctant participant in his conversion from "us" (the vulnerable outsider) to "them" (the streetwise city dweller).

"Wingfield"

The power of this optimistic story resides in its brevity and simplicity. Told by a first-person narrator looking back on his experience of army boot camp and the Vietnam War, the story introduces a soldier named Wingfield, with whom the narrator trained in boot camp. An emblem of youthful innocence, Wingfield is held in contempt or punished by the soldiers around him who have lost this quality in themselves. The story is about the narrator's recovery of this innocence, of a part of himself he believed he had largely relinquished even before arriving at boot camp and that he was certain had been destroyed later in Vietnam, when his platoon was massacred in a night attack.

The narrator, like many other soldiers in boot camp with him, comes to despise the sleepy-headed Wingfield. Wingfield pays no attention to the training that will be vital to his survival in battle. He drifts through it all, a chuckle-headed farmboy tired from chores and oblivious to his need for this masculine wisdom. A somnambulist, he symbolizes a boyish lack of guile, and so remains in the background as an incomprehensible object of derision by the more worldly-wise recruits.

During a training exercise the narrator attacks Wingfield, asleep and vulnerable, the epitome of innocence, and at that moment feels brutally superior in his mastery of the knowledge of boot camp. His training has created someone capable of the desire to kill the pitifully weak Wingfield. And in that moment the narrator despises Wingfield as a victim. His strength of mission and purpose places him in a hierarchy as victor to Wingfield's victim. "From now on [Wingfield's] nights would be filled with shadows like me, and against such enemies what chance did Wingfield have?" (*Garden*, 120).

Yet there are levels of innocence and levels of experience. This manly world of recruits involving deadly lessons in ambush and patrol is itself only a boy's game of playing soldier. The night of the training maneuvers the narrator talks of the "dead" soldiers as shot from behind and sent to the parking lot, which had become "no longer a parking lot but the land of the dead" (*Garden*, 119). Later, in Vietnam, the narrator is awakened to a more deadly reality: the carnage of the "real" war, where the dead do not come back to life at the conclusion of the game. After the massacre, one of the narrator's fellow soldiers, named Parker, writes to the narrator from the hospital, where, recovering from malaria, he has escaped the slaughter. The narrator refuses to answer Parker's inquiry, suppressing the names of those who died in the massacre. In hiding the devastation from Parker, he cloaks it with his own soul.

Almost a decade after the narrator's part in the war ended, Parker and his family arrive at his home unexpectedly. The narrator, who lost any vestige of youthful innocence in Vietnam and has become prematurely old in his habits, perceives that Parker will want "an accounting" (*Garden*, 120). Parker—himself "a jovial uncle of the boy he'd been" (*Garden*, 120)—thinks that the narrator should marry and that he is too serious about things. Parker's wife comments, "You remind me of my grandfather" (*Garden*, 121). Then the beginning of the narrator's rediscovery of his battered innocence begins as Parker forces him to speak of their dead comrades, "name after name into the night" (*Garden*, 120). But it is Parker's incredible news of Wingfield's survival, the survival of that half-awake boy, that changes the narrator at the end of the story. Wingfield, glimpsed by Parker only six months earlier in a train-station waiting room, his mouth open in his usual peaceful sleep, survived not only the pranks of boot camp but the terrors of Vietnam. He appears unscathed, a constant among the levels of shattering experience capable of drawing a contemptuous finger (in training) or hard steel (in battle) across a person's throat.

The narrator reaches a conclusion about himself after the Parkers leave his house: "Then I rummaged through the garbage and filled the dogs' bowls with the bones and gristle Parker's wife had thrown away. As I inspected the dishes she had washed the thought came to me that this was a fussy kind of thing for a young man to do" (*Garden*,

121). Outside, in the backyard, he acknowledges the presence of those things that bring death and make victims of us all (with his finger to Wingfield's throat, he had once seen himself as this force): "I sensed the wings of the bats above me, wheeling in the darkness" (*Garden*, 122). But now he can recoup a portion of that innocence he thought he had completely lost. He feels himself "a soldier on leave," "careless and go-to-hell." He toasts the whole world around him that is full of experience and innocence, things active and terrifying, asleep and peaceful: bats in the dark, insects, the "snoring earth," "closed eye of the moon" (*Garden*, 122), nodding and sighing trees. Now at peace with himself, no longer the prematurely old man, having relieved himself of the names of the dead and having received the incredible news of Wingfield's continued presence in the world, he falls back on the grass to sleep and dream.

The first story in the collection to exhibit an unalloyed optimism at its conclusion, "Wingfield" offers a complete connection between the narrator and his life. In "Face to Face," one character triumphs, but another is defeated. In "An Episode," Brooke's adultery inflicts pain on his innocent wife as it heightens his sensitivity. In "Worldly Goods," innocence is perceived as outmoded and ridiculous in its inability to provide Davis with survival skills. Here, in "Wingfield," there is no ambiguity. Innocence is alive in the world; Wingfield has survived Vietnam. The seemingly lost simplicity of the narrator's childhood is recovered. As in Marcel Proust's *Remembrance of Things Past*, time has been regained. It is interesting to compare "Wingfield" with "Smokers." In the latter, the young boy is desirous of becoming more sophisticated and less naive; in "Wingfield," the unnamed man celebrates his renewed return to feeling like "[a] boy who knows nothing at all" (*Garden*, 122).

"In the Garden of the North American Martyrs"

The title story of the collection is in many ways not typical of the others. Though set in academia, as is "An Episode in the Life of Professor Brooke," it is a much stronger indictment of the cruelties inherent in that world. By enlarging on this theme, Wolff criticizes all who abandon love and charity for power and pride. Unlike the other stories, "In the Garden of the North American Martyrs" turns on a rather surprise ending; on reflection, though, it is not hard to recognize the archetype of the "worm turning."

The best-known story of this type is James Thurber's "Cat's Cradle." There, as in Wolff's "In the Garden," the central character, who is usually shy and inoffensive to a fault, gathers sudden and surprising strength of character and triumphs over the situation at hand. More artfully crafted than most such stories, Wolff's takes on the form of a parable—this also setting the story apart from most others in the collection, written in the tradition of modern realism. The symbolism and humor are painted broadly, in unmistakable strokes most nearly approaching the parable qualities of "Maiden Voyage" and farthest from the more subtle techniques of a story like "Wingfield."

Mary, meek and risking nothing, is repressed. Fearful of the challenges and uncertainties of the world, she has ensconced herself in academia, where risk taking is minimized, though, ironically, egotism, territoriality, and the will to power can be menacing to the modest and the shy. But she has learned to camouflage herself with ridiculous eccentricities and corny, hackneyed humor. She forms herself into "something institutional, like a custom, or a mascot—part of the college's idea of itself" (*Garden*, 124).

When Brandon College is bankrupted by a financial officer's speculation—a risk Mary cannot imagine taking—she finds herself across the country in Oregon. From here to the end of the story, the landscape plays a symbolic role, much as it does in "Hunters in the Snow" and "Maiden Voyage." Oregon, where she gets a job teaching at an unnamed "experimental college" (*Garden*, 125), is foreign to Mary, practically deadly in its damp, chilly weather, which begins to bring on in her an unspecified malady. When in her third year there Mary receives a letter from Louise, a former colleague in history from Brandon, mentioning a job opening where Louise now teaches, near Syracuse, New York, Mary decides to apply (note that since 1980 Wolff has taught at Syracuse University). Later, arriving in Syracuse, she senses a vague connection with the landscape, feeling as if she has come home. In a book on the Iroquois and the Jesuits that she will put to effective use at the story's conclusion, Mary "read about the area with a strange sense of familiarity, as if the land and its history were already known to her" (*Garden*, 126). When Louise picks Mary up at the airport, Mary tells her she has a feeling of déjà vu. Later she imagines herself at home in this landscape, with "a silver moon shining through bare black branches, a white house with green shutters, red leaves falling in a hard blue sky" (*Garden*, 129). The landscape holds more than one meaning for Mary. It is connected with the primitive brutality of the wilderness; it also represents her hope for a secure job and a home.

The reader immediately recognizes Louise's symbolic dimensions. She is an academic egotist who dismisses Mary chiefly because she is a "nonentity" as a historian and a person. For her, Mary is a comfortable, unthreatening confidant. The greatest cruelty Louise perpetrates against Mary is her failure to forewarn her that her job candidacy is a sham, that a university regulation requires an interview with at least one woman candidate. When she does admit this, Louise still harps on her own vulnerability and unhappiness, not caring about her betrayal of Mary's trust. Indeed, in a rather broad stroke, Wolff makes Louise the author of a biography of Benedict Arnold, the betrayer of West Point, the very synonym of traitorous egotism. Interestingly, Arnold is also connected to New York State, the landscape of his betrayal and the site of his earlier glory during the French and Indian War. In fact, some of his supporting forces against the French would have been the Iroquois about whom Mary is reading. And, ironically enough—and most fitting in Wolff's discussion of power, exploitation, and cruelty— the Iroquois, important supporters of the British, will be destroyed by the internecine warfare caused by the political divisions among them during the American Revolution.

Just prior to Mary's presentation to the faculty, Wolff convenes the unsavory academics. Louise, the most fully realized academic, is joined by an unnamed scholar who pompously denigrates Brandon College, and by the history department chair, Dr. Howells, a bombastic and dishonest man. Each is complicitous in the heartless betrayal of Mary's trust and expectations, which recalls the sacrifice of Davis's antiquated automobile on the altar of survival in "Worldly Goods." Microcosmically, Wolff presents a lacerating view of the supposed humanists of academia who exploit those weaker in character and lower in professional rank than themselves and who prove to be dishonest, unfeeling, self-aggrandizing, rude, and pompous.

Wolff extends his horizon beyond the meanness of academia to include all who prey on the innocent, the less strong. The story becomes an excoriation of such egoistic brutes. The college is a copy of a college in England—still one of the most class-conscious of countries, once an exporter of empire and exploiter of weaker nations. The college motto is "God helps those who help themselves," the maxim used by the robber-baron alumni who "helped themselves to railroads, mines, armies, states; to empires of finance with outposts all over the world" (*Garden*, 131). These same men managed to deny their services to their country in times of war. "There were not many names [on the plaque honoring the dead]. Here, too, apparently, the graduates had helped themselves" (*Garden*, 131). In truth, the soul of the college is a vast inhuman power generator, which Mary sees on a student-conducted tour of the campus. The student calls it "the most advanced in the country" (*Garden*, 131), and Mary sees that for him "the purpose of the college was to provide outlets for the machine" (*Garden*, 132).

Mary's mixed feelings about the landscape (as wild and domesticated), her betrayal by Louise and the other academics, and her insight into the machine-like nature of the college and the rapacious nature of its graduates all spur this normally weak woman to bravery, the "turning of the worm." The Iroquois exerted their force over the weaker, innocent Jesuits. In turn the Indians were subjugated, exploited, and ultimately eradicated by the English colonists, many of whom themselves would be victimized by generations of graduates from this very college, who exploited men and nature. The motto "God helps those who help themselves," translated as image, becomes the victim with a boot always on his throat.

Mary's triumph actually begins when she concludes that part of her faculty lecture drawn from the images and words of others and starts to speak for herself. Usually shy, never original or thought-provoking, she simply blurts out the injunction at the story's end: "Mend your lives" (*Garden*, 135). Speaking as a victim, she implores her shocked and angry audience to renounce pride and strength. "Turn from power to love. Be kind. Do justice. Walk humbly" (*Garden*, 135). She sermonizes, refusing to be called down by the crowd, turning off her hearing aid against their cries for her silence. Always silent before, she continues her sermon. We sense the seething of an uncivilized audience. The wilderness has long ago given way to the domesticated garden, and the martyrs are no longer openly, physically tormented. Still, there is cruelty, exploitation, domination—the modern methods of torment, only more subtle.

The title story of the collection, "In the Garden" provides some interesting insights to consider. Throughout the collection, in numerous ways and subtleties of degree, characters have been faced with the possibility of mending their lives, of turning from potentially harmful attitudes toward expressions of love through humility, kindness, and justice. Sometimes the need to mend has been perceived only vaguely, as in "Next Door," "Smokers," and "Passengers." But at times the mending seems impossible because it is the reader, not the characters involved, who comprehends the need for the advent of love and kindness; such is the case in stories like "Hunters in the Snow" and "Maiden Voyage." Throughout the collection, though, some characters seem to have taken Mary's injunction to heart: Brooke in "An Episode," Virginia in "Face to Face," and, most forcefully, the unnamed narrator in "Wingfield."

Self-betrayal is a theme in several of the stories. It is dominant in "Smokers" and "Worldly Goods," in which protagonists distort their own lives in reaction to the world around them. In this regard, "In the Garden" serves to reinforce even more strongly the message of the story preceding it, "Wingfield." For in "Wingfield" self-betrayal is reversed and a life is mended by the reintroduction of an innocence that cannot be obliterated by the world's cruelties.

Like a spiritual jeremiad, Mary's words are both a warning and a prescription for behavior. A weak, lonely, powerless creature, Mary becomes powerfully vocal and insistent. The message she delivers reverberates throughout the story collection and so defines Wolff as a moralist, taking part in a tradition in fiction that encompasses such diverse writers as Graham Greene, Albert Camus, Andre Dubus, and Flannery O'Connor.

"Poaching"

"Poaching" is the story of Wharton—nervous, imaginative, self-conscious—on the threshold of middle-aged change but hesitant and fearful. The central conflict in the story is symbolized by the two cartoon characters he draws. Wharton believes that Pierre the Trapper is like his father, but this character is also expressive of Wharton's virtues and vices. Like Pierre, Wharton is antimaterialistic and prone to smugness and sermonizing. Unlike Pierre—and, we suppose, his father—Wharton is aware of his irritating habits and is critical of them—though not often given to self-censorship. This awareness is the reason Wharton finds Pierre "obnoxious" and has grown "mortally tired of the Trapper and his whole bag of tricks" (*Garden*, 143). This ability to see himself clearly is a virtue crucial to the theme of "Poaching." His self-awareness makes him desirous, but also fearful, of change.

Though Wharton is too much the officious adult with his son, George, he tries to temper his interference. "[Wharton] stopped himself. George was not a man, he was a boy, and boys should not be hounded all the time. They should be encouraged. . . . Wharton decided that he should let George see his lighter side more often" (*Garden*, 142). He admits to his failures with his estranged wife, Ellen, when she castigates him for "his nagging, his slovenliness, his neglect of her. . . . The other charges she had brought against him were true and he did not challenge them" (*Garden*, 143). When she picks the perfect present for George, Wharton's smugness about materialism surfaces, but he admits "[t]he world of things was not alien and distasteful to her. . . . He despised his possessions with some ostentation; those who gave him gifts went away feeling as if they'd made Wharton party to a crime. He knew that over the years he had caused Ellen to be shy of her own generosity" (*Garden*, 145). When Ellen accuses him of thinking himself better than she, he does not deny it. "During most of their marriage he *had* imagined that he was too good for Ellen. He had been wrong about that and now look at the mess he had made" (*Garden*, 146).

The counterpoint to the comfortable and profitable but static world of Pierre the Trapper is Wharton's creation Ulysses, a dog searching for his master in the goldfields of the Yukon. Ulysses of legend is much like Pierre. He is cunning, self-assured, a master of men and situations. But he is, in addition, the searcher, the wanderer, the restless adventurer. Here Wolff may be making use of the Ulysses of the Tennyson poem and the image of the old sailor urging his retired crew to imagine another voyage of possibilities, where "[s]ome work of noble note, may yet be done."[11] Where the legendary figure is desirous of change, Wharton is more human in his dimensions, more fearful and hesitant. "Pierre still paid the bills, and Wharton could not afford to pull the plug on him" (*Garden*, 143).

Wharton recognizes his faults but sees no way of changing without risk. Indeed, he is afraid of change. He fears the complications of George's developing personality; he is concerned about Ellen's move to Victoria. All of this is dramatically intensified when Wharton hears rifle shots outside, coming from somewhere on the land he and George live on, and assumes that a poacher is taking aim at his wildlife.

The supposed poacher becomes emblematic of an obstacle that must be confronted but that magnifies one's dread of it. A poacher, by definition, is one who takes what belongs to another, who trespasses on another's property. To pass on to something else, to another stage in his life, Wharton must confront the poacher. To strike out for new horizons with Ulysses and leave the static and boring Pierre behind, Wharton must stir himself from his inertia. Wharton is the creator of Pierre and the author of his own familial dilemma, and, as it turns out, he is also the creator of the poacher. "He even knew what Jeff Gill [the suspected poacher] would look like: short and wiry, with yellow teeth and close-set, porcine eyes. He did not know why Jeff Gill hated him but he surely did, and Wharton felt that in some way the hatred was justified" (*Garden*, 152).

Having awakened to rifle shots down at the pond "pale and trembling" (*Garden*, 151), Wharton sets off unarmed—a most reluctant Ulysses, "afraid to walk his own land" (*Garden*, 152). There are no sirens to overcome, no Scylla and Charybdis; his mud-caked boots offer the only physical challenge. But an anger rises in him over his own impotence. And though he earlier expressed reservations about carrying the rifle as "a sign of weakness" (*Garden*, 141), he now thinks that if he had brought the rifle he would be capable of using it. "He had felt foolish and afraid for so long that he was becoming dangerous" (*Garden*, 152).

With delightful humor, Wolff deflates the tension of the ending without making it any the less significant. Indeed, without irony at Wharton's expense, the ending, in which the poacher is discovered to be an elderly beaver, the rifle shots his tail slapping the surface of the pond, becomes a statement on how the worry and fear invoked by the unknown can waste considerable energy. Later, when Wharton slips in the mud, Wolff further humanizes the theme by having Ellen tell him "he ought to take a roll in the mud every day, that it would be the making of him" (*Garden*, 153). Surely Pierre would have sidestepped the treacherous ground.

Wolff concludes by tempering the jubilant moment at the pond. Having conquered his fear, Wharton wants to see the future spread out before him in some certainty, along the patterns of his own expectations—a course, naturally, the future cannot be made to take. The lesson of Ulysses, after all, is the lesson that setting forth brings with it the unexpected and unplanned for—this is the adventure of the future and its attendant risk. For Wharton, the beaver "had been sent to them; they had been offered an olive branch and were not far from home" (*Garden*, 154). The jetty that thrusts out into the beaver's pond appears to move like a ship of discovery, "sliding forward like the hull of a boat" (*Garden*, 154).

Wolff, however, refuses to romanticize the future as Wharton would have it. Though George's subsequent maturity frees Wharton from worry and Ulysses liberates him from Pierre, the decrepit beaver is shot as an environmental nuisance, and Ellen and Wharton never live together again after these few days. Realistically, the conflict between the desire for a secure present—projected forward into an expected future—and the trepidations over the uncertain and unknowable is always present; even the moment of Wharton's triumph is the moment of his very human wish for a comfort so certain in its qualities that it will last forever.

This is again an optimistic story, as were the two immediately preceding it—"Wingfield" and "In the Garden"—and as are others throughout the collection. "Poaching" is most comparable to "Next Door." In the latter, the narrator vaguely understands his predicament in terms of two movies. In the one on television, the expected occurs and the conclusion is unsatisfactorily pessimistic. The narrator's imagined movie is unclear, but in it the people are explorers and their final discovery is hopeful and appears fulfilling. With Wharton, Pierre represents inertia; he is tired of the stagnation of his life. At the same time he is afraid of taking risks, of the fundamental uncertainty of the future. Wharton rises to the challenge of the poacher only to find that his fears are the major obstacle to new achievements. Here the gentle and humorous irony of the ancient beaver-as-poacher serves Wolff's purpose well.

"The Liar"

This last story in the collection shares similarities with the title story. Each ends with the positive self-assertion of the protagonist. And each moves beyond the qualities of realism into an almost mystical, transcendent state. Like "In the Garden of the North American Martyrs," "The Liar" delivers a larger philosophical theme than most of the other stories. The story of James, the first-person narrator, is the story of a young boy achieving an epiphany with slightly delayed consequences, which will determine much of the direction of the rest of his life. Examining a theme much explored in Western literature, Wolff places the boy's parents at opposite ends of responses to life.

The father is much admired by James, who comes to understand and share his father's fear of life. His father is a cynic whose "jokes were how he held himself together" (*Garden*, 166). He is bright but egotistical and opinionated—"a curser of the dark" (*Garden*, 162). He loves to read the newspaper and rail at the foolishness in the world. He encourages James's cleverness, his intellectual glibness, with word games at the dining-room table. The father's condescending and worldly attitude, expressed in his "fixed and weary smile" (*Garden*, 163), helps shape James's personality.

Very much a social misfit, James's father is occupied with his own opinions. He has few friends, and those who come to dine are victimized by his terrible cocktails, given names that deride honorable professions. One of his friends, Dr. Murphy, concludes quite correctly that James's father took a mediocre path in life so as never to test his limits. His easy intellectual cynicism is attractive to his son, especially as it contrasts with his mother's attitude.

James's mother is antithetical to his father. Not a reader, she is puzzled and uneasy about the word games at the table; she often feels she might be the butt of family jokes. A devout Catholic, she prays by rote and does not "consider originality a virtue" (*Garden*, 156). She is, however, a compassionate person of action. During an outing at Yosemite with the whole family—James, his brother, and two sisters—it is she who scares away the bear in a significant scene. The cynical and intelligent father cannot act because he imagines the consequences of the bear's violent reaction. Fearful of action, full of doubt, he remains frightened at the picnic table. The mother, oblivious to the danger, knowing something must be done, throws rocks at the bear, simply, directly, and successfully. At this moment, James cleaves to his father, whose fear of life's consequences he shares. But it is his mother who saves his life.

After the father's death, the mother's actions and optimism hold the family together. "She made lists of chores and gave each of us a fair allowance. . . . She told us frequently, predictably, that she loved us" (*Garden*, 165). Having once attempted to channel her husband's energy away from condemnation and contempt—"to take up causes, to join groups" (*Garden*, 163)—she now tries to get James to help others and so take his mind off too constant an examination of his feelings. When Wolff writes that James's mother has always wanted him to sing in harmony with the others, he has chosen the perfect activity in which to express her desires for her son. Singing in harmony requires the ability to blend in with others, to take part in a communal activity. It is a worthwhile expenditure of energy, enriching the singer and the audience. It is a sharing of oneself with others, something James's mother does most strikingly with Frances, a woman at church whom she understands has need of attention, a sympathetic ear—the same woman James disparagingly categorizes as paranoid.

Soon after his father's death, James develops the unhealthy habit of telling morbid lies. Although his father seemed to achieve some sense of serenity before he died, his death undoubtedly magnifies James's fear of life's risks. Intuiting more than verbalizing James's frailty, his mother encourages him to "think more about other people" (*Garden*, 169) in an attempt to correct in him the self-absorbing despondency she failed to correct in her husband. But it must be James who comes to this realization, and he does so in a moment of epiphany following their discussion of Frances: "I thought of Mother singing 'O Magnum Mysterium,' saying grace, praying with easy confidence, and it came to me that her imagination was superior to mine. She could imagine things as coming together, not falling apart" (*Garden*, 172).

This epiphany, however, is an intellectual realization; the real proof of change is an emotional and practical application of a realization. James's mother decides to send him to stay a few weeks with Michael, his older brother, who now lives in Los Angeles, where he works helping the unfortunate. When the bus breaks down on the road, James begins to tell his fellow passengers lies. But these lies are not morbid; instead, they are lies about his helping refugees to find jobs and housing. Though these stories are not true and the song he sings to the passengers is, in its words, a fabrication of language, his offerings to the riders are honest attempts to transcend his egotism, to please others, not to call attention to himself.

Wolff concludes by giving us a composite in James of both his parents. The stories he tells the passengers are clever lies learned through the parlor games, a tribute to his father's intellect. But they are meant as solace to the weary passengers, and his comfort does take the form of a song. And though he is not singing in harmony, he is sharing himself openly. In the cathedral of the bus James becomes voice transcendent of body, communion lifted above self.

"The Liar" bears some resemblance to "Smokers," the only other story in the collection concerned with an alienated boy. Each boy is striving to find his individual voice. In "Smokers," the narrator strives to increase his distance from his middle-class parents through stories that remake his parentage and past into something more grand and romantic. The reader leaves the boy vaguely aware of the sacrifice of his virtue to achieve his goal and can only hope the boy will eventually realize his mistake.

In contrast, the lies James tells at the conclusion of "The Liar," and the language he fabricates into a song, soothe the bus passengers. Here the boy seems to have conjoined his parents' divergent personalities into his own redemptive message. Though still lies, like those of the boy in "Smokers," these are not self-aggrandizing. Instead, they are manifestations of James's earlier intellectual epiphany that clearly defined for him the destructive nature of his father's personality and the constructive nature of his mother's. Here a lie that consoles and obliterates egotism appears as a truth worth singing. The language literally transcends meaning and becomes a language of love, what Wolff calls "an ancient and holy tongue" (*Garden*, 175). Selfish lies can mask oneself and pervert development; unselfish lies can allow a person to recognize his own true voice.

Apprehending the diverse and subtle themes generated in a collection of 12 stories can be a daunting task. Yet rendered in Wolff's lucid prose certain elements are quite transparent. Often irony plays an important part. Sometimes gentle and humorous, at times mystifying, the literary device serves Wolff's realistic purposes. His irony is lifelike in its dimensions; it arises from a fundamental contradiction in the human condition: the inability of intelligent human beings to comprehend their lives.

In "Next Door," "An Episode," "Smokers," and "Passengers," the characters yearn to alter their lives after contact with others whose lives seem more dangerous and vital. There is macabre irony in "Hunters in the Snow," where superficial friendship is rekindled over the expiring body of a former friend. Sometimes the irony appears cosmic in nature, as when the foolish, unprepared Wingfield safely muddles through the Vietnam War as more canny men perish. The irony is situational in "In the Garden," where the once meek Mary roars out her admonitions. And in "The Liar," a young boy's lies provide more comfort than truth.

The title story also provides a way of understanding the themes at work in the collection. By choosing to title the book after a single story, Wolff emphasizes the theme of "In the Garden," causing it to reverberate throughout the collection and demanding that the reader see the stories in relation to Mary's jeremiad. When she cries out to her hostile audience, she demands that they mend their lives through the exercise of love, kindness, and justice practiced with humility. And the stories in the collection can be interpreted as stories about the need to reform and improve one's life. At their most bleak, in such stories as "Hunters in the Snow" and "Maiden Voyage," mending seems impossible. In "Next Door" and "Passengers," the protagonists are only vaguely aware of the need for change. In "Smokers" and "Worldly Goods," the central characters have betrayed themselves and so are left in uncertainty. Brooke in "An Episode" and Virginia in "Face to Face" manage to improve their lives, though the process of change is costly: Brooke becomes an adulterer; Virginia loses Robert. Only in "Wingfield," "In the Garden," "Poaching," and "The Liar" are the characters' lives thoroughly mended.

The reader should notice the existential dimensions of Wolff's mending process. Two of the basic tenets of twentieth-century existential philosophy are the alienation of people from one another and from themselves. An existentialist like Camus (a favorite writer of Wolff's), writing in *The Plague*, states that only through reconnecting with ourselves and one another—through communal contact and loving sympathy—can we recognize our human potential. Mary's struggle to achieve her voice, and the struggles of Wolff's other characters—successful, partially successful, unsuccessful—define the collection as illustrative of the need to overcome personal and social alienation.

The arrangement of the stories within the collection further emphasizes Mary's admonitions and serves to conclude the book on an optimistic note of connection. The first eight stories offer varying degrees of mending, but, beginning with "Wingfield" and continuing to the end, Wolff imbues the stories with unalloyed hope. The narrator of "Wingfield" recoups a boyhood innocence almost obliterated in a brutal world. Mary's meek voice gives way to the prophet's profundity. Wharton casts off his stagnant past and emerges into a satisfying future. And, in "The Liar," James finds that the melody of communion outweighs the truth of the lyrics. The book opens in "Next Door" with the narrator's vague notion that something in his life needs changing. *In the Garden of the North American Martyrs* concludes with James's triumph. Lives can be mended.

Back in the World

Introduction

> The desire to subvert and to probe and to question and to dig
> the foundations out from under everybody and to represent
> fraudulent selves to the world, all that is contained and legiti-
> mized in imaginative acts. What is destructive and also self-
> destructive is transformed. You don't give it up. You just find
> a way of using it.
>
> Tobias Wolff, from an interview with Bonnie Lyons and Bill
> Oliver

Between the publication of *In the Garden of the North American Martyrs* in 1982 and *Back in the World* in 1985, Tobias Wolff had been generously recognized. *In the Garden* had received the St. Lawrence Award in fiction and been published in England as *Hunters in the Snow*. His novella, *The Barracks Thief*, had won the PEN/Faulkner Award. And Wolff had been honored with a Guggenheim and a National Endowment for the Arts fellowship. His individual stories had been published in prestigious magazines and collected in anthologies of prize-winning fiction.

Just as stories within collections are compared with one another, critics naturally compare story collections. Some reviewers admired the obvious differences between Wolff's two books; others were disconcerted and argued that the first collection was the better of the two. Overall, the reactions were favorable. If some were hesitant, none despaired of Wolff's talent and so looked forward to his third collection.

Mona Simpson found the stories in *Back in the World* to be "in a more somber mode. . . . A plainer, more subdued quality of language is immediately apparent."[12] She thinks the opening sentences of the stories display voices that "feel omniscient, universal, with biblical resonance" (Simpson, 38). She notes that "Wolff works with the same thematic concerns, the same passion for moral questions, but his fictional canvas is sparer and simpler. He has, for the most part, abandoned the domestic, the familiar righteous citizen, and all his incumbent irony. He has chosen more dramatic, emblematic characters" (Simpson, 38).

What Mona Simpson says is true. Wolff's gift for probing the paradoxical, commonplace mysteries of life is intact. His stories are still modern in approach, though more of them are downright pessimistic, particularly "Sister," "Soldier's Joy," and "Leviathan." But many of the stories resonate with themes of duty and responsibility for the lives of others: "Coming Attractions," "The Missing Person," "The Poor Are Always with Us," "Desert Breakdown, 1968," and "The Rich Brother." And among these last stories, Wolff has created his most obvious moral parables. Taken together they are like a jeremiad; they amplify the words of Mary in "In the Garden of the North American Martyrs": " 'Mend your lives' " (*Garden* 135).

Wolff was aware of the differences between the collections. "I think the stories [of *Back in the World*] are connected by subject matter and style. The two collections seem to me to be different. . . . I wanted a unity of voice and perspective from one story to the next. I wanted you to read it like a novel, with the same kind of narrative presence in each story."[13]

To achieve this "narrative presence"—what Simpson describes as "omniscient"—Wolff eliminated stories told from the first-person point of view. Where four of the dozen stories in *In the Garden* were in the first person, all of the stories in *Back in the World* are in the third-person limited omniscient. This definitely shades the thematic concerns and voices in the collection.

The title of the collection originates in a phrase American soldiers in Vietnam used to refer to their lives back home. Wolff explains the curious use of a phrase from a single story to title an entire collection: "It wasn't just Vietnam. 'The world' is what people in religious orders—nuns and priests—call secular life. That's the way Jesus talks about it: The world's yoke is heavy, my yoke is light. So 'back in the world' is an expression which has many connotations. I thought it was an expression that caught the spirit of a lot of the stories" (Lyons and Oliver, 9).

"Coming Attractions"

As in previous stories with children as central characters—"Smokers" and "The Liar"—Jean in "Coming Attractions" is precariously balanced between childhood and maturity, at the juncture of the self and its relationship to the world beyond it. "Smokers" concludes with "the boy" having just betrayed his conscience to enact his plan for personal power. James in "The Liar" turns his lies outward for the benefit of others and so shows promise of breaking the grip of destructive self-absorption.

Ensnared between the worlds of childhood naivete and adult complexity, Wolff's children are further confused by the conditions of their home lives. In "Smokers" the young boy actively denies his middle-class past by reinventing his parents. In "The Liar" it is the death of James's father that precipitates his elaborate lies.

Jean's rite of passage begins as the reader learns the details of her 15-year-old life. Alone in the movie theater where she works, Jean is a confusion of child and adult. We learn that she and her friend shoplift "everything else that wasn't bolted down," in what for Jean must be a means of asserting herself as well as disdaining adult conventions.[14] Yet when she pretends an abandoned coat is a body, she is scared by her own imagination.

A victim of volatile teenage sensibilities, Jean locks herself in the absent manager's office for safety, only to open the door when she begins to feel trapped. Uncertain, insecure, lonely, bored—a tumult of emotions—Jean phones her father but reaches his new wife, and the reader understands a source of Jean's confusion.

At first the cruel thoughtless child, Jean remains silent when Linda answers. But then "she heard the fear in Linda's voice like an echo of her own . . . she couldn't do it" (*Back*, 5). Her quite sudden sympathy for Linda's fear, her ability to recognize her own weakness in another, lies in sharp contrast to her earlier playacting and silly, risky shoplifting. The story now very much becomes one of the seesaw actions of a young child/woman.

Debunking the myth of the cruel stepmother, Wolff presents a woman who is nice and understanding. Still, it is her father to whom Jean wishes to speak, and it becomes apparent that he will not allow himself to be disturbed by serious problems. Linda reminds her that her father is "more of a good news person" (*Back*, 7). More mature at this moment than her father, Jean realizes the truth of what Linda says. With this exchange Wolff introduces a further thematic complexity. Jean's father, her mother, Mr. Love, and Mr. Munson are adults who exhibit childish tendencies. Wolff reveals the selfish, uncertain, confused sensibilities residual in many adults.

Thwarted, trapped by her father's foolish rules, Jean slams down the receiver only to phone her home a few moments later. In a conversation with Tucker, her younger brother, Jean learns of her mother's irresponsibility. Out on a date with "Uncle Nick," she has yet to return home. Jean soothes the boy, and her wisdom of the moment helps maintain Tucker's calm. She provides him with the emotional comfort her mother, the adult, should have supplied.

Failing to find the number of her English teacher—with whom she has either had an affair or has fantasized about having one—she chooses a name for a prank call. One moment the responsible adult with her brother, she turns her anger with her parents—her sense of being victimized and trapped—on a stranger over whom she can exert some juvenile power.

Having phoned a Mr. Love (an interesting choice), Jean pretends the man has won a prize. When the man grows wary of Jean's personal questions about his love life, she suddenly blurts out her transgressions to the stranger—her thefts and her licentiousness. Mr. Love, like Linda, doesn't conform to expectations. Instead of slamming down the receiver, he becomes Jean's confessor, the perforated telephone receiver the grille in the confessional.

Becoming childish himself at times, admitting his naivete has caused others to take advantage of him, he listens to Jean's tale of adultery with Mr. Hopkins. When Mr. Love suggests she attend church, Wolff lambastes the contemporary Catholic mass by having Jean disparage an Easter service where the priest played "a tape of a baby being born, with whale songs in the background" (*Back*, 11).

For a while completely honest, Jean drifts into playacting again with stories of the cruel games she plays with Mr. Hopkins, her tattoo, and her motto "live fast, die young" (*Back*, 12). Then, desirous of an adult's attention, she says she's "totally out of control" (*Back*, 11) and asks Mr. Love to bawl her out.

When the arrival of Mr. Munson, the theater manager, interrupts her phone call, Wolff resumes his theme of confusion between the worlds of adults and children. Once a good, athletic skater, Mr. Munson comes from skating at the mall with a broken ankle and bandaged forehead. Upset with himself, his age, his lost grace, Munson foolishly blames his karma. As with the other adults in the story, Mr. Munson is not a very good model for a 15 year old. If the usual initiation story involves the progression of a childish perspective to a more mature one—the progress from simplicity to complexity—then Wolff wishes to redefine this particular progression in "Coming Attractions." In Wolff's view adults often regress: they act childishly out of selfishness, despair. Children, then, on the cusp of adulthood, sometimes act with a spontaneous sensitivity, courage, and selflessness. Perhaps the *tendency* of adults is to act like adults and children like children, but chronological age is no sure marker of maturity.

The last scene begins with Jean's unsympathetic reaction to Mr. Munson's pain and anguish. Insensitive for the moment, incredulous of such silliness in an adult, Jean dismisses his pleas for understanding, pleas not dissimilar to those she just made to Mr. Love.

At home alone, with Tucker in bed, Jean reads the love letters her father still sends her mother, letters that betray Linda. Disgusted by the correspondence, baffled by her own sexuality, Jean undresses and playacts a prostitute in front of a mirror. Interrupted by the awakened and frightened Tucker, she becomes comforting and sensible, promising him a special day tomorrow if he'll go back to sleep.

Jean goes outside and descends into the icy water of the apartment complex's pool to retrieve a discarded bicycle Tucker had mentioned to her earlier. This is the first *action* the reader sees Jean undertaking for another. The scene is reminiscent of D. H. Lawrence's "The Horse-Dealer's Daughter," where the reluctant doctor enters the pond to save Mabel from drowning and emerges in a moment of baptism and rebirth for them both: "At last, after what seemed an eternity . . . he rose again . . . gasped . . . and knew he was in the world."[15] Jean's descent into the numbing water and struggle with the dead weight of the bike, her emergence, choking from the cold grip of the pool, is a symbolic rite of passage, of rebirth, that Wolff has prepared for throughout the story.

But Wolff eloquently leaves Jean only half-reborn, still suspended on the edge of the pool, half in, half out of the water. "In a little while she would pull it out. No problem—just as soon as she got herself back together" (*Back*, 16). The reader has great hope for Jean, and yet Wolff has argued that life's "Coming Attractions" are an uncertain mixture of childish and adult sensibilities in a state of flux. The reader believes that Jean will leave the pool, the bicycle in tow, but children-as-adults and adults-as-children, Wolff says, are ways of the world.

Though the central characters in Wolff's three stories about young people—"Smokers," "The Liar," and "Coming Attractions"—are confused and often resort to lying to create supposed adult personae, "Coming Attractions" provides more insight into the complexity of the dilemma. By exploring Jean through her relationship with the adults around her, Wolff conveys a sense of how muddled the adult-child world really is. And yet within his realistic method, Wolff concludes the story with an emblematic baptism evoking the more parable-like qualities of "In the Garden" and "Worldly Goods." The rite of passage aspect of the story compares well with John Updike's "A & P," James Joyce's "Araby," and Sherwood Anderson's "I Want to Know Why."

"The Missing Person"

One of the longest in the collection, "The Missing Person" is a religious story. On one level, it concerns Father Leo, a "missing person" who repurchases the loving kindness he has misplaced over years of bitter career disappointments and the resultant cynicism. On another level, Wolff uses Father Leo's plight as a means of expressing what Wolff considers to be missing from the contemporary American Catholic Church.

As a youth Father Leo chose the priesthood as a vocation for its lure of romance and ministration to the suffering. Only slightly less extravagant than Emma Bovary in her love of the mystical and exotic in religion, Leo imagined himself a self-sacrificing missionary among the Aleuts, creating "a life full of risk among people who needed him and were hungry for what he had to give" (*Back*, 19). But shortly after his ordination he is sent to Seattle to manage Church bazaars and to visit the infirm. After serving the senile parish priest for years, Leo is pained to see among the priest's papers scathing and often false reports of Leo's abilities. Despairing, Leo considers his youthful love of a woman he would have married "if he had not felt even greater help-lessness before his conviction that he should become a priest" (*Back*, 20). For Leo, as for Emma Bovary, love and religion are mysteries. But where Flaubert condemns Emma's confusion of the two, Wolff seems to encourage their confluence in Father Leo. The priest has turned the mysteries of his heart into an answer to God's call. His love has become his religion, and his religion—at least at the outset—is loving self-sacrifice. Where Emma's desires are always voluptuously egotistical, Father Leo's are to aid the needy.

Passed over to replace the parish priest, Leo is chosen to teach religion in a Church school. Beginning uncertainly, he soon comes to flourish among the children he recognizes as needing his direction. Unfortunately, Leo does not keep up with the changing curriculum and is fired after an overseer finds his "ideas . . . obsolete and peculiar"

(*Back*, 22). Here Wolff begins to portray Father Leo as antithetical to the worldly concerns of the modern Church. Ministering to the students, a good teacher who makes contact with them, he is fired because he sees no reason to update his methods. When Leo is sent to the dead-end job of chaplain at the convent of Star of the Sea, the reader learns that the previous chaplain ran off with a nun. Embittered at reaching the end of his career while still a middle-aged man, and surely far from his romantic early goals, Leo knows that this is "a job for an old priest, or one recovering from something: sickness, alcohol, a breakdown" (*Back*, 22).

It is through the antics of the nuns at the convent that Wolff takes his sharpest jabs at the contemporary Church. "Something had gone wrong at Star of the Sea" (*Back*, 22), Wolff writes, where nuns are either decidedly sad and silent or elated and boisterous. Though Leo is to be their confessor, many of the nuns meet his presence with open derision. The nuns, once cloistered in meditation, now go forth in the world and become local disc jockeys and travel agents. "The director of novices described herself as a 'Post-Christian' " (*Back*, 23).

Perceiving the depths of the trouble, Leo complains to the Mother Superior, who quickly tires of him. Instead "she lived in her dream of what the convent was . . . a perfect song, all voices tuned sweet and cool and pure, rising and falling in measure" (*Back*, 24). (This harmony of song, with voices "tuned" and "perfect," is reminiscent of "The Liar," in which James's mother wants him to sing in harmony with the family and in which he does sing a solo that soothes the passengers on the bus.) Irritated with him, the Mother Superior first suggests he might want another job—both of them knowing this position is the last he will ever be offered. She then recommends that Leo begin helping Jerry, the convent fund-raiser. Leo is glad to accept this strange offer, for "he would be getting out every day, away from this unhappy place" (*Back*, 25).

Certainly Wolff is taking a religiously conservative view of the Church. Where Easter Mass in "Coming Attractions" had degenerated into a tape of a baby crying and a whale singing, the convent here is replete with worldly nuns who ignore their spiritual duties. Wolff's opinion that the Church has lost the ideals of self-sacrifice and ministration to those in need is an abstract generalization he uses Father Leo to represent. Feeling himself at the end of a mostly useless career and in an untenable job, Leo abandons the Church for the world when he becomes Jerry's partner in extorting money from contributors.

Part 1

A professional confidence man, Jerry reminds the reader of Mr. Tweed in "Maiden Voyage." Tired and dispirited, Leo warms quickly to Jerry's ebullient personality. When Jerry tours the dilapidated convent with Leo in tow, the reader perceives the decay of the Church— "cracked foundation," "old pipes," "scummy water in the vast basement" (*Back*, 25–26). As Jerry schemes for the improvement of the convent, he becomes Wolff's outlandish savior of the Church—from the Church's modern point of view. Who better to represent the Church in the world than a huckster?

Like the cynical Tweed, Jerry is gauche and crass, a money changer in the temple with "rings spark[ling] on his thick, blunt fingers" (*Back*, 25) and his face made over with "little scars under his eyes" (*Back*, 26). He is artful, with a rather crude ability to lie to donors directly and outrageously. Never as urbane and glib an evil as Tweed, Jerry is the essential "root of all evil." Overt, insatiable, delighting in manipulation, submerged in public and private lies, he has obliterated his person for money; indeed, he is one of the three "missing persons" in the story, along with Leo and, later, Sandra. That the Church would select such a person, oblivious to everything but his power to bring in cash, is one of Wolff's strongest indictments of the modern Church.

Thwarted by circumstances, Father Leo allows Jerry to become his corruptor. Jerry likens them to outlaw partners fleecing the foolish. As Jerry lies to wealthy patrons by playing on their own disappointments and weaknesses, Leo sits silently by, head bowed, the official sanction to the extortion. Leo likes Jerry, who *acts* in the world and gets something done, and so is very unlike Leo, who has been unable to realize even the simple dream of becoming a good and useful priest. Soon he is rationalizing Jerry's conduct. "They [the donors] had plenty of money, too much money. . . . Anyway, Jerry was a performer, not a liar. Lying was selfish, furtive, low. What Jerry did was reckless and grand, for a good cause" (*Back*, 28). Further corrupted, "Father Leo came to need these pleasures, most of all the pleasure of watching Jerry have it his way with people who were used to having it their way" (*Back*, 29). He thinks that people, seeing him happy, now say of him: "*What a jolly priest.* . . . He wanted to look like someone with good news, not like someone with bad news" (*Back*, 31).

After Jerry tells Leo he is bad as Jerry and fills Leo's head with a mixture of lies and half-truths about his own life, Leo tells Jerry that he became a priest because he murdered a man who was beating a woman. The reader can compare this outrageous lie with the opening of the story and the two real reasons the young romantic chose the Church: to sacrifice himself and to serve suffering humanity.

If at this point Father Leo has begun to "go missing" as a person himself, it is his trip with Jerry to Las Vegas that allows him to recover himself and, by extension, his hope for the Church. And there is no better place than Las Vegas at Thanksgiving as a backdrop for the story's end. A city created and controlled by mobsters, an artificial city of the plain devoted entirely to Mammon, Las Vegas lives on the weaknesses of the flesh, the flagging of the spirit. It is the abode of "missing people." As Sandra, the third missing person in the story, later says about Las Vegas, "When you reach a certain point it's the logical place to come" (*Back*, 49).

With Jerry quickly gone missing completely, absorbed into the garish, debilitating city, Leo soon encounters another of the city's visitors, Sandra. Repelled by the badly sunburned older woman, who is in obvious need of conversation, Leo is too self-absorbed with his concern for Jerry to pay her any attention. The second time she seeks him out, Leo, who is not wearing his clerical collar, tells her his name is Slim and again puts off her need to confide in him. But on returning to his room Leo experiences a crucial event that redirects his attention. Victimized by a hotel burglar who has stolen the money Leo had saved by not gambling, Leo "sat on the bed. The hollowness spread downwards into his chest and leg. . . . He began to talk to himself. . . . He struck himself over the heart. He gripped his shirt in both hands and tore it open to his waist. He struck himself again. Back and forth he walked" (*Back*, 42). Later he decides not to call the police, because "[t]hey would ask him questions; he felt uneasy about that, about explaining his presence in Las Vegas" (*Back*, 43). And Leo is concerned that if he brings Jerry into it, the police would become interested in the con man with an alias.

Though he has not had a complete epiphanic revelation of his straits, when he next meets Sandra, he expresses his concern for her for the first time by suggesting she get in out of the sun. Then, perceiving her loneliness, he sees "no reason to hurt her feelings" (*Back*, 44) and keeps up his end of the conversation. When he tells her he is a priest, her angry, disbelieving response is confirmation of how far he has gone missing himself and how much a part of Las Vegas he seems. "You're no priest. . . . If you were a priest, you wouldn't have let me go on like I did. You wouldn't have let me make a fool of myself" (*Back*,

45). Previously unable to explain to anyone why he is in Las Vegas, Leo can only admit, "I'm a little confused right now" (*Back*, 45).

When Jerry calls Leo and admits he has lost all his money and much of the convent's, Leo begs the con man to return with him to Seattle, where Leo says he will take the blame. Jerry refuses and so remains a missing person. Immediately after, Sandra calls, frightened of the hotel burglar and noises at her door. She asks Leo, as a priest, to come to her aid. Reluctant, Leo pounds his pillow and then tells her he is on his way. Thus Wolff has Father Leo recover himself as he tries to help another missing person. Alone with Leo, Sandra confesses her previous lies about being happy in Las Vegas. When Leo admits it is an awful place, Sandra points out that many people wash up here finally; it is a repository for people gone missing.

When Leo grows more vitriolic in his condemnation of Las Vegas—and by extension, the world—as a "dangerous" place where "everything is set up so you can't win" (*Back*, 50), Sandra tries to temper his anger by reminding him that some do win. Leo counters that he has yet to see any winners.

But coming quickly away from a wholesale jeremiad, Leo thinks of his newfound notoriety with the nuns as a murderer and smiles. Then, swiftly, he becomes intimate in his conversation with Sandra. At first pitying her, when she asks if, hypothetically, he could love her, Leo cagily admits he could. Then he admits he admires her spirit in coming to such a city alone. When they share a laugh, the human connection is finally made between them. Leo continues to talk to her. "He did not think, he just listened to himself. His voice made a cool sound in the stuffy room" (*Back*, 53). Leo's words become the litany of a priest, the soothing comfort of a ritual, his presence more important than what he says (like the song of James in "The Liar"). All through the night, Father Leo stands watch over the sleeping woman like a spirit intervening between the world and the vulnerability of innocence. He imagines, finally, a coyote out in the desert beyond with a rabbit in its mouth. Although this image is part of his earlier romantic view of the priesthood—suffering in an exotic place—he has fulfilled the most important, and up to now unrealized, obligation he first set for himself: to live a "life full of risk among people who needed him and were hungry for what he had to give" (*Back*, 20).

This story is one of Wolff's most religious. It takes the form of a diatribe against the Catholic Church in America with an illustration in Father Leo of how the Church can be saved. With its obviously parabolic qualities of moral instruction, the story can be compared with "Worldly Goods," "In the Garden," and "The Liar." For Wolff, the modern Church is in decay. Too involved in the fashions of the world, the Church must anchor itself in the solid nature of men like Leo— that is, men like Leo as he is at the story's end. Instead of abetting missing persons, like Jerry and the worldly nuns, the Church must recover the lost through priests like Leo. Unless this happens, the Church becomes, collectively, missing—lost to itself and its suppliants.

The story of the Church's recovery is embodied in the personal narrative of Father Leo's rehabilitation, his recovery of the lost ideals of his youth. For Christianity begins with one person suffering for another, with one brother serving as another's keeper. How else to bring home a wayward Church than through the redemption of one person's soul?

"Say Yes"

One of Wolff's shortest stories, "Say Yes" carries an interesting variation on one of his most prevalent themes—the inability of one person to know and understand another fully and the resultant mystery that enshrouds and often romanticizes the unknowable. This story is reminiscent of several permutations of this theme in *In the Garden of the North American Martyrs*—notably "Next Door," "Face to Face," and "Smokers." But the brevity of "Say Yes," its understated style and cryptic tone recall the works of minimalists such as Mary Robison and Raymond Carver, Wolff's close personal friend and colleague.[16] While the theme is certainly historically one of Wolff's concerns, his minimalist tendency toward terseness and the symbolic expansion of the most mundane of objects and events clearly reflects contemporary literary influences.

The reader of *Back in the World* has only to compare this story with the preceding one, "The Missing Person," to see the differences between Wolff's usual attention to character and thematic development in scenes and this quick evocation of the same. Wolff, a writer of modern short stories that dismiss nineteenth-century introductory explications and usually achieve closure shy of completely explaining themes, is no Peter Taylor who writes from this earlier tradition. But neither is Wolff a protégé of the minimalist school begun with Hemingway and most recently manifested with Carver and Robison. And yet "Say Yes" does remind the reader of a more quotidian version of the battle between the two lovers in Hemingway's "Hills Like White Elephants," in which brevity is achieved through the ruthless paring away of extraneous details. In both, the sparse background becomes symbolically meaningful; the dialogue is rendered in terse sentences; the core of the dilemma remains unspoken. All of this, like the theme itself, remains cryptic and elliptical, demanding that the reader take an even more active part in supplying the missing information.

The unnamed husband helps his wife wash dishes. He is arrogant in his complacency and self-assuredness. He believes he understands her completely and so can interpret the smallest nuances of her facial expressions. He is confident and certain of his role in their marriage, though a bit manipulative, as if he is the more intelligent, more orderly of the two.

When the complication is introduced that will bring about the resultant crisis—should blacks and whites marry—the husband is firm in his conviction that only people of the same culture, people who share the same language, can find understanding and familiarity together. "A person from their culture and a person from our culture could never really *know* each other" (*Back*, 58).

Angered by what she terms his "racism" and speaking out for the power of love to diminish such differences, her growing tension is symbolized by the handling of the dishes she is washing. The increased distance between them is represented by the dishwater, which "had gone flat and grey" (*Back*, 58).

When Ann cuts herself on a submerged knife, the husband springs into action, but it is a patronizing and studied response and recalls his earlier thoughts about his predictable role in the marriage. "He hoped that she appreciated how quickly he had come to her aid. He'd acted out of concern for her . . . but now the thought occurred to him that it would be a nice gesture on her part not to start up the conversation again, as he was tired of it" (*Back*, 59). For him, their relationship should be one of quid pro quo in which each understands the nuances of the other.

Not only does Ann not drop the subject, but she brings it to a head when she asks him if he would have married her had she been black. Seeing himself as the voice of reason in both a patronizing way and, for Wolff's purpose, reacting against her passion—always the darker, more dangerous, and uncontrollable part of the self—the husband gets

Ann to admit that this is an impossible hypothetical. "He took a deep breath. He had won the argument" (*Back*, 60).

But Ann, adamant and unbending before his powers of logic, continues until he admits that he would not have married her had she been black, and thus from an unfamiliar background. Indeed, what is at play here is the old saw, "Familiarity breeds contempt." But with Wolff it is not contempt as much as it is stasis.

Upset by the event, the two begin obvious shows of indifference. The husband, wishing for the status quo to return, a bit rattled by the vehemence of her reactions, cleans the kitchen until it reminds him of when it looked new, "before they had ever lived here" (*Back*, 61). When he takes out the trash he feels "ashamed that he had let his wife get him into a fight" (*Back*, 61) and thus, the reader understands, upset his controlled response to their relationship. When he considers their marriage he denies the faintest shadow of difference and recalls instead "the years they had spent together and how close they were and how well they knew each other" (*Back*, 61).

Coming back inside to a dark house, which symbolizes the advent of something unusual, the husband wants to recapture the security of familiarity. When he tells her through the bathroom door he will make it up to her, she asks what it is he will do. Surprised by her demand, he is perplexed by her tone of voice. "But from a sound in her voice, a level and definite note that was *strange* to him, he knew that he had to come up with the right answer" (*Back*, 62; emphasis added). Uncomfortable with her sudden "level and definite note," which both upsets his control of their situation and promises something "strange," the husband says that he would marry her if she were black. Ann's response—"we'll see"—continues the new note of indefiniteness in their relationship.

No longer in control, the husband waits anxiously in bed in the darkened bedroom. And, as Wolff did in "Coming Attractions," he truncates the close of the story. The husband is literally "left in the dark." He is obviously sexually aroused by the possibilities to come, but he is also frightened by his loss of control. The reader leaves him nervously awaiting some promise of the extraordinary. "His heart pounded the way it had on their first night together, the way it still did when he woke at a noise in the darkness and waited to hear it again—the sound of someone moving through the house, *a stranger*" (*Back*, 62; emphasis added).

A lighter permutation on a recurrent theme, "Say Yes" speaks to the necessity of the out of the ordinary to awaken the heart. Too self-assured, too intellectually ordered and controlling, the husband is comfortable only in the security of the familiar. He believes that he fully knows his wife and that his expected role in their relationship is empowered by this knowledge. Yet when Ann becomes unfamiliar and "strange," his heart reacts as it did to the passion and suspense of their wedding night, when he did not know her. Wolff, who often writes of the yearning people have for the mystery and romance of the unknowable in the lives of others, here writes about the damage done when another's life is taken for granted, when what is strange or unique has long been submerged by the manageability of the familiar.

Making use of a term the writer D. H. Lawrence would have used in describing their unbalanced relationship, Ann has been "obliterated" by her husband's stronger, more dominant role in their marriage. But when Ann becomes unknown again and "a stranger," and so introduces into the fearful husband's life the variable of mystery, she acquires power as the one in the relationship able to insert the startling pleasure of the unpredictable.

"The Poor Are Always with Us"

Beginning with a title paraphrased from the New Testament with the corollary themes of responsibility for others and the perils of wealth, Wolff's story is an almost religious parable on the duties of the able toward the less fortunate. Though not as directly expressive of a religious attitude as many Flannery O'Connor stories, or, more recently, "A Father's Story" by André Dubus, "The Poor Are Always with Us" reminds the reader that Wolff is a moralist.

Where materialism was castigated in "The Missing Person" and was an aspect of the dilemma in "Passengers," in this story it describes the essential nature of the characters. The story begins with the line, "The trouble with owning a Porsche is that there's always something wrong with it" (*Back*, 65); the central character, Russell, is quickly drawn as a Silicon Valley whiz kid of the 70s with far more money than wisdom.

The conflict begins at the Porsche mechanic's garage, where the spirit of the times is Bruno, mechanic to the wealthy, whose patrons smoke marijuana in his office while he works on their expensive cars with the skill (and probably expense) of a neurosurgeon, "wearing starched white smocks and wielding tools that glittered like surgical instruments" (*Back*, 65). Here Russell manages to irritate Dave, another customer. Once a Silicon Valley computer genius, himself, Dave has run out of ideas while still a young man. Lonely, Russell interjects a self-righteous pronouncement into a conversation between Dave and his African-American companion Groves, castigating an acquaintance who has been fired for selling technology to the Japanese. Dave is immediately antagonistic toward Russell, whom he calls "a little weenie." Though Groves attempts to mediate between the two, their exchanges continue until, in a moment of foolishness, Dave wagers his car against Russell's over the identity of a singer on the radio, and he loses.

The conflict initiated, Wolff elaborates on the character of Russell. Young and with more money than he needs, Russell is reminiscent of Glen in "Passengers," who may have already lost himself in the quest for material self-gratification. Like Glen's, Russell's milieu is the essential "me" of those times. His apartment complex is peopled by childless couples whose dogs have been trained not to bark so they won't intrude on others' lives. Yet Russell has not gone as far as Glen. Attacked earlier as immature, with no right to an opinion, Russell tells Dave, "I know the difference between right and wrong" (*Back*, 67). And later Russell recalls a roommate who disparaged his "uptight" attitude because Russell refused to indulge in the sex and drugs so readily available. Russell keeps in mind a man named Teddy Wells, now 50, who has been divorced six times, spends most of his money on cocaine, and cruises for teenagers. Wolff writes that "Russell just wanted to keep his bearings" (*Back*, 72). Now Russell knows he will not yield to his desire to keep Dave's car, though he rationalizes his right to it. "But all of [his excuses to keep the car] sounded like lies to Russell—the kind of lies you tell yourself when you already know the truth" (*Back*, 70). He feels foolish about the events of the afternoon, and, though he dreams "of being a magnanimous person, openhearted and fair" (*Back*, 71), he knows that most people, like his roommate, would "think he was being fussy" about his values (*Back*, 71).

Prepared to do the right thing and in doing so to keep his "bearings" intact, Russell is thwarted by the neurotic anger of Dave, who sees Russell as some sort of scavenger feeding off the ideas people like him originated. For Dave, Russell represents a thankless progeny unaware of the gratitude they owe to the first Silicon Valley geniuses like himself. Afraid of Dave's belligerence, Russell reluctantly agrees to a second wager, this time the toss of a coin, and wins Dave's station wagon.

Wolff adroitly finishes the scene with Dave stalking down the street on foot followed by his girlfriend, seemingly as unsettled as Dave, screaming after him at the top of her lungs. Luckless, a victim of his character, Dave is now the ultimate California outcast—a man on foot in the most mobile, car-oriented state in an automobile-crazed nation.

When Groves shows up at Russell's apartment to mediate a second time, Wolff provides more insight into Russell's character. Lonely, without a roommate or girlfriend, indeed, it seems without friends at all, Russell lives a monastic existence in an apartment with no pictures, stereo, or television. After Russell sees through Grove's elaborate excuse for Dave's behavior—the Vietnam veteran's syndrome in all its hackneyed aspects—Groves tells the truth about Dave's professional failure. Admitting his fear of Dave, Russell signs the car title over to Groves so he will have no further contact with Dave.

But Groves absconds with the car, now legally his, and Russell is stalked by Dave for a year, all the while preparing for a confrontation by practicing "again and again the proofs of his own decency" (*Back*, 79). Such a showdown never materializes, however, and Wolff collapses the final scene into a brief tableau in which Russell, parked in his Porsche, sees Dave attempt to cross a major street in heavy traffic. Though Russell's life seems to have improved—he is awaiting a date buying liquor for a party—Dave's has not. He is on foot and vulnerable. When he twice "tests his luck" (*Back*, 79) against the traffic, he has none and is forced back to the curb. For Dave there is no help—"no light nearby" (*Back*, 79)—and he is the only pedestrian. Russell expects to see Dave's anger flare up in defiance of the circumstances, but Dave is calm, "wait[ing] his chance. . . . He accepted this situation, saw nothing outrageous in it" (*Back*, 79).

For a moment Russell pities Dave, thinks he would do anything to help him. But just as quickly he denies the possibility of aiding him. "It didn't make sense trying to help Dave, because Dave couldn't be helped. Whatever Russell gave him he would lose. It just wasn't in the cards for him to have anything" (*Back*, 80).

The title of the story is a rendition of an injunction appearing at least twice in the Bible. When Christ rebukes Judas Iscariot for his attempt to prevent Mary from anointing His feet, Christ, recognizing Judas's condescending concern for the poor, says, "Let her alone: against the day of my burying hath she kept this. For the poor always ye have with you; but me ye have not always" (John 12:7–8). Here Christ echoes a passage from the Pentateuch, when God instructs,

"But thou shalt open thine hand wide unto him [the poor], and shalt surely lend him sufficient for his need, in that which he wanteth. For the poor shall never cease out of the land. Thou shalt open thine hand wide unto thy brother, to thy poor, and to thy needy, in thy land" (Deuteronomy 15:8–11).

Often related piecemeal to the layperson as a statement of rather bleak fact, "the poor are always with us," taken in context it is rather an injunction reminding the more fortunate that, according to Scripture, there are always among them those in need of help. Indeed, other than these two versions of the origin of Wolff's title, both testaments are replete with admonitions concerning the right-living person's attitude toward the unfortunate. Taken in context, the caution serves not as a reminder of pessimistic fact but instead a warning that there is always work at hand if one will only take notice.

The reader knows that Russell has a good heart and intentions. He lives a separate, monastic existence in an attempt to "keep his bearings" (*Back*, 72) in a time and place antagonistic to such. Yet simply not becoming one of those lost in the culture of materialism is not the same as actively helping one already engulfed. At the story's end the reader is aware of some slippage on Russell's part. To his Porsche he has added a girlfriend, drinking, and parties. Seeing Dave ensnared in the traffic, vulnerable, car-less, a potential victim of the more powerful all around him, Russell feels his heart go out to him. In an interpretation of the scriptures as statements of pessimistic fact, Russell denies any ability to help, to intercede. There is no risk in the abstraction of pity, of charity of the heart without action. But how much more difficult and dangerous would be an actual, active intervention into Dave's life that would force a confrontation with the frayed personality Russell fears? Indeed, earlier, when Russell might have interceded, he chose the unreliable Groves to shield him from Dave's aggression, thus exacerbating the conflict further.

Perhaps Russell will never become a degenerate, promiscuous Teddy Wells, but he has damaged himself already. He has refused to see himself as Dave, once a talented man, now unbalanced by his bad fortune. Russell sees in Dave's acceptance of his fate no need for intercession. So he tells himself that he is not his brother's keeper, that such unfortunates will always exist on the fringes of society.

But like Glen of "Passengers," trapped in a basement closet and remembering his youthful freedom, Russell feels uneasy. He, too, recalls his childhood, and feeling "a little lost," attempts to locate himself (*Back*, 80). But he is able only to pinpoint a geographic, not a moral, reference. *"I'm on El Comino"* (*Back*, 80), he says, and on his way to a party. He has, it seems, "lost his bearings." Russell reminds the reader of the self-betrayal in "Smokers" and, even more so, in "Worldly Goods." The story also contrasts with "The Missing Person," in which Father Leo recovers his errant self by aiding Sandra.

"Sister"

In "Sister," Wolff, the frequent moralist, lambastes the egoism of the 1970s and early 1980s "me generation." He focuses on the loneliness and despair of a young woman, Marty, by exposing the predatory aspects of her generation's sexual practices. As a secondary issue, he speculates on the new role of women enmeshed in an aggressive approach to sexuality once practiced only by men. Wolff, who through his characters and thematic concerns often reminds readers of their responsibilities toward one another, in this story concentrates on the failure of Marty to succeed; her story becomes the story of Robert in "Face to Face" rather than Virginia, who salvages her life.

At the beginning of the story, Marty is an anxious, excited player of the sexual game. When from her kitchen window she notices two men in the park, she quickly gets ready for playacting, allured by one man in particular, especially the "deep brown color of his skin" (*Back*, 83). She is very conscious of her dress but also worried that she might appear too eager. When "[f]or a few moments she [loses] her image in the mirror" (*Back*, 83), she brings to mind Russell in "The Poor Are Always with Us," "lost" to himself on the roadside amidst the material trappings of the world, as well as Jerry in "The Missing Person." Wolff intensifies this undercurrent of insecurity when, going out, Marty is frightened by a neighbor's dog, which she believes is "trying to get at her" (*Back*, 84) from behind a door. Marty continues on to the park to engage the two men, her inner doubt and vulnerability made apparent by Wolff.

To underscore Marty's self-doubt, Wolff has her take comfort in imagining her brother's hunting trip with his buddies. Antithetical to the cruel, disastrous hunt in "Hunters in the Snow," the one Marty imagines is romantically bucolic, similar to scenes from nineteenth-century novels involving characters like Levin in *Anna Karenina* and the narrator in Turgenev's *Sketches from a Hunter's Album*. She envisions victorious hunters triumphantly drunk and completely at ease in their

situation. Her association to the imagined scene is one of relation—
she defines herself as her brother's sister and, as such, feels vulnerable
and uncertain as she descends the hill to engage the men in pursuit
of sex. Though her generation has attempted to equalize the struggle,
she still feels herself the potential quarry, the victim to the victorious.

When she enters the park, Marty notices some boys playing football.
Wanting nothing more than to turn and run back home so as not to
engage in the playacting that will be necessary between herself and
the tanned man, she watches the young boys, already mimicking adults
by "hunching up their shoulders and shaking their wrists as they jogged
back to the huddle, grunting when they came off the line as if their
bodies were big and weighty" (*Back*, 84). And though their antics make
her laugh, the reader understands her tone as uneasy.

The game, the hunt, the sexual sparring begins with a jolt when
Marty recognizes Jack, the tanned man's friend, as someone who recently abandoned her in a local singles' bar. His vague recollection of
her contributes to the undercurrent of tension, though Marty is too
attracted to the tanned man to flee. While he looks Marty over blatantly,
she notices his "chest . . . covered with little curls of glistening golden
hair" (*Back*, 85). She realizes the two have been talking about sex
when she arrived and that it is "still in the air somehow, with the ripe
smell of wet leaves and the rain-soaked earth. She took a deep breath"
(*Back*, 85–86).

When the three talk, the conversation is superficial and sexually
charged. The two men talk about bikini-clad women and desire, while
Marty makes light of their allusions with banal chatter. The meaningless conversation becomes more complicated in its disingenuousness
when Jack, still vaguely suspicious of Marty, lies about his name. Then
they all exchange false names to protect themselves. Like actors in
roles, they are now free to resume the sexual game without fear of
personal involvement.

Willing to lie, to playact, to manipulate, to take part in the impersonal
singles' bar scene, Marty takes little notice of the tanned man's wedding ring. But when the hood of his jacket falls, revealing a balding
head carefully combed over from one side, Marty does notice this. The
reader is reminded of both the staginess of the encounter and the
vulnerability of everyone involved in it. Where now the man is ashamed
of his bald spot, earlier Marty was afraid her feet would look too big
in her new tennis shoes. Artificially glib in their sexual games, they

nonetheless remain human and fearful of ridicule, of victimization, of the many small details that can betray vulnerability.

But their conversation fails to acknowledge anything remotely personal and remains silly sexual banter. Only when Marty professes her belief in reincarnation—reflecting a Western trend of adopting Eastern religious myths—does the reader see her real despair. "She wasn't even sure she actually believed in it. . . . She had serious doubts, sometimes. But at other times she thought it had to be true; this couldn't be everything" (*Back*, 89). But she could not possibly admit to such a deep concern in the deceitful atmosphere of this conversation; it would leave her too exposed.

Marty's scheme to double-date is thwarted by an errant frisbee that separates her from the two men and places her in the path of a skidding automobile. For a few terrifying moments, Marty sees the careening car in slow motion; unable to move, she believes she is about to be run over. At the last second the car's tires catch on dry pavement and she is saved. But she has dramatically displayed her vulnerability, which is supposed to be carefully cloaked in idle chat and casual sex. "Marty turned toward the park and saw the two men looking at her. They were looking at her as if they had seen her naked, and that was how she felt—naked. She had nearly been killed and now she was an embarrassment, like someone in need" (*Back*, 90). Marty is no longer welcomed in the park, in the superficial dialogue, the theatrical play-acting because she has appeared "naked," vulnerable and human.

Such sympathy and understanding are not available in her world, so Marty walks back to her apartment feeling ghostly, insubstantial. The earth, earlier associated with sex, now "smells of decay" (*Back*, 91). Weakened, unable to pass the snarling dog in her apartment building, she sits on its steps. She realizes she has no one to comfort her, to listen to her fears, to tell her "everything is going to be all right" (*Back*, 91). Her epiphany is as chilling as Eveline's in James Joyce's story by that name. There the protagonist actually flees her chance at a fresh start in life and sets "her white face to him [her lover], passive, like a helpless animal. Her eyes gave him no sign of love or farewell or recognition."[17] Marty believes there will never be anyone for her, and so she never again has to put herself at risk as she did with the men in the park. Very much like Robert in "Face to Face," who looks at Virginia "with sudden panic . . . deciding at that moment always to be alone" (*Garden*, 72), Marty rejects everyone. And like a Hemingway character coming to the realization that a reduced and simple state of existence, no matter how isolating, is best because it exposes one to the least harm, she feels "empty and clean, and did not want to lose the feeling" (*Back*, 91).

At the close of the story, Marty imagines her brother and his buddies, who seem to her, in her romantic way, in charge of their lives, full of masculine camaraderie, while their dogs, like Marty, are left in the cold car, "whimpering to themselves" and "watching the bright door the men have closed behind them" (*Back*, 92).

One of Wolff's most pessimistic views of modern culture, "Sister" recalls "Hunters in the Snow" and Robert's failure in "Face to Face" to reconnect to life. Indeed, Marty differs greatly from Virginia, the protagonist in that story, who is able to salvage a life that might well have gone the way of Robert's. "Sister" contrasts with "Coming Attractions" and "The Missing Person," where central characters are saved from selfish despair through their acceptance of duty to others. And the lies told by Marty and the two men to protect themselves remind the reader of the lies told in "Smokers," "The Liar," and "Coming Attractions," where they serve the purpose of creating an image thought to be more robust and less vulnerable to the world's onslaughts. Marty comes to embody those who resign themselves to defeat and are quite beyond help: Robert in "Face to Face," Jerry in "The Missing Person," and Dave in "The Poor Are Always with Us." Previously, Wolff has made this type of character peripheral, but in "Sister" it is central.

Wolff tells us that Marty feels "empty and clean" (*Back*, 91) and that, at the story's conclusion, she wants to retain this feeling. But where this sort of stoicism of defeat might make sense for a character in Hemingway, a writer whose moral universe dictates that knowledge of limitations is power, for a character in Wolff it is an indictment. Marty has yielded to exclusion from the world. She takes the course of least resistance, as does Robert in "Face to Face" when he decides to retreat into himself and deny the struggle life often demands. By acquiescing to her perceived role as a sister, a woman, even a bitch dog left alone in a truck (by Marty's brother and his friends on their hunting trip)—all controlled by the whims of men—Marty consigns herself to victimhood. Clearly, Wolff is trouncing the societal mores of the times (the 1970s and early 1980s, before the advent of AIDS slowed the sexual revolution). He is also investigating the difficulties women have in adjusting to sexual games whose rules have, for centuries, been imposed by men. But the single most important theme is one seen throughout Wolff's fiction: the difficulty of making genuine, intimate contact with others when to do so is to expose oneself to the possibility of ridicule. It is an indictment of Marty's times that sex is less intimate than straightforward conversation, that actually being naked is less risky than uncovering one's vulnerable humanity.

"Soldier's Joy"

"Soldier's Joy" is Tobias Wolff's fourth treatment of soldiers and his second short story about the reintroduction of the Vietnam War veteran into American society. It also provides the title of the collection in the phrase "back in the world," the soldier's shorthand for civilian life. The phrase resides at the core of this story. Hooper, a veteran of Vietnam now serving stateside, reveals his cast of mind in a monologue of self-revelation that precipitates the murder of the soldier Porchoff: "Back in the world we were going to have it made. But ever since then it's been nothing but confusion" (*Back*, 116).

The dilemma of the Vietnam veteran's reintroduction to society has become a contemporary cultural focal point worthy of such movies as *The Deerhunter* and *Born on the Fourth of July*, numerous novels such as Stephen Wright's *Meditations in Green*, and short-story collections such as Tim O'Brien's *The Things They Carried*. The theme occupied Wolff in an earlier story, "Wingfield." But in that story the narrator is finally able to confront his confusion and to experience a cathartic moment through the story of the soldier Wingfield's survival of Vietnam, representing a survival of innocence that frees the narrator's vestigial innocence to emerge. At that epiphanic moment, the narrator of "Wingfield" becomes "a soldier on leave . . . a boy who knows nothing at all . . . a carefree and go-to-hell fellow" (*Garden*, 122).

But in this story the confusion wins out. Innocence, represented by the soldier Porchoff, is murdered. To Hooper, "contact" does not mean the touch of flesh or spirit; it means the destruction of the enemy, the mindless and stultifying task of sanctioned killing, which bonds fellow soldiers. Hooper tells Porchoff that there is "nothing wrong with you that a little search-and-destroy wouldn't cure" (*Back*, 116). Hooper believes love and faith are formed in the crucible of battle. "Everything was clear" (*Back*, 116). The soldiers in Vietnam "were not separate men anymore, but part of each other" (*Back*, 117). Hooper tries to comfort the startled Porchoff by assuring him that another war is imminent. "I can feel it coming. . . . All you need is a little contact. The rest of us too. Get us out of this rut" (*Back*, 117).

This "rut" is evident at the start of "Soldier's Joy." Hooper is listless, the peacetime military routine enervating in its monotony. He oversees men digging the base commander's pool by hand—obviously just for something to do. Since he has already put in 20 years and has just been broken down from corporal to PFC, his top sergeant tries to convince him to retire. Being "back in the world" is not at all what had been expected by someone who has depended on the military for discipline, for routine, for a direction in life.

Though Hooper has a wife and has a son, the reader learns this obliquely, for they matter little to the soldier. In fact, Hooper seems to have failed as husband and father since his return—another manifestation of the world's confusion. His sex life is as much a routine as his base duty. His lover, Mickey, is utterly and frankly faithless to her husband, a supply sergeant, to Hooper, and to Briggs, another soldier on the base. Even Mickey's bedroom is military—lamps made from brass shells, sheets of parachute silk; Hooper observes that "everything around him" was "stolen" (*Back*, 97). But despite this and the fact that he is a poor sexual performer, Hooper continues his affair with the promiscuous Mickey, because it, too, is a routine. "It was just something he did, again and again" (*Back*, 97).

The action of the story begins when Hooper is paired with Captain King on night-guard duty at the base. King himself is much like Hooper, who realizes that the old captain "regarded him . . . as a comrade in dereliction, a disaster like himself with no room left for judgment against anyone" (*Back*, 99). But Hooper is critical of the captain's lackadaisical attitude. He obviously does not consider himself as far gone as the hopeless King. For Hooper, a "lifer" is still a "grunt," not an officer, and so he believes that he is still connected to the camaraderie of his fellow enlisted men.

In his own element, with common soldiers around, Hooper is able to take charge. He delivers two soldiers to guard the communications center—Porchoff, derided as "Porkchop" by the others, and Trac, who has been to Vietnam and whose face Hooper finds oddly familiar, as if in Vietnam Trac had been a child "running alongside Hooper's APC with a bunch of other kids all begging money" (*Back*, 100). This confusion, one of many in Hooper's life, is a striking one. For in it he blurs young soldiers and childish innocence. The two are confused, as they were in Vietnam, where young, inexperienced boys took on duties that destroyed their innocence. This theme is also expressed in Tim O'Brien's short story "Spin," in which a soldier named Azar straps a claymore mine to a puppy and detonates it. When his comrades look amazed, Azar shrugs his shoulders and says, "What's everybody so upset about? I mean, Christ, I'm just a *boy*."[18] This shattered innocence, which the narrator in "Wingfield" is able to regain, has been completely lost by Hooper; furthermore, he thinks the loss worthwhile if it brings him faith and love through esprit de corps and so centers his life in battlefield activity.

For Hooper, the army supplies an additional incentive. He believes that he behaves better when he is being watched by others and so abrogates his ultimate responsibility for his actions—war is made by politicians; soldiers perform their duties without criticism, mindless as to consequences. Theirs is a brotherhood of honor and duty to others; there is a blood bond that directs enlisted soldiers' lives through the adrenalin rush of combat. Here the grunts follow the orders of officers and make deadly contact with the enemy. And here in battle all is directed toward killing and surviving in a very simple, neat package of duty without responsibility.

Despite this attitude, on this particular night Hooper deserts his duty and goes temporarily AWOL to seek out the licentious Mickey. Hooper seeks "contact" even though it is sexual, something he isn't good at, and with a woman whose favors are liberally dispensed without much pleasure on her part. Still, Hooper has abandoned his post, the base—the companionship of other soldiers—and is seeking something that he can find only "back in the world." On the drive into town he sinks into memory, but Wolff withholds his thoughts from the reader. Are they of civilian life? Of his wife and son? Of Vietnam? At Mickey's, Hooper spies a car belonging to yet another lover he cannot place. He skulks around her house without a definite purpose until one of Mickey's neighbors confronts him. Like some peculiar conscience, the woman berates Hooper for sniffing after a whore. She carries an army pistol and looks menacing and strange, a harridan in a prom dress. "She wore glasses with black frames, and she had on a white dress of the kind girls called 'formals' when Hooper was in high school—tight around the waist and flaring stiffly at the hip, breasts held in hard-looking cups. Shadows darkened the hollows of her cheeks. Under the flounces of the dress her feet were big and bare" (*Back*, 108). This odd apparition is a blurring of high school innocence armed with a deadly weapon. Acting as his conscience, forcing Hooper to obey, the woman practically drives him back from "the world" to his duty on the base. When the woman's husband appears and learns that Hooper is a soldier, he becomes curiously formal and gallant, as if Hooper were a soldier from another era. He, too, thinks Hooper should be at his post. "The man gave a slight bow with his head. 'To base with you then. Good night sir' " (*Back*, 109).

The reader feels that whatever vague possibilities Hooper had sought off-base have been completely closed to him. The odd civilian couple, representing his blurred conscience and the romantic attitude only civilians can have toward military life, has forced Hooper back into the narrow confines of his soldier's life. The neighbor expects Hooper to maintain his soldierly conduct, if for no other reason than to keep up the illusion of the military her husband believes in. "There've been disappointments enough in his life already and God only knows what's next. He's got to have something left. . . . Why are you still here? Get back to your post" (*Back*, 110).

Confused and thwarted by the civilian world, Hooper is secure and assertive once he is back on the base and "out of the world." Waving at soldiers in a passing jeep, "Hooper felt a surge of friendliness toward them. He followed their lights in his mirror until they vanished behind him" (*Back*, 111). Walking in the rain, "Sweet, almost unbreathable smells rose from the earth" (*Back*, 111). Though the peacetime army is lacking in many ways, it is less daunting to Hooper than the outside world. His attitude expresses a posture as old as soldiering. The young soldier Nikolai Rostov expresses exactly the same sentiments in Tolstoy's *War and Peace*: "[A]fter taking leave of his liberty and letting himself be nailed down within one narrow inflexible framework, Rostov experienced the same sense of peace, of moral support, and the same sense of being at home. . . . Here was none of that turmoil of the world at large in which he found himself out of his element and made mistakes in exercising his free will."[19]

Back on the base events cascade quickly and dramatically toward the story's conclusion. At the communications center, Porchoff has supposedly gone berserk and threatened to shoot Trac. Hooper considers waking Captain King, but here, among the enlisted men, the threat of violent contact quickens his pulse and clearly directs his attention. The uncertainty of the world gives way to the certainty of Hooper's duty.

Inside the fenced compound, Hooper dismisses Trac's offer of assistance. Alone with the armed and nervous Porchoff, Hooper, who minutes before was himself confused and unhappy, is now in his element and cannot understand why Porchoff is upset. Not sure of what could be the matter, Hooper guesses homosexuality and drugs. As a lifer to a recruit, Hooper condescends to Porchoff in a fatherly way. But Porchoff's crisis is one of identity in the faceless sameness of military life. His is an articulate rebellion that Hooper, safe from the confusion of the outside world, refuses to acknowledge. Porchoff says he has no friends. "It's like I'm not even there. So what am I supposed to act like?" (*Back*, 115).

Hooper correctly identifies Porchoff's problem as part of the rut they are all in and offers him hope of impending change. When Porchoff pursues this possibility by asking Hooper to tell him about the best time in his life, Hooper speaks of the freedom of Vietnam. Up until this part of the story, the reader has sided with Hooper, the central character through whose perceptions the narrative has progressed. But in a sudden and chilling dislocation, as Hooper reveals the startling damage Vietnam has done to him, the reader identifies with the alarmed and dismayed Porchoff. The anxious recruit is asking the correct questions; Hooper is supplying insane answers.

In Vietnam, friendship was replaced by camaraderie; human contact corrupted into battle skirmishes; introspection annihilated by concerns for simple survival. When Porchoff refuses to hand over his rifle and says Hooper is indeed the crazy one, the reader agrees. Hooper hopes for combat, where life is reduced to the simplest of terms, killing and surviving. Hooper offers himself to Porchoff as an example of what, if he is lucky, he will have the chance to become. After reacting in defense against the insanity that confronts him, Porchoff is killed by Trac in the sort of contact the two Vietnam veterans best understand, and it immediately refreshes them. Trac mumbles in Vietnamese; Hooper sees him as the child/soldier that he must protect. Their hands lock in an understanding of the combat situation. The moment is one of bloody bonding, and the dead Porchoff is forgotten as Hooper consoles the frightened grunt. Immediately the battle-hardened Hooper begins to clear away any incriminating evidence; he takes charge of the situation. He calls Trac "son" and says they must get their stories straight for Captain King. Such, according to Wolff's dark story, is the stuff of "soldier's joy"—the contact of battle has been made, the enemy destroyed, and camaraderie established. All this is comprehensible to Hooper, direct and simple, without the confusion of civilian life. He is far from the world now and an inhabitant of the simplicity of the battlefield.

Wolff has thus written a story almost exactly antipodal to "Wingfield." In that story, the Vietnam veteran's life has been shattered by the ambush that killed many of his fellow soldiers. He has refused to name the dead, to acknowledge his past. Instead, he has become prematurely old, his youthful innocence destroyed. But when he learns of Wingfield's miraculous survival, hope is rekindled. At the story's end, the suffering veteran regains his innocence in a moment of epiphany.

Hooper, too, was psychologically maimed in Vietnam. Love has been usurped by camaraderie; human contact has been perverted into search-and-destroy missions. Porchoff, the story's emblem of hopeful normality, of innocence, in a way, is murdered by Trac, who thinks he is saving Hooper's life. And battlefield comradeship, their only form of sympathy, provides them with their bond. The corrupting influence of practiced brutality has deformed the human being in Hooper, who must now depend on such contact to supply meaning in his life. Love, hope, innocence, compassion—all have been exchanged for his simplified life in the military; the confusion of "the world" beyond the gates of the army post has made impossible Hooper's reentry into an existence infinitely more fruitful in its human possibilities. Like Marty in "Sister," Robert in "Face to Face," and Jerry in "The Missing Person," Hooper cannot mend his life.

"Desert Breakdown, 1968"

Unlike any story in either of Wolff's collections, "Desert Breakdown, 1968," uses a dual-character point of view that divides the narrative almost equally between Mark and Krystal, a young married couple. While this is a point-of-view technique of some long-standing use—as in "Unlighted Lamps" by Sherwood Anderson (*The Triumph of the Egg*) and "The Shadow in the Rose Garden" by D. H. Lawrence (*The Complete Stories*)—for Wolff it is unusual. He used it most extensively in his 1975 novel, *Ugly Rumours*.

A simple event gets the story going: the breakdown of the couple's car in the desert. Often fiction writers introduce such fate-altering opportunities only to have them rejected by characters disabled by their past, incapable of grasping at even the most seductive of futures (Katherine Mansfield's "The Ladies' Maid" and James Joyce's "Eveline" come to mind). But Wolff, making use of this device in a more modern, cinematic fashion, effectively "splits the screen," showing Mark defeated by his choice and Krystal triumphant. As a result of the breakdown, both are exposed to the enticing and erotic lives of others, and both temporarily abandon their family and immerse themselves in the pleasure of self-gratification, turning their backs on responsibility and duty. Mark ends up rejecting this experience completely, with the result that he is plunged back into a life he finds bitterly frustrating. Krystal, however, repudiates only part of the experience and is changed for the better because of it.

Inhabiting Mark's consciousness first, the reader quickly learns of his boyish insecurity and ill-fashioned plans. Krystal, disheveled and huge with child, is unattractive to him. They are headed toward California, the perennial land of milk and honey, with fruit always hanging just outside the window for plucking, where Mark has vague plans of a career in entertainment. His parents, back in Phoenix, have offered him sound advice on remaining there and selling real estate, but to the young man just out of the army with aspirations of stardom, their plans smack of complacency. Mark "always looks discouraged" (*Back*, 123) in the photographs Krystal constantly snaps, and his only talent is to cruelly mimic his companions and parents. When Hans, Krystal's child with her first husband, awakens, Mark tries to soothe him with a phrase that is repeated later and is emblematic of Mark's own insecurity: " 'Pretty soon,' he said, 'pretty soon, Hansy,' not meaning anything in particular but wanting to sound confident, upbeat" (*Back*, 125).

The landscape itself becomes a symbolic backdrop for the actions of the characters. Barren, sterile, unforgiving, the terrain is like that of the desert world in the short story "The Guest" by Albert Camus— "plateaux burned to a cinder month after month, the earth shrivelled up little by little, literally scorched, every stone bursting into dust under one's foot."[20] And perhaps this resemblance is no coincidence, given that this story, like "The Guest," exhibits the existential qualities of alienation and lack of commitment. Both Mark and Krystal are "doomed to freedom"; at the story's end, they will have to exercise their free will to reestablish their lives. For Mark, the topography is threatening, seeming to discourage his ethereal plans for the future: "The road went north . . . leading them toward a solitary mountain far away that looked to Mark like a colossal sinking ship" (*Back*, 127).

Just prior to their car trouble, Mark and Krystal pull into a service station. They park out front, where, rooted to an ancient plank bench, is a chorus of old men looking as if "they had been there forever" (*Back*, 127). Like the chorus in a Greek tragedy, the old men reflect the predominant values of this desert. Xenophobic, they are critical of outsiders, seeing them as targets for their mumbled derision. Webb, the choragus, leers at Krystal's heavy body as the others utter lewd remarks and chuckle. Mark sees her now as these old men see her—made grotesque by her pregnancy, an obvious target for sexual slurs by the withered, impotent old men. In the presence of these men, Mark begins to repudiate his current life, which is already undermined by his insecurities. He is ashamed of his wife, of Hansy's unusual name, of the battered car that looks ridiculous beside the men's practical pickups. Krystal's reaction is to laugh at the men and then startle them by suddenly taking a snapshot.

When the car fails to start, the literal breakdown occurs and the story begins. With Mark ready to "lower his head to the wheel and give way to tears" (*Back*, 130), the reader is introduced to the hard-edged Hope, Webb's lover, who runs the service station and offers her assistance. The old men, like relics of ancient gods, remain unmoved and uncaring, forcing Mark into the decision of walking to the highway to catch a ride to retrieve a car part.

Alone with Hope, Krystal feels "heavy and vaguely ashamed." She watches Hope with "innocent, almost animal curiosity" (*Back*, 133). Hope refers to Mark as a "boy," and when Krystal explains their California plans to her, she smiles at their naivete. But Krystal thinks the smile is too tight and appears "painful somehow" (*Back*, 134). Outside the old men continue their ceaseless muttering. Webb enters brusquely for a beer and abruptly takes Hans away from the women.

Miserable in the heat, foolishly afraid of snakes at midday, Mark "wanted to be cheerful" (*Back*, 136) but is dismayed by the disruption of his plans. His feelings of boyish defeatism run rampant in the desert: "Whatever [he and Krystal] did, it always turned out like this. Nothing ever worked" (*Back*, 136). He tries to console himself by imagining his success on stage at the Sands in Las Vegas, where he plans to invite his parents only for the purpose of humiliating them for their failure to help him.

What Krystal meanwhile has begun to learn from Hope is to adopt her attitude toward men. Rough and masculine herself, Hope defines manliness as a commitment to stand up for a woman; indeed, to kill for one if need be. Hope tells of how Webb beat her husband and followed her around town with his wife in the car. As Krystal listens to the story, she is soothed by the "dim, peaceful, cool" bedroom that has become "pleasant. . . dark." As Hope works on a motorcycle in the middle of the floor, Krystal thinks Hope's defiance is "like Beethoven shaking his fist at the heavens" (*Back*, 140). But when she learns that Hope abandoned her two sons, she says that she could never do such a thing. Hope says she is sure Krystal could. Children "crowd you out of your own life," she says. And she adds: "They'll do all right. . . . They're both boys" (*Back*, 140). Lulled by the dark coolness, Krystal drifts off to sleep. And though she remembers that Hans is outside with the old men, she cannot fight off her drowsiness.

Mark, like Christ tempted in the wilderness, is about to be offered worldly delights and an unbelievably lucky break that could make his career. All he must do is abandon his family. In the pattern prefigured in the story by Hope and Webb, and which Krystal has begun to slip into by neglecting Hans, Mark's test appears, appropriately enough, in the form of a speeding hearse pulling over to give him a lift. Inside is a zany and lusty trio of Hollywood moviepeople: Barney sports a Mohawk haircut; Nance is sexually alluring, with full lips and a gold nose-ring; and the unnamed driver mumbles nonsense rhymes.

Initially uncomfortable in such an alien atmosphere, Mark quickly adapts. His wit is appreciated. Cool inside the automobile, like Krystal in Hope's bedroom, Mark vaguely recalls the desert heat and feels "glad to be right where he was" (*Back*, 143). He forgets about Krystal and Hans and becomes enraptured with the exotic lives of the moviepeople, which are so unlike his unhappy domesticity. They call him Marco instead of Mark; they offer him a trip to the mountains to a remote movie location, a place they refer to as "partyville." Barney guarantees Mark a job. Redheaded, Barney becomes the tempter in the wilderness and recalls the less devilish, but still provocative, Riley, who reveals an alternative life to Brooke in "An Episode in the Life of Professor Brooke." As in that story, red hair evokes that of the agent of lust in Thomas Mann's "Death in Venice" and, perhaps, the hair of Judas Iscariot, who betrays Christ. "What have you got to lose?" Barney asks Mark. And tells him, "Don't disappoint me" (*Back*, 146).

Feeling "rushed" and "a little wild" (*Back*, 146), Mark considers how to work Krystal into the plan without losing the current momentum, but can't. The foolish boy Hope knows him to be surfaces as Mark imagines his future success and thinks Krystal better off without him. Considering abandoning his family, Mark tells himself: "He could leave them. . . . It was a terrible thing. But it happened and people survived, as they survived worse things" (*Back*, 148). His fantasy grows so elaborate that he begins to dismay over how quickly Krystal will recover from his absence. Echoing Hope, Mark concludes that marriage forces one "to give up one thing after another. . . . You had to give up your life" (*Back*, 149). Deciding on his course of action, Mark agrees to Barney's proposal to invest in his own aspirations, having used a boy's egotistical logic.

Simultaneously, back at the service station, Krystal begins to regret her lost life in Germany and becomes aware of the unbearable desolation of her surroundings, in which "she count[ed] for no more than a rock or a spiny tree" (*Back*, 150). She realizes that Mark will never be important in her life.

Past the town of Blythe and the auto parts store, Mark becomes "uncomfortable" with the hurtling hearse and the mumbling, Charon-like driver, who "changed lanes without any purpose" (*Back*, 151). Growing frantic over the terrific speed at which they are traveling, Mark peers over the seat and is stunned by what he sees. Though Wolff leaves the details to the reader's imagination, we deduce some kinky ménage a trois. "He had never seen anything like that before. It took the wind out of him" (*Back*, 152). As the car presses forward at high speed and animal noises are emitted from the front, Mark demands to be let out. Barney reminds him of his decision to go with them, while Nance invites him up front to partake of their pleasures. Desperate, Mark raps on the driver's head until she slams to a stop in the middle of the road. "I want out" (*Back*, 152), Mark tells them.

Almost immediately, Marco becomes Mark again. No longer an adventurer, an explorer of the exotic, he lands back in his unbearable rut. Once at the parts store, he discovers that what he needs costs more than he can pay; the situation thus echoes his earlier lament that everything conspires against him. Outside in the heat again, Mark "could smell himself. He remembered the coolness of the hearse and thought, *I blew it*" (*Back*, 154). Further frustrated by being unable to contact an army buddy on the phone, Mark considers dialing people in Los Angeles until he gets "a human being on the other end. There had to be someone sympathetic out there" (*Back*, 155). Instead he phones his parents in Phoenix, and, considering this a defeat, imagines that he will mimic a police officer and terrify them with cruel details of their son's death in a traffic collision. But when his father answers, Mark's plan vanishes as he declares himself the caller.

For Mark, the desert breakdown has been a bitter defeat. Full of elaborate, boyish fantasies of abandoning his responsibilities for the freedom of an entirely egotistical existence and emerging as the exotic Marco, he is instead forced to depend on his parents and to acknowledge his familial duties. Is it probable that Krystal was accurate earlier, when she understood that Mark would never be valuable in her life. The reader can see him returning to Phoenix to sell real estate, pessimistic and bitter, thinking that he once had a chance to radically alter his future but discovered himself to be too conventional to grasp the opportunity.

But where Mark is defeated, Krystal triumphs. She realizes the dangerous selfishness of her situation when she turns on the light in Webb and Hope's bedroom. What had been cool, dark, and narcotizing, allowing her to forget Hans, suddenly becomes vulgar, like a bedroom in a bordello. Exposed to the light, the "love nest" is all red, with "red tassels" dangling from the lampshades and "pillows . . . shaped like hearts and covered in a satiny material that looked wet under the light . . . they had the appearance of real organs." Thinking "It was horrible, horrible" (*Back*, 156), Krystal echoes a chilling line from another story about the dreadful machinations of the human heart, Joseph Conrad's *Heart of Darkness*, in which the protagonist, Kurtz, repeats "The horror! The horror!"[21]

Where Mark is debilitated by his rejection of a new life, Krystal is energized. She rushes outside to retrieve Hans, finding him happily covered in dirt. When she attempts to gather him up, he calls her a bitch, something he has learned from the old men and at which they laugh. Taking this rejection as a physical blow, Krystal slaps the child and, picking up a plank, attacks the old men, agents of vulgarity and the status quo of this desert service station. In a Teutonic rage befitting a character from Wagner, ranting in German, she forces their surrender of the bench. Then, finding Webb asleep in her car, she smacks him cruelly across the soles of his feet. Watching them cower, she almost smiles.

Where Mark is embittered and uncertain about his denial of a more exotic life, Krystal is charged with the acceptance of her duties to Hans and her unborn child. Though rejecting Hope's selfish advice about abandoning her children, Krystal does draw from her strength of will. Krystal has shaken off the numbing qualities of self-absorption. And it seems doubtful that this new and stronger Krystal will be satisfied with the pessimistic, frustrated Mark. They have traveled in antipodal directions from the single event of the desert breakdown. Mark remains a child; Krystal has become an adult.

Both Krystal and Mark have been briefly exposed to the alluring, mysterious possibilities of the lives of others, a theme Wolff explores often, in such stories as "Next Door," "Say Yes," and "The Missing Person." Yet "Desert Breakdown" more closely resembles "Face to Face," another story about a couple in which the woman triumphs and the man is defeated.

"Our Story Begins"

Unlike any other short story by Tobias Wolff, "Our Story Begins" is about writers and the nature of short fiction. In truth, this single story can serve to illuminate in many ways all of Wolff's other stories. If "back in the world" is the phrase that best describes the general, overarching theme of the collection, "Our Story Begins" offers the reader Wolff's thoughts on the subject matter and intent of realistic short fiction.

"Our Story Begins" seems an illustration of Nadine Gordimer's comparison of short fiction to the "flash of fireflies," in which moments of revelation present brief insights into characters' lives.[22] But art whose subject matter is the composition of art is often a chancy proposition. Stories, novels, documentaries, movies often dwell on the life of the artist, which provides more engaging material for drama, especially if that life was tumultuous, with marital discord, wartime backdrops, or the like. Such events often enliven an otherwise tedious topic. Since the inception of art is cerebral and the execution most undramatic, works about the modes of perception and means of composition are inherently unexciting. Such intellectual pursuits are often left to scholarly articles with their attendant audiences. Neither is Wolff a postmodern writer engaged in self-referential writing that describes or questions the labyrinthine roles of writers, characters, and readers.

Eschewing the postmodern and wanting to enliven a potentially tedious subject for the majority of readers, Wolff conceals the fact that the central character in "Our Story Begins" is a writer until its end. The story itself is traditionally framed. Charlie, a busboy in a meaningless job where he is invisible to other employees, walks down a fog-enshrouded street in San Francisco to a café. From the mist emerges a "three-legged dog" (*Back*, 163), which unsettles the young man. Near the conclusion of the story a Chinese woman "appeared beside him," holding a lobster "waving its pincers" (*Back*, 177). Both images emerge and vanish like the "flash of fireflies" of which Gordimer speaks. They are strange occurrences that present Charlie, the writer, with potential material. What is the story of this dog? This Chinese woman with a lobster? Like the nature of the short story, they appear and disappear, discrete moments of mystery, lyrical moments of potential revelation.

The central moment of illumination is the story within the story Charlie overhears in the coffeehouse, which he frequents because of its romantic association with Beats Jack Kerouac, Allen Ginsberg, and Neil Cassady. Charlie is aware that he somehow taints this shrine to that rebellious pantheon with the fish odor he has brought from work. The "sweet smell of coffee" (*Back*, 163) is disrupted by his reek and reminds him of his failure as a writer and nonentity as a person (note the similarity to Mark's awareness of his odor in "Desert Breakdown, 1968" [*Back*, 154]). In combination with the overheard story, the fish smell serves to debunk Charlie's romantic view of the writer's life and to force him, at the end, to realize and accept its actual nature.

The story overheard concerns the nature of love (and reminds the reader of the wide range of such presentations, from Raymond Carver's "What We Talk about When We Talk about Love" to Plato's *Symposium*). As it is told, Charlie, the protagonist, disappears, as would an author who allows his characters to occupy center stage. Like the narrator as agent in framed stories, Charlie intrudes only to offer a moment of transition or, in this case, to counterpoint the discussion by describing the reaction of some old Italian men to the opera playing on the café record player. Quickly, he slips back into eavesdropping and voyeurism—character traits of writers and readers alike.

The story is about a Filipino named Miguel and his unrequited love for a woman named Senga. Seated at the table are two men and a woman. One of the men, Truman, is married to the woman, Audrey. The reader and Charlie realize that the man telling the story, George, is Audrey's lover. Through his comments we learn that Truman is indifferent to his wife and hostile to women. Audrey, meanwhile, finds Truman boorish and predictable. The tale-teller, George, is debonair and sophisticated. Truman takes the side of the beleaguered Senga, and the two lovers champion Miguel's adventurous quest. At the conclusion of the story, Audrey suggests that George tell Truman about their affair; Truman, upset and refusing to hear any more, leaves the coffeehouse, with George and Audrey in tow.

The two love stories are themselves the stuff of the opera playing in the background—sentimentality, melodrama, beauty, love, obsession, egotism, betrayal. But unlike opera, a prolonged narrative that reaches a conclusion (usually bloody and despairing), the stories of Miguel and Senga and of Truman, Audrey, and George are unfinished. For us, the readers, and for Charlie, the writer, they are the lyrical "flash of fireflies" that, like the deformed dog and the woman with a lobster, appear only to disappear; they have materialized, for a moment, from the fog of surrounding events. They have stood out clearly, discretely from the world.

Charlie leaves the coffeehouse and finds the street "foggy and colder than before" (*Back*, 175). Now the reader discovers that he is a forlorn, struggling writer without friends, trapped in a demeaning job. His novel has been returned from one editor with this comment: "Are you kidding?" (*Back*, 176). He had almost decided to give up his work, but somehow the experience of the last half-hour has changed his mind. He recognizes the sadness around him, but he enjoys his part in it, his complicity as a writer, a chronicler of fragmentary insights into the lives of others. Charlie pictures himself on watch in the prow of a boat with a lantern in hand: "All distraction gone. Too watchful to be afraid. Tongue wetting the lips and eyes wide open ready to call out in this shifting fog where at any moment anything might be revealed" (*Back*, 177).

It is interesting to note that Wolff makes Charlie a novelist and yet the nature and duration of Charlie's revelations, illustrating Gordimer's point, are those lyrical moments of mystery inherent in short fiction. Perhaps that is why Charlie's novel is rejected. He may be, by disposition, a short-story writer, a miniaturist like Wolff himself. If this is so, then maybe the end of the story can serve him as an epiphany (another device of short fiction) signaling his need for a change in direction. After all, this narrative about Charlie takes the form of a short story; the overheard story of Miguel and Senga is the material of a short story. Finally, this story about the nature of short fiction and its inherent material requirements can be applied to Wolff's best fiction as well— almost all of which is short (excluding the novella, *The Barracks Thief*, and the early novel, *Ugly Rumours*).

The reader always gains only glimpses into Wolff's characters, entering the story in medias res, in the middle of things. Quickly something develops, a revelation surfaces. Then, just as rapidly, the lights go out, the story ends. There is little explication, and unanswered questions often linger. Like the afterimage on a retina, the story's residue is there for readers to make out as best they can. Wolff's stories emerge from the fog to be beheld by the reader for a moment. Then they are over, until Wolff, like Charlie, with lantern in hand, discerns another emerging figure.

"Leviathan"

One of Wolff's more pessimistic stories—in much the same vein as "Sister" and "Soldier's Joy"—"Leviathan" offers its title as a biblical allusion key to the theme of the story. The description of the leviathan as a powerful submerged beast best left undisturbed is borrowed from the Book of Job. In Job, the writer is mightily impressed by ferocious crocodiles and marvels at what power must issue from an even more powerful creator.[23] The passages devoted to the behemoth picture an awesome submerged force. "None is so fierce that dare stir him up" (Job 41:10), the Bible warns, concluding, "He maketh the deep to boil like a pot. . . . Upon earth there is not his like, who is made without fear" (Job 41:31–34).

For Helen, the story's protagonist, the leviathan is both literal and figurative; it is the whale she confronts in what she considers her finest moment, and it is the despair she has tried to suppress over her unhappy marriage, which she cannot escape because of her devotion to orthodox Catholicism. The beast is the source of the mystery and the enlightenment, the dread and what small resolution there is to be, like some "vast image out of *Spiritus Mundi*" in Yeats's poem "The Second Coming."[24]

This particular beast's hour of birth comes around at the tail end of Helen's thirtieth birthday party, when she and her husband, Ted, and another couple, Bliss and Mitch, exhausted after a night of cocaine snorting, cast about for something to say as the sun rises on a workday morning. At this juncture in her life—and with her comedown from cocaine doing its depressant work—Helen sees her husband and her friends in a new light. To her surprise, she learns that Mitch is 40 and has had a face-lift. Later she learns that Bliss is despondent because her former husband, who has custody of her children, may be moving farther away. Helen is incredulous of Mitch's surgery and cruel about Bliss's predicament. "Still, Bliss should have thought about that when she took a walk on them, right?" (*Back*, 183). The reader comes to see four yuppies who are comfortable, self-indulgent, fashionable, cynical, and fairly hollow. But both Mitch and Helen perceive that something is wrong with their lives. For Helen, whatever has been submerged is making its way toward the surface. At one point, when she looks down into the apartment's pool, she sees a girl from upstairs on a float and "the long shadow of the air mattress glide along the bottom of the pool like something stalking her" (*Back*, 184).

When Helen's critical gaze falls on her husband, she sees his narcissism. She admits to herself that he looks great, but she "didn't understand why he had to be so obvious and crass" (*Back*, 185). And, as the two men try to comfort Bliss, who in selfish fashion is now crying because she could not bring herself to visit one of her children in the hospital for an operation, Helen begins to find all of them repellant. It is Mitch who first verbalizes Helen's thoughts when he says he regrets not having done much with his life. Typically, though, he wishes he had been less a milquetoast and, like Ted, more cynical and aggressive. Then, as in "Our Story Begins," Mitch relates a story illustrating his kindness toward a hanger-on who eventually ruined his marriage. Mitch wishes he had murdered the man, but his real regret is having let himself "drift into things" he didn't like (*Back*, 186). Mitch believes that "Sometimes it's better to do something really horrendous than to let things slide" (*Back*, 188).

Whereas Helen is piqued by Mitch's story—the shadow along the bottom is coming closer to the surface—Ted delights in the idea of telling stories about the worst things they have done. Quickly Helen parries his predictably crass and cynical idea into something positive. She says they must tell the thing they're most proud of. Ted and Mitch laugh at the preposterous notion.

During her story, Helen reveals her dilemma. We hear her talk of how contemporary Catholicism has been "watered down" (*Back*, 189) since Vatican II, so we have more context in which to understand her cruel comment earlier about Bliss's abandonment of her family. She goes on to admit that she once wanted to become a saint, to live a Godly life; she even considered becoming a nun. This meets with a derisive laugh from Bliss, who says Helen would not have lasted two hours and calls her "Sister Morphine" (*Back*, 190). Helen counters sharply by saying she knows Bliss can't comprehend, but that if she had decided to become a nun nothing would have stopped her. "To me a vow is a vow" (*Back*, 190).

The story she tells is about taking a child with Down's syndrome out on a bay to watch for whales. A whale bumps up against the boat, and Helen fears that the child will become unmanageable and dive into the sea. When her audience tries to defend the animal's behavior, Helen calls it a "monster," saying "He was horrible and huge and he stank." When the whale scraped the boat, the sound was "like people moaning under water" (*Back*, 192). She admits her fear, and when Ted, Mitch, and Bliss interrupt to predict that the boy did dive in and that Helen dove in to save him, Helen tells them to be quiet. She says she simply "talked him down" (*Back*, 193) by mastering her own terror. Confronting and controlling her fear, she says, is what she is most proud of. That once, nine years ago, when she was still a young woman searching for some meaning in her life, when everything was still possible—being a saint or a nun—before the drift into what she and Mitch perceive as their present doldrums, a leviathan rose from the depths and she defeated it by turning her own fear into courage.

Only Mitch is moved by the story. Bliss is incapable of anything but a glib response, and Ted is sound asleep. But now, for a moment, the leviathan rises again to rock the frail boat that is Helen's present married life. In an act of anger and defiance, Helen slaps Ted's sleeping face. Insensitive, Ted only groans in his sleep and turns over. But when Bliss flippantly calls Ted a "slug," Helen must defend him and her current life. She upbraids Bliss, reminding her, "Ted is my husband. Forever and ever." And when Mitch tries to get her to talk about her unhappiness, Helen says, "There's nothing to talk about . . . I made my own bed" (*Back*, 194). She then tries to obliterate her sorrow, pouring Ted's secret stash of cocaine across the table. The story closes with Helen, Mitch, and Bliss smiling up from the cutting mirror like merry carolers outside a festive Christmas window.

Once an idealistic young woman defeated what had threatened her. But now the submerged and lurking behemoth must not even be allowed to breach, for Helen no longer has such resilience; her strict adherence to Catholicism won't allow her certain freedoms. Helen sees her marriage as a duty; she detests Bliss's failure to be responsible to her family. Yet this sense of duty has yoked her to a crass and cruel man. Instead of confronting her feelings, she desensitizes herself with more cocaine. The final smile on Helen's face is a terrible one in a world freezing up all around her.

Helen's realization of her frustrated life recalls that of other Wolff characters, in "Next Door," "Passengers," and "In the Garden." Yet it is most like the story "Sister," in which a realization offers little hope of alteration. Unlike Krystal in "Desert Breakdown," Helen does not triumph as a result of her newly gained insight. Instead she clings to her conservative Catholicism, which she believes has been weakened over the years by liberal interventions (as do the characters in "Coming Attractions" and "The Missing Person"). Once as romantic about Catholicism as the young Father Leo, her faith yokes her forever to Ted, whom she despises. And she is not the unnamed narrator of "Wingfield," who is able to retrieve a vestige of his innocent childhood. Instead Helen is more like Nora from "Maiden Voyage," destined to remain with Ted out of a debilitating sense of duty and obligation.

"The Rich Brother"

"The Rich Brother," the last story in *Back in the World*, anchors the book in one of Wolff's more persistent themes: the obligation of one person to another. Indeed, in this story the actual situation between two brothers of opposite character illustrates the ancient precept that one is surely another's keeper. Wolff renovates the biblical parable of Cain and Abel, diverting it from its usual course of bloodshed and banishment. In several stories in *Back in the World*, a character wrestles with egotistical self-gratification in a struggle to extend him- or herself outside that confining carapace. Often this act of moving away from self results in a crucial, liberating shift of values or the recouping of lost or obscured ones. In this way, "The Rich Brother" connects with the first story, "Coming Attractions," to illuminate the idea. There the troubled teenager is finally able to overcome her self-absorption by plunging into an icy pool to retrieve a bicycle for her younger brother.

Pete, the rich brother, is a successful California realtor, somewhat like Russell in "The Poor Are Always with Us." But Pete is Russell a few years later, a bit softer and more willing to change. He is also like Glen in "Passengers," as Pete, too, will be affected by another person along for the ride. In fact, this is not only the story of Pete's revelation concerning his responsibilities toward his brother, but it is the story of Pete's salvation. For Wolff, the accumulation of material wealth deadens the soul. When Father Leo of "The Missing Person" ministers to Sandra, a lost soul, he redeems himself. For Jerry, the confidence man consumed with greed for riches, it is too late.

"The Rich Brother" is a simple moral tale. "There were two brothers, Pete and Donald" (*Back*, 199), Wolff begins. And the two brothers represent polar opposites. Pete is comfortable in his materialism; Donald is thrashing about in his spiritual dilemma. He is a troubled character, long on courage but short on practicality—which, of course, infuriates Pete. Once a member of an ashram in Berkeley, Donald has now been thrown out of a Pentecostal communal farm. There he has managed to give a load of groceries away to migrant workers and nearly burn the place down while cooking dinner.

The story begins when Pete, in his Mercedes, picks up Donald to take him home. Having reviewed Donald's life on the drive up, Pete is angry even before Donald gets in the car. Matters are intensified when Donald spills orange soda on the leather upholstery and then wonders what was wrong with Pete's old car that he should have bought this new one.

Later on, Donald, dressed in a hooded sweatshirt and looking like "an inquisitor" (*Back*, 205), admits he is not good at coping in the real world. "You have to be practical. You have to be kind to yourself" (*Back*, 206), he says, and tells Pete he is thinking about getting into some sort of business. But soon they are arguing again, and Donald reminds Pete of how much he used to hate him, of how he often struck Donald on the scars of an operation. This Pete dismisses awkwardly, saying it never happened or, if it did, it was kid stuff, though the reader acknowledges Pete's jealousy of Donald, who was obviously sickly and so received more attention than he did. As in the biblical parable, there is a long-standing but submerged uneasiness between the two brothers, generated, it seems, by differences in habit and character. Pete, like Cain, feels his sacrifices have not been acknowledged, whereas Donald seems blessed but unaware. Donald, like Abel, lives in some sort of natural rhythm whose harmony infuriates Pete, who is left to smooth over Donald's improprieties.

The story is complicated by the catalyst of a passenger, Webster, whom the brothers pick up at a restaurant. As with Bonnie in "Passengers," the hitchhiker precipitates the action of the story. Webster is a confidence man, out to take the two brothers for money. A glib talker, he completely fools Donald, who thinks the perspicacious Pete is cruelly indifferent to the tale of loss and tragedy Webster tells as he relates his search for lost Peruvian gold mines.

Later, when Pete awakens to find Webster gone, he discovers that Donald has given him the $100 Pete had handed to his brother earlier. Donald defends himself by telling Pete that he didn't give any money away; since he is trying to become more practical and to start a business, he explains, he invested in Webster's gold mine. When Pete explodes with anger, Donald slowly begins to understand what he has done. At this moment, Pete, like Cain, begins to realize the connection between them: "And it came to him that it would be just like this unfair life for Donald to come out ahead in the end, by believing in some outrageous promise that would turn out to be true and that he, Pete, would reject out of hand because he was too wised up to listen to anybody's pitch anymore except for laughs. What a joke. What a joke if there really was a blessing to be had, and the blessing didn't come to the one who deserved it, the one who did all the work, but to the other" (*Back*, 218–19).

For Pete/Cain, life is unfair; blessings might actually accrue to Donald/Abel, who, Pete believes, is unworldly, impractical, and spiritual, who has not labored nearly as hard as he has. Like Cain must have, Pete "felt a shadow move upon him, darkening his thoughts" (*Back*, 219). But Pete does not reach for the stone yet. Instead, he seems resigned to his role as Donald's keeper. "You can't work, you can't take care of yourself, you believe anything anyone tells you. I'm stuck with you, aren't I" (*Back*, 219). But then Donald demands to be let out of the car, and Pete warns him that this will be the end of their relationship.

Outside, on the shoulder of the road, Donald enrages Pete by first absolving him of any blame: "Blame me? What the hell are you talking about? Blame me for what?" (*Back*, 220). Then Donald adds the final straw by blessing Pete. This benediction is more than Pete can stand, and he drops to his knees searching for the murderous stone. "He didn't know what he was looking for; his hands would know when they found it" (*Back*, 220). But when Donald touches him on the shoulder, Pete rises and drives away, muttering about his brother's incompetence. He plays a tape and pretends he is "at liberty," has "finished his work," and "settled his debts." He rehearses what he will tell his wife when she, like God (in Genesis 4:9–10), asks "Where is he? Where is your brother?" (*Back*, 221). To this Cain, the murderer, answers, "I know not: Am I my brother's keeper?" But Pete is not the murderer of his brother; he will not even maroon him. He is his brother's keeper, and all the time he is mumbling and upset he realizes that he is already slowing the car to turn around. He recognizes both the injustice of the world and his burden and obligation.

Wolff concludes *Back in the World* on a resoundingly positive note. Harboring one of his most persistent themes (as in "In the Garden," "Liar," "Coming Attractions," "The Missing Person"), this refreshened parable of Cain and Abel answers the question asked but not acted on in "The Poor Are Always with Us": "Am I my brother's keeper?" Instead of picking up the stone, Pete acknowledges his duty to his brother, who will most likely be the one blessed, while his own onerous role is ignored. Yet in his heart he cannot answer God by pretending he has no obligation. This story works in odd contrast to the pessimistic sense of duty to Ted that Helen has in "Leviathan." In that story, her duty is as ignoble and stultifying as the loveless 50-year-old marriage between Nora and Howard in "Maiden Voyage." But in "The Rich Brother," the reader understands the duty as done out of love, of acceptance of an assignment in accordance with human nature. It is liberating in its responsibilities, not demeaning and personally damaging. Pete feels he must answer his wife's questions with "the right answer" (*Back*, 221), and the rightness of the answer has to do with the sacrifice of self out of human decency and love that will, in turn, expand the humanity of the one sacrificing.

Back in the World is unlike *In the Garden of the North American Martyrs.* In her review of *Back in the World*, Mona Simpson, comparing the two, finds Wolff's second collection "more somber" than his first, and his characters less ordinary and domestic and more symbolic and dramatic. Wolff himself says that he perceived the stories as sharing subject matter and style, more like a novel than a collection.

One of the obvious differences between the two books is reflected in Wolff's choice of titles. The title story of *In the Garden of the North American Martyrs* is an optimistic one, in which the protagonist, Mary, finds a sudden strength of voice with which to issue a warning to her audience about the need to mend their lives through love, kindness, and justice. The story becomes one way to interpret the entire collection. *Back in the World* takes its title from the bleak story of Hooper's failure to alter his life along more human lines. Wolff wants the stories to share a sense of the heavy yoke the world imposes through the burden of responsibility.

Another difference between the collections is Wolff's use of point of view, which in *Back in the World* produces the emblematic quality of the characters noted by Simpson. In Wolff's *In the Garden*, four of the dozen stories are told in the first person, the intimate point of view, which reduces the distance between the reader and the character as if the story were being related directly to the reader. In *Back in the World*, however, all ten stories use the third-person limited omniscient point of view, which causes the characters to remain more removed from the reader. This sustained point of view results in a consistent tone that is less confessional in places and more oracular, more "story-like" throughout.

The overall tone of *Back in the World* is less hopeful than that of *In the Garden*. Even the optimistic stories are more parabolic, less domestic, as Simpson points out, and therefore more emblematic. Missing, too, is the gentle humorous irony of the first collection; instead the irony becomes more the cosmic irony of the desperate nature of the human situation: People are intelligent, but intelligence does not often lead to significant change in character.

Certainly the themes present are those expected from Wolff: Lives are in need of repair; mending comes about through self-awareness and/or a responsive action toward another, a denial of the egotistical self in favor of a reconnection with others; the lives of others are alluring, exotic, and seductive but fraught with danger.

The opening story of *Back in the World*, "Coming Attractions," and the closing one, "The Rich Brother," are two of Wolff's most transparent calls to the importance of becoming more human by abandoning egotism for brotherly concern. But overall, the tone of the collection is not hopeful; there are fewer stories that leave the central characters open to the possibility of change. In *Back in the World*, "Say Yes" is the only story that comes close to "Next Door," "Smokers," or "Passengers." Though "Coming Attractions," "The Missing Person," "Our Story Begins," and "The Rich Brother" are optimistic, the central portion of the collection contains "The Poor Are Always with Us," "Sister," and "Soldier's Joy," which are not. *In the Garden* concludes with four positive statements about human beings' capacity for growth and change, beginning with "Wingfield" and including "In the Garden," "Poaching," and "The Liar." *Back in the World* closes with less optimism. In "Desert Breakdown," as in "Face to Face," the woman triumphs where the man fails. "Our Story Begins" is more about writing short stories than anything else. "Leviathan" portrays the ignoble face of duty, as opposed to the optimism of "The Rich Brother."

Wolff's voice has become less hopeful in *Back in the World*; when characters fail, they do so more completely. Wolf indicts the contemporary Catholic Church in several stories. His fictional jeremiads are more intense, more pronounced, his voice more clarion in its insistence on the need for mending through brotherly and sisterly compassion. The yoke of the world must be borne, Wolff says, but the difficulty of the task seems more evident in this second collection, and the consequences of failure less mitigated.

Published but Uncollected Stories

Introduction

> When I sit down to write, I discover things that I have, for one reason or another, not admitted, not seen, not reflected on sufficiently. And those are the things that I live for in other people's fiction as well as my own.
>
> Tobias Wolff, from an interview with Jay Woodruff

Since the publication of *Back in the World* in 1985, Wolff's fiction has been well served in the reprint market. *The Barracks Thief and Other Stories* (including Wolff's novella plus six stories from *In the Garden*) and *The Stories of Tobias Wolff* (issued in England and incorporating *In the Garden*, *Back in the World*, and *The Barracks Thief*) have been published. Wolff has also tried his hand quite successfully at memoir with *This Boy's Life*, which was made into a motion picture,[25] and, most recently, with *In Pharaoh's Army: Memories of the Lost War*, which offers poignant testimony to a young lieutenant and his country's loss of innocence.[26]

A deliberate craftsman who produces work slowly, Wolff has continued his artistry in short fiction as well. As was true at the inception of his career, his work appears in first-rate magazines and journals—*Esquire*, *Harper's*, the *Atlantic*, *Granta*—and is often anthologized with the nation's choice stories in *The Best American Short Stories* and *Prize Stories: The O. Henry Awards*. The three stories analyzed in this section of the book represent a sampling of the work to appear in Wolff's forthcoming collection.[27]Always his most severe critic, Wolff admits to the difficulty of arriving at a collection he wishes to issue. In 1991 Wolff told an interviewer that he "had enough uncollected stories to make a couple of collections, probably. At least one. But I won't collect them. Now and then I'll go back and reread them, wondering if I was just being too hard on myself. And I'll say no, I wasn't" (Woodruff, 24).

From the following sampling and from the many others available in anthologies and magazines, the reader can see where Wolff has continued his traditions and where he has broadened his vision. Soldiers, in Vietnam and stateside, remain a focal point. The uneasy relationship between parents and children, the damaging constraints of failed imaginations, the duty people owe themselves and the responsibility they owe others, the sometimes transcendent nature of common existence, which may, if one is only aware, become a moment of true epiphany— these are the recurrent and developing themes of Tobias Wolff's short fiction. People who are cowards may become saviors; the moment is always about to transpire. What Wolff admires in Chekhov can be said of his own short fiction: "If he could not write at length then he would write in depth, making every detail suggest others, capturing a moment of someone else's life in such a way that we intuitively trace that life beyond the story, drawing the circle from the arc."[28]

"The Other Miller"

Wolff's view of military life is invariably dispiriting. In "Wingfield," the recruits intimidate and threaten one another, the strong victimizing the weak. In "Soldier's Joy," the central character has rejected the reality of the civilian world outside his base in favor of the insulating rigidity of military routine. In "The Other Miller," a young man named Wesley Miller has fled his home to join the army and so punish his mother for her remarriage, which has made her less attentive to him.

At the onset, Wesley is an obnoxious sort, hardly a sympathetic character. He is an anxious, neurotic mess of a young man, obviously more child than adult. A training skirmish inflicts him with a physical misery exceeded only by his mental turmoil. Mired in a muddy foxhole, Wesley is already apprehensive. Worries have swamped him in an egotistical world of self-deprecation, a motif that appears in each of Wolff's collections. Though surrounded by fellow soldiers caught in the same deplorable inclemency, Wesley imagines the attacking soldiers blessed with perfect weather, light packs, and ideal sleeping conditions. He probes his broken bridgework, giving himself pain, and worries about his ulcerous stomach, all the time reminding himself of an unspecified dread that he defines as his luckless life in which things only get worse.

When he is mistaken for a W. P. Miller in another company, Wesley seizes the opportunity to escape the physical misery of the field exercise. He goes along with the Red Cross announcement that his mother has died, trying hard not to laugh aloud at the fortuitous mistake. He believes this to be "the luckiest he has ever been."[29] And, like the characters in "Coming Attractions" and "The Liar," Wesley comes to relish the act of lying. He enjoys the attention and commiseration of the other soldiers. Full of self-pity, having defined himself as an "outsider," he feels that this time "everybody is on the outside" but himself ("Miller," 32). He justifies the mistake as the army's; he rationalizes his behavior by telling himself he is delaying the other Miller's painful news. To the reader, it seems that such a delay could cause the other Miller to miss his mother's funeral.

Wolff executes a deft move at this point in the story. Realizing that the reader may soon figure out that Wesley may indeed be the rightful recipient of the death notice, Wolff introduces a voice that mixes the authorial tone with Wesley's own to produce a number of ambiguous possibilities. "This is what happened" ("Miller," 32), Wolff states directly, before Wesley's voice intrudes to continue the exposition of an earlier and similar mix-up concerning the death of the other Miller's father. It serves Wolff's theme well that the reader at this point in the story likely dismisses the potential irony. Indeed, Wesley, who believes himself luckless and is fearful of the future, does not arrive at this possible conclusion, though one might suspect he would. He does not because he cannot yet confront the possibility. The reader does not because it would mean yielding to an acceptance of Wesley's unappealing point of view.

Wesley, like the boy in "Smokers," becomes quickly engaged in his own lies to the two soldiers with whom he rides back to the base. He understands that he can get pity and attention; he can debase himself through lying and cajole the soldiers into expressing the sympathy he believes he rightly deserves: "From now on he can say anything" ("Miller," 33). So, in the jeep, he launches into a far-fetched string of sentimental recollections he recalls from a country song. The soldiers, genuinely moved at first, offer him pop-psychological advice about confronting his feelings. This scene foreshadows Wesley's epiphany at the story's conclusion.

In this serving of lies resides a portion of truth about his troubled relationship with his mother. His father having been killed in a ludicrous accident while a soldier, Wesley believes his act of joining the service will cause her more profound pain. Nothing more than a tremendously upset child, Wesley punishes his mother for finding a life with a new husband. Typical of such a mentality, he believes that the grief

Part 1

he is inflicting on himself is greater than hers. A petulant and egotistical boy, he has imprisoned himself in misery in order to torment her.

A disconsolate person, Wesley is like Hemingway's Nick Adams in "Big Two-Hearted River: Part II," who avoids confronting the cost of his psychological wounds by refusing to think about anything but the immediate and palpable: "Beyond . . . the river went into the swamp. Nick did not want to go in there now."[30] Wolff, who says he is indebted to Hemingway "first and last" (Ross, 496), has Wesley forbid himself thoughts of the future and the possible consequences of his cruel and selfish actions. The other soldiers talk Wesley into eating a burger, but when they decide to visit a nearby fortune-teller, Wesley is terrified. The "less you know, the better off you are," he cautions them ("Miller," 37). Unable to change their minds, he whines like a child, demanding they take him straight home. And the implication is that he does not mean the army base.

But they proceed to a fortune-teller, and the palmist at the door is a child's nightmare. A harbinger of the future Wesley refuses to confront, she has a wandering eye and black teeth. She "beckons" him inside ("Miller," 38); her hands, covered with flour, are ghostly. He imagines returning with a rabble, like the mobs in horror movies, torches in hand, to drive her from town. It says little of Wesley's character that he would return at night with other men to take arms against a solitary old woman. The horrified boy demands that she leave him alone and flees. He smells his own body odor, a device Wolff uses in "Desert Breakdown, 1968," and elsewhere to objectify fear, a sense of mortality, an awareness of weakness. Wesley curses himself, the gypsy, and the army.

Back in the jeep alone, Wesley excoriates those who would think of the future. With childish superstition, he believes that something foretold is certain to happen, that the future is an "ambush" where "everything gets worse" ("Miller," 39). He was once secure, but then his father died and his mother remarried and so displaced him. The future is change, alteration, mortality, loss—all beyond his ability to control and so best not even thought about.

In the moment before his epiphany, Wesley believes himself to be unafraid of his own death—indeed, better prepared for it than anyone he knows. But fear of death is not what he has been repressing. "Behind his eyelids he is wide awake and fidgety with gloom, probing against his will for what he is afraid to find, until, with no surprise at all, he finds it. A simple truth. His mother is also going to die" ("Miller,"

40). And with this, all is out in the open both to consider and to dread, since to acknowledge the possibility is, for him, the same as activating the inevitable. His newly minted thought gives him mental anguish.

Valuable, sometimes essential, almost all epiphanies are painful and unsettling. Consider the sorrowful but enlightening epiphany of Gabriel in James Joyce's "The Dead," who ponders his own mortality: "His soul had approached that region where dwell the vast hosts of the dead. . . . His own identity was fading out into a grey impalpable world: the solid world itself which these dead had one time reared and lived in was dissolving and dwindling" (Joyce, 225). Very much like Gabriel, Wesley listens to his own breathing, a sign of life, of humanity, which has replaced his earlier concern with his odor of fear. If his mother dies, he wonders, where will his home be, to whom will he offer forgiveness? In this moment of painful revelation, during an epiphany that is also a rite of passage from childish simplicity to adult complexity, he feels the necessity of human contact, the "almost muscular ache of knowing that he is beyond his mother's reach" ("Miller," 40). He recognizes that his foolish punishment of her is "killing him" ("Miller," 41).

But when Wesley decides to use the mistaken furlough to go home to visit his mother, he imagines the cruel, cosmically ironic possibility that perhaps his mother is already dead and that he is the "right" Miller. The reader, too, perceives this as a possibility, not just a vestige of Wesley's cynicism. He has had no letter from her for more than a year; there is no way of knowing that those letters he returned did not contain news of her declining health. But Wolff has carefully prepared the story for just such a predicament. The future is full of uncertainty, some of which is dreadful. It could be that Wesley's mother is dead and that he will have no opportunity to pardon her and so exonerate himself. His epiphany may have come too late to be of use. But this is to yield to Wesley's superstition that to think about future tribulations is to ensure their occurrence. Neither Wesley nor the reader can predict what he will find once he reaches his door. But even in his pessimistic imaginings he finds himself in familiar, comforting territory, welcomed with outstretched arms. Whether there is to be joy at homecoming or mourning at loss remains to be discovered. Living involves such uncertainties.

"The Other Miller" is comparable with many of Wolff's stories in which characters are uncertain about their future: "Next Door," "Face to Face," and "Passengers." But the closest comparison is with "Poaching," in which Wharton is very reluctant to confront the future.

"Memorial"

For a writer who often tells moral tales against the setting of a realistic world, Wolff has perhaps created his most interesting and complex moral story in "Memorial." The theme of the story is the complicated relationship between the spiritual and the corporeal, between savior and saved; it takes on the paradoxical heart of the Christian mystery— that one must lose one's life to gain life eternal. Reminiscent of Oliver Stone's film *Platoon*, which uses the backdrop of the Vietnam War to ask fundamental questions about the nature of good and evil, "Memorial" also uses soldiers in Vietnam to portray thematic concerns. In an interview conducted in 1989, Wolff was asked why he had not "dealt directly" with the war in his previous work (the interviewers did not seem to know about *Ugly Rumours*, Wolff's 1975 novel set in Vietnam during the war). Wolff answered by applauding the works of Philip Caputo, Michael Herr, and Ron Kovic, and especially Tim O'Brien's short story "The Things They Carried." He argued that another story about Vietnam would need "an enormous amount of invention to arrive at something fresh, something that people don't already know, to tell the story in a way that is redolent of the place, that grows from the ground of that particular experience and not from some other" (Lyons and Oliver, 16).

"Memorial" does and does not fit Wolff's qualifications. *Ugly Rumours*, his only other piece of fiction set in Vietnam, shares similarities with "Memorial." Neither work provides a realistic evocation of place. Unlike the writers he mentions (and others like Stephen Wright), Wolff is not interested in capturing the Vietnam War in precise detail, whether realistically or surrealistically. Instead, Wolff uses Vietnam as a moral backdrop, much as Joseph Conrad uses the world of sailing ships and sailors. Both that world and Vietnam are microcosms that test characters' cowardice or courage—spiritual loci where characters exhibit the spectrum of human emotion and conduct. Just as Conrad does not instruct the reader in the details of rigging, navigation, and the like, neither does Wolff provide a detailed accounting of the lives of officers and grunts. In short, Wolff's work is not "redolent of the place."

In both *Ugly Rumours* and "Memorial," Wolff explores the moral states of several different characters, using the nineteenth-century convention of the omniscient narrator, who distributes the point of view unevenly among the characters. *Ugly Rumours*, however, is unsuccessful as a novel, whereas "Memorial" is one of Wolff's best short stories. Norman Friedman's essay "What Makes a Short Story Short" may be too prescriptive, but it does have its salient points. Friedman argues that "a story may be short, to begin with a basic determination, for either or both of two fundamental reasons: the material itself may be of small compass; or the material, being of broader scope, may be cut for the sake of maximizing the artistic effect."[31] *Ugly Rumours* is a perfect example of the material of a short story stretched so tightly onto the frame of a novel that the fabric tears, destroying the intended effect. In "Memorial," the material fits the frame perfectly. The theme that was an important part of the novel is realized in the short story.

"Memorial" begins with an homage to O'Brien's "The Things They Carried." In O'Brien's story, the soldiers are evoked through a catalogue of what they carry with them, emotionally and physically: "they carried whatever presented itself, or whatever seemed appropriate as a means of killing or staying alive" (O'Brien, 8). In "Memorial," the central character, B.D., "carried certain objects. . . . There were certain words he said to himself at certain moments, power words. Sometimes he really believed in all of this; other times he believed in nothing."[32] Both B.D. and his friend Ryan are short-timers with only a few weeks left in their tours. Their unit has been relatively free of casualties, and their lieutenant lets short-timers stand down from dangerous duties like night ambushes.

When this officer is replaced by another who refuses to continue this practice, the story's conflict begins. Ryan, who is a mimic and a joker, cannot help infuriating the new officer. Slowly developed as a curious Christ figure in the story, Ryan, because of his nature, comes into inevitable conflict with the lieutenant. Not portrayed by Wolff as virtuous or mild, not even a fool out of place like Dostoyevsky's Prince Myshkin in *The Idiot*, Ryan is simply being himself. And this figure of Christ, as somehow unmanageable, defiant, unable to act in any other fashion, reminds one of the inimitable protagonist in the Kafka story "The Hunger Artist," who begs not to be pitied or admired, saying, "Because I have to fast, I can't help it."[33] When B.D. begs Ryan not to anger the lieutenant any more and so save himself from a second night ambush, Ryan says, "The thing is, I can't. I try but I can't" ("Memorial," 178). He tells B.D. that someone has to show the officer what sort of person he is. "Somebody's got to take responsibility" ("Memorial," 178).

B.D.'s concern is not only for Ryan. It is primarily for the uncomfortable position that Ryan's behavior puts him in. Looking over Ryan's high school yearbook the night of Ryan's first ambush patrol under the new officer, B.D. recognizes the young boy, the human being he wishes to save from putting himself in harm's way. But earlier, when B.D. tried to intervene by complaining to the lethargic sergeant, the sergeant condemned B.D. for looking out for himself. "You been duckin' ever since you got here, you and Ryan both" ("Memorial," 177).

As Ryan's attitude continues to put him in danger, B.D. grows more desperate not only to save his friend's life but also to save himself from the gnawing realization that he could help Ryan by volunteering when the lieutenant asks if any other short-timers would like to take on the ambushes (B.D. and Ryan are the only short-timers in the unit). At one point, B.D. steals a fragmentation grenade with the idea of "fragging" the lieutenant, of killing him in his tent and in this way saving Ryan and himself. But such an action is impossible; B.D. believes that he has not killed anyone yet, and he recalls a specific incident where he had a man in his rifle sights but did not fire because the man was blind. But even here his compassion is complicated by the uncertainty of whether the man was actually blind or whether B.D. misread the situation.

B.D. seeks out their former lieutenant to beg him to intercede on Ryan's behalf with the newly assigned officer. Hoping for some intercession that will prevent him from placing his own life in danger on Ryan's behalf, of removing himself from his moral predicament, B.D. takes strength from the mere presence of the officer. He breathes in the smell of the man, "taking comfort from it as he took comfort from the man's bulk, the great looming mass of him" ("Memorial," 181). Yet here, too, he is disappointed. As is the way with officers, the lieutenant will not intercede for an enlisted man. He tells B.D. to forget his "personal problems" and asks, "If you're so worried about him, why don't *you* volunteer?" ("Memorial," 182).

All of this leaves B.D. with a heightened sense of consternation. Only he can intervene to save Ryan's life, and by doing so he will be forced to jeopardize his own. B.D. knows himself to be a coward on any real, demonstrable level. He believes he can perform some romantically heroic act, something "he'd heard and read about, and in which he thought he recognized the possibilities of his own nature.

But this was different" ("Memorial," 183). For unlike Ryan's nature, B.D.'s is understandably timid. And this action is something to be done with consideration beforehand, not impulsively. This act of sacrifice involves acceptance "in advance" ("Memorial," 184). The more B.D. thinks about the possibilities of losing his life for Ryan's, of sacrificing it on his behalf (which Ryan has done for B.D. but completely in keeping with Ryan's obstinate nature), the more B.D. realizes the weaknesses of his flesh to make such a commitment. "He didn't know if he could do this. He just didn't know" ("Memorial," 184). Then, as with Peter's denial of Christ, B.D. begins to construct differences between them. "He didn't know Ryan all that well, when you came right down to it" ("Memorial," 184).

When Ryan is mortally wounded in a sniper's attack on the base, B.D. rushes to his aid only to find him gone, ascended in a medical evacuation helicopter. In a flash-forward technique Wolff has used before, B.D. tries to tell his girlfriend what he thought that day, but he is unable to do so. B.D. believes that since leaving Vietnam he has lived the life of a good man, caring friend, and son; but that moment of doubt exposes all the deficiencies of the flesh: "he felt . . . weak, corrupt, and afraid" ("Memorial," 185). Years later, B.D. still cannot find the words for his feelings that day in Vietnam and falsely claims that "grief was impossible to describe" ("Memorial," 186). But Wolff, the intruding narrator, brutally attacks this conclusion. It is not grief B.D. felt: "He had felt delivered—set free" ("Memorial," 186). With the ascension of Ryan in the helicopter, B.D. was absolved of making any commitment that might have threatened his own life.

Wolff then turns to Ryan's experience of that day. On the helicopter, he is in the charge of a nurse who is allowed only to change a minor dressing; she is not allowed to touch his wound until he reaches doctors at their destination. As with the crucified, stigmatized Christ, Ryan is in a transmogrified state, which the nurse must respect. But as Ryan dies, the nurse, like B.D. before her, is captivated by a reverberation of the same dilemma. When the unconscious Ryan grasps her hand and says "Come on in" ("Memorial," 187), the nurse is startled. His phrase seems an invitation to death (and the Christian paradox of having to die to obtain eternal life), but it also echoes entreaties of salvation: "Come unto me all ye that labor and are heavy laden" and "Behold I stand at the door and knock" (Matthew 11:28–30 and Revelation 3:20). Like B.D., the nurse is frightened by this contact with death. She quickly removes Ryan's hand from hers and places it in the hand of another wounded soldier. Upset, she asks another nurse for drugs to calm her fright (something she has obviously done before, owing to the tremendous strain of her duty), but is refused. She looks out a window, down to the East China Sea, and imagines herself on a cruise ship, clean and comfortable among friends, removed from the trauma of her job. Surely she is as relieved to be away from Ryan's cryptic words as was B.D. to be set free of his presence.

The theme of "Memorial" is the quandary of Christianity: The nature of Christ was the admixture of the flesh and the spirit; though incarnate, he was predestined to overcome, with difficulty, this defect. The flesh, the human in B.D. and the nurse, yearns for comfort, wishes to be rid of such troubling puzzles. In the abstract, B.D. believes himself able to overcome the fear of death and act heroically in obscure, romantic situations. But confronted with the actual choice in fact, the corporeal is proverbially weak, as Matthew 26:41 reminds the reader. The flesh struggles for reprieve from such questions, taking succor in the real and practical ways of a tangible world.

"Lady's Dream"

"Lady's Dream" is an interesting contrast to an earlier story about a married couple from *Back in the World*, "Say Yes." In that story, a domineering husband and his wife become alienated during a foolish argument, and the husband thrills, at the story's conclusion, to the sudden allure of mystery about his wife. In "Lady's Dreams," the husband, Robert, has, to use a D. H. Lawrence term, "obliterated" his wife's personality, forced her own character to serve chiefly in reaction to his dominance. But unlike "Say Yes," this story is the wife's, and there is nothing to thrill at when the story ends. It concludes with her reiteration of the bleakness of her marriage and her and her children's position in it. The wife in "Lady's Dream" can only summon a nostalgic farewell to her youth, when her girlish love for her husband seemed as untrammeled as her future.

Now Lady finds a moment of freedom from Robert in her pretense of sleep as they travel by car. In an archetypal motif that stretches from the blind soothsayer Tiresias in *Oedipus Rex* to the narrator in Raymond Carver's "Cathedral," Lady is most perspicacious when her eyes are closed to the actual world around her: "She's beginning to see things in the lengthening moment when her eyes are closed, things more distinct and familiar than the dipping wires and blur of trees and the silent staring man she sees when they're open."[34]

What she perceives is her unfortunate subservience to Robert, who is principled, considerate, and unaware, but who numbers the vacuum-cleaner bags for her and "wears a hard hat when he works around the house." A man who questions her only "about his own self" and who "loves her name. Lady. Married her name. Shut her up in her name. Shut her up" ("Lady's," 75).

Wolff divides the point of view to investigate both characters' thoughts during their courtship years before. Robert, a young soldier stationed in the South prior to being shipped off to the Korean War, sees Lady as symbolic of southern attributes he dislikes. Though he wants to marry her as an act of rebellion against his father, who seems to have been as domineering and opaque as his son, Robert believes it will take him years to educate Lady by eradicating an upbringing he finds "Irrational. Superstitious. Clannish" ("Lady's," 77).

What Robert failed to understand was the essential nature of the young girl her name contradicts. For she is brash and sassy, open and emotional, a product of the South. Here Wolff is playing off an expected motif in European and American literature, and that is the delineation of northern and southern temperaments and their antithetical composition. Robert wishes to behave along rational, logical lines. He judges Lady to be too passionate and frivolous. He concludes that these characteristics will have to be worn away in time to produce a "quiet and dignified" wife "respectful of life's seriousness," so creating a "pure Lady" ("Lady's," 77). It is painfully apparent that the wife in the car may be endowed with all of these qualities now, but what has been eroded, Lady believes, is her elemental nature.

In her reverie, Lady places herself in her family home prior to the moment of irrevocable commitment. There, with her mother and sister, her father no doubt on the road selling paint, she relives her naive last hour of freedom, unaware of what would become of her once entrusted to Robert's husbandry. But through the filter of her marriage, she now sees the three women in her home as "waiting but not waiting. . . . Sufficient unto themselves. Nobody has to come" ("Lady's," 76)—certainly not Robert, who would alter her life in unhappy and unimaginable ways.

But at the moment of his arrival, both she and Robert are transported on a flood of passion. Ironically, Robert has decided to break off their relationship, aware that it is unfair to use Lady to rebel against his father. He has determined he will face up to him. But his intellect gives way to his desire when he imagines the dessert of strawberries Lady and her sister may serve him. Using the fruit, so often used as avatar of the sensual and voluptuous (Thomas Mann increases its venereal significance by making it overripe and a potential host of contagion in "Death in Venice"), Wolff has Robert rush forward to partake of it in strikingly sexual terms: "He'll be lucky if he gets any tonight" ("Lady's," 78).

Reacting to Robert's passion—her reaction to his instigation a harbinger of her unhappy future—the young woman touches Robert's face. Here, too, there is irony, for Lady reaches out only to wipe away a smudge of shoe polish, but Robert thinks otherwise. They yield to one another. Now, daydreaming in the automobile, the married woman would like to warn the young girl of the consequences of a misunderstood touch.

Of course, that is impossible. For the girl would not have listened to her; on the porch she reacted to Robert out of love. Now recalling the intervening years of Robert's mastery, of his efforts to "patiently school [her] to death" ("Lady's," 78), she answers to his voice out of habit. In the last moment of her reverie, before she must open her eyes and pay attention to his demands, Lady says a benediction for that innocent girl acting out of naive motives; she imagines her family's home a ship on an open sea, amidst boundless possibilities.

"Lady's Dream" is the doleful story of a woman's loss of identity in marriage. Now the wife can only lament her past, visit it in reveries where irrevocable moments have not yet transpired, where possibilities still remain viable.

In "Say Yes," the husband's complacent dominance of his wife is overturned by her sudden mysterious allure. For Robert and Lady, no such possibilities appear. Where the dock in "Poaching" became Wharton's symbolic ship sailing into a promising future, Lady's ship, her childhood home, has taken her nowhere but nostalgically recalls her youthful freedom, before the rush of passion that entangled her and her husband forever.

Notes to Part 1

1. Jay Woodruff, *A Piece of Work: Five Writers Discuss Their Revisions* (Iowa City: Iowa University Press, 1993), 33; hereafter cited in the text.

2. Richard Orodenker, review of *In the Garden of the North American Martyrs*, *North American Review* 267 (June 1982): 60.

3. Anatole Broyard, "Books of the Times," review of *In the Garden of the North American Martyrs*, *New York Times*, 25 November 1981, C21:1.

4. Tobias Wolff, introduction, *Matters of Life and Death: New American Stories* (Green Harbor, Mass.: Wampeter Press, 1983), x; hereafter cited in the text as *Matters*.

5. Tobias Wolff, introduction, *The Vintage Book of Contemporary American Short Stories* (New York: Random House, 1994), xiii; hereafter cited in the text as *Vintage*.

6. Tobias Wolff, introduction, *Broken Vessels*, by Andre Dubus (Boston: David R. Godine, 1991), xv.

7. *In the Garden of the North American Martyrs* (New York: Ecco Press, 1981), 4; hereafter cited in the text as *Garden*.

8. Thomas Mann, *Death in Venice*, trans. David Luke, in *The Norton Anthology of World Masterpieces, Volume 2*, ed. Maynard Mack et al. (New York: W. W. Norton, 1992), 1556; hereafter cited in the text as Mann.

9. F. Scott Fitzgerald, *The Great Gatsby* (New York: Charles Scribner's Sons, 1953), 60.

10. Fyodor Dostoyevsky, *The Idiot*, trans. Henry and Olga Carlisle (New York: New American Library, 1969), 596.

11. Alfred, Lord Tennyson, "Ulysses," in *Norton Anthology, Volume 2*, 689.

12. Mona Simpson, "The Morality of Everyday Life," review of *Back in the World*, *New Republic*, 9 December 1985, 38; hereafter cited in the text.

13. Bonnie Lyons and Bill Oliver, "An Interview with Tobias Wolff," *Contemporary Literature* 31, no. 1 (Spring 1990): 4; hereafter cited in the text.

14. *Back in the World* (Boston: Houghton Mifflin, 1985), 4; hereafter cited in the text as *Back*.

15. D. H. Lawrence, "The Horse-Dealer's Daughter," in *The Complete Stories* (New York: Viking Press, 1971), 450.

16. Tobias Wolff, "Raymond Carver Had His Cake and Ate It Too," *Esquire*, September 1989, 240ff.

17. James Joyce, "Eveline," in *Dubliners* (New York: Penguin, 1992), 34; hereafter cited in the text.

18. Tim O'Brien, *The Things They Carried* (New York: Penguin, 1990), 40; hereafter cited in the text.

19. Leo Tolstoy, *War and Peace*, trans. Rosemary Edmonds (New York: Penguin, 1978), 462.

20. Albert Camus, "The Guest," trans. Justin O'Brien, in *One World of Literature*, ed. Shirley Geok-lin Lim and Norman A. Spencer (Boston: Houghton Mifflin, 1993), 531.

21. Joseph Conrad, *Heart of Darkness* (New York: W. W. Norton, 1963), 79.

22. Nadine Gordimer, "The Flash of Fireflies," in *Short Story Theories*, ed. Charles E. May (Athens: Ohio University Press, 1976), 180; hereafter cited in the text.

23. Roy B. Chamberlin and Herman Feldman, *The Dartmouth Bible* (Boston: Houghton Mifflin, 1961), 463.

24. *Selected Poems and Two Plays of William Butler Yeats* (New York: Macmillan, 1966), 91.

25. *This Boy's Life*, dir. Michael Caton-Jones, Warner Bros., 1993.

26. Tobias Wolff, *In Pharaoh's Army: Memories of the Lost War* (New York: Knopf, 1994).

27. Letter from Tobias Wolff to James Hannah, 12 July 1994. As noted in the preface, at this volume's time of printing, Wolff was expecting to publish a third story collection in late 1996.

28. Tobias Wolff, introduction, *A Doctor's Visit: Short Stories of Anton Chekhov* (New York: Bantam, 1988), xiii.

29. Tobias Wolff, "The Other Miller," *Atlantic*, June 1986, 31, hereafter cited in the text as "Miller."

30. *The Short Stories of Ernest Hemingway* (New York: Charles Scribner's Sons, 1966), 231.

31. Norman Friedman, "What Makes a Short Story Short?" in *Short Story Theories*, ed. Charles E. May (Athens: Ohio University Press, 1976), 133.

32. Tobias Wolff, "Memorial," *Granta* 44 (Summer 1993): 173; hereafter cited in the text as "Memorial."

33. Franz Kafka, *The Complete Stories*, trans. Willa and Edwin Muir (New York: Schocken Books, 1983), 277.

34. Tobias Wolff, "Lady's Dream," *Harper's* (December 1992): 75; hereafter cited in the text as "Lady's."

Part 2

THE WRITER

Introduction

I'm still a liar, really, and I don't mean just in terms of telling
stories and being a story writer. I wouldn't ever want to be
held to a literal version of the facts when I tell people a story.

Tobias Wolff, from an interview with Jean Ross

Tobias Wolff is a modern short-story writer who eschews both the
traditional, plot-driven story and postmodern experimentalism. Like
Anton Chekhov, the "father" of the modern short story for whom Wolff
often expresses admiration, Wolff is interested in stories that illuminate
character rather than construct plot or indulge in experimental elaboration. The three interviews that follow reveal much about Tobias Wolff,
modern story writer.

In the Jay Woodruff interview, attention is first focused on the genesis and revision of one story in particular, "In the Garden of the North
American Martyrs." Here the reader learns how Wolff combines autobiography with his reading of history to produce fiction. He discusses
the numerous revisions he made and the design problems he had to
overcome before he was satisfied with the story. Wolff continues by
talking about other stories of his and about contemporary writers he
admires, especially André Dubus and Raymond Carver. He elaborates
on the publishing experience of these two and on the whimsy of critics
and reviewers. One of the most interesting exchanges in the interview
occurs when Wolff speaks of his writing as a process of discovery, of
illumination. When he begins a story, he very often has no idea where
it will end; remaining open to the possibilities is what he enjoys most
about the writing of fiction.

The opening of the interview by Bonnie Lyons and Bill Oliver
concentrates on Wolff's first memoir, *This Boy's Life*. The reader learns
about Wolff's childhood and the ways that his most important themes—
telling the truth, lying, reinventing oneself—emerge from his personal
history. He also discusses his preparations for writing and the moral
value of some of his best fiction. Using autobiography as a base, Wolff
offers insight into several specific stories.

Part 2

In the third interview, by Jean W. Ross, Wolff discusses his fiction as an optimistic act and the writers who have most influenced his art. He concludes by talking about his role as teacher of creative writing and his students' attempts at publication.

The three interviews overlap at times, but together they present a valuable mosaic. While a writer is best known through his fiction, discussions of method, subject matter, literary influences, and autobiographical ingredients provide the reader with a more profound understanding of the original works and the mind that produced them.

Jay Woodruff

JW: How did ["In the Garden of the North American Martyrs"] get started? What was its genesis?

TW: Well, there are a few things that I can trace it to. One is a job interview I had several years ago which was not, it turned out, a serious interview. That is, I had been brought across the country in order to fulfill a requirement of the college that so many people be interviewed for each position. And when I found this out it really burned me up. I tried writing the story a couple of times from a personal point of view, my own point of view. This never really took. It sounded whiny, "poor me." After all, I live a rarified life, one that's lucky compared to almost everybody else's. This didn't seem to be the stuff of tragedy.

I'd had the experience of watching my mother struggle and have a harder time of it than she would have had if she were a man. It occurred to me that this was the kind of experience women have a lot more often than men. And once I was able to make that leap, get out of my own case and see the whole question of injustice in a larger way, then this story began to take. I began to feel its possibilities. I went back to it and worked on it for several months. And this is what I came up with. I was ransacking my files here, hoping to find some remnants of that original draft. But I couldn't find it, so I must have thrown it away. Anyway, I put it through many different versions. That's the genesis of the story.

JW: How long did you struggle with those first attempts before you put the story aside?

TW: I'm a very slow writer. If people knew how hard it was for me they'd think I was crazy to be a writer. I suppose a couple of months, anyway. It usually takes me that long to give up. I'll usually even finish a bad story and then not send it off rather than not finish it, because I'm terrified of developing the habit of giving up on stories as I write

Reprinted from *A Piece of Work: Five Writers Discuss Their Revisions*, edited by Jay Woodruff, by permission of the University of Iowa Press. Copyright 1993 by Tobias Wolff.

them. I've had trouble with even my best stories along the way, and I've been tempted to quit on them. So I know from experience that if I see it through I might end up with a good story. Then again I might not. But it's the only chance I've got to finish the thing. I did finish a story—it just wasn't a story that I liked, that's all. But that took me a couple, three months to write. And then I went back and worked another three months on the version you're reading now.

JW: Once you'd made that leap and knew this was going to be in the third person with a female point-of-view character, how much at that point did you know about the story?

TW: Well, by no means everything. I was surprised, as I often am in writing a story, by many of the things that came up. For example, the appearance of the Jesuit martyrs in the story was a late thought in the process. You ask, what's the genesis of a story? Almost everything a writer is doing at a given time can be part of the genesis of a story. I was reading Parkman's wonderful book, *The Jesuits in North America*, and I was riveted by his description of the martyrdom of Brébeuf and Lalement. I dreamt about it a couple of nights. It exerted itself on the story I was writing in a strange way, because it helped me to see that much of what the story was about had to do with power. It illuminated that for me. There are so many forces at play in the writing of a story. Take "The Dead," Joyce's story. Why did he write that story in the first place? Because somebody scolded him about *Dubliners*, told him he'd left out something essential to the people of Dublin, their great sense of hospitality. And he agreed. He went back and he wrote, I think, the greatest thing he ever wrote. Somebody said something that illuminated his own work for him.

When I made the peculiar juxtaposition that allowed the Jesuits to spill into the story, I knew that there was something right and even necessary about it. I wrote this story thirteen or fourteen years ago now, and it's hard to recover all the stages of its evolution because I don't keep rough drafts.

JW: Why don't you keep drafts?

TW: They embarrass me, to tell you the truth. Many writers seem to have a tremendous confidence in their futures and a certain assumption that generations to come are going to be interested in what they've written at every stage. I guess I really don't have that feeling. I only want people to see my work at its very best. I don't even let my wife look at things I'm writing until I'm done with them, or at least until

I've brought them as far as I can. I come very slowly to the ends of my stories, and the work I do to get there is rough. It's often very false. It's awkward. It's not interesting to me. It might be interesting, I suppose, to somebody who wanted to see just how dramatic a difference revision can make to a hopeless writer, to give everyone else hope. But I think part of my reluctance is that people would think I was crazy, really, to be a writer, if they could see my early drafts and see how hard it is for me to get from one place to another.

JW: Do you get terribly discouraged?

TW: Less and less so because I know now that it will finally work out. It used to be much harder for me because it seems such a strange way to write. And I knew that other people weren't writing that way. I thought there must be something wrong with me. But now I've learned that this is the way I write. And I can't imagine doing anything else. I love finishing a good story. Or finishing what I think is a good book. No feeling can compare. And then it's all been worth it. But it's hard as it goes, sometimes. Once I get a first draft down, once I really know where I'm going and what the story is about, and what I'm trying to do, then a kind of playfulness enters in to my writing that I absolutely live for. It's getting that first draft out that's very, very hard for me.

JW: Do you ever get a draft out and get stuck with it? Like not know—

TW: How to crack it?

JW: Yeah.

TW: Once in a while that happens to me. It does happen sometimes. And then I just throw the story away. I'll fool with it for a while and then throw it away. Once in a while I'll finish something that I like but don't really think is a serious story. That happened to me last year. I'm going to let the story be published, but I'm probably not going to include it in a collection. I think it's a funny story, and it's an odd story. I like it. But in the end it really doesn't earn its keep for me, so I probably won't collect it.

JW: So you have a good number of uncollected stories?

TW: Oh yes, I have enough uncollected stories to make a couple of collections, probably. At least one. But I won't collect them. Now and then I'll go back and reread them, wondering if I was just being too hard on myself. And I'll say no, I wasn't.

JW: It must be a difficult position to negotiate. I mean to be at a point in your writing life where you could, I would assume, get a story published just about anywhere you want.

TW: I wish.

JW: Am I completely naive about that? I would assume that most magazines would be very happy to publish your work.

TW: I've been very lucky. But there's a lot of competition. Don't forget, Saul Bellow had won the Nobel Prize before he was ever able to place a story in the *New Yorker*. "The Silver Dish" was the first story he ever had in the *New Yorker*. Magazines are run by editors with tastes of their own. And that's the way it ought to be. What other way could it be? Some editors seem hospitable to my fiction; others don't. It isn't a question, though, of my being able to finish a story and send it out and be sure of selling it, because that really isn't the case. I've got a story right now I really like that I'm sending to quarterlies, because I know I can't place it with large-circulation magazines because of the things that go on in it. André Dubus has an essay on being a writer, in which he says that there's a moment when something happens in a story he's writing, something untoward or violent, and he thinks to himself, Well, there goes the *New Yorker*. And the moment he has that thought, a wonderful sense of release and freedom comes over him— that it is no longer even possible to think about responding to some editor's taste. He's beyond the pale already and it gives him freedom. And I think that's exactly where you start becoming interesting as a writer, when you give up trying to second-guess some editor somewhere into taking a story, which you can never count on anyway. It doesn't do to try to figure it out. You just write the best you can and hope that somebody out there is going to hear you.

I know that Ray Carver's stories were submitted to the *New Yorker* for years before they began to publish them. And I know that some of his best stories were rejected by the *New Yorker* before they began to take his stories. Why? I'm not attributing corruption to them just because he got well known in the interim. I honestly think that at some point they began to like his stories, though they hadn't liked the others. But why? Where's the line that was crossed there? I don't see it. So it's a very whimsical business. You become especially aware of it as a short story writer. Novelists will characteristically work for three or four years before they have something to send out. But story writers have something to send out every few months, so they're much more aware of the caprice of response. Also, when you publish a collection of stories and the reviews start coming in, one reviewer says this is a wonderful collection and the story that's obviously the best story in here is such and such. And if only such stories as, and then he names the obviously worst one, would live up to this level . . . blah-blah-blah. Then you get another review which names a completely different set of stories as the obviously best ones and the obviously worst ones. And you suddenly realize that what Edmond Wilson said is true—"No two readers read the same book." In the end you have to be the arbiter of your fiction, the judge of your fiction, the harshest judge of your fiction, as you are your own best reader. Who else is there in the end that you have to please? I have an acquaintance who is a very successful novelist commercially. I happen to know that she hates her own work. She's an absolutely miserable person, a really unhappy woman. And she's defensive. She talks a lot about how much money she makes and all this. She's clearly made miserable by her feelings about her own work. I know another woman who is also very commercially successful whose stuff is crap. But she doesn't believe that her stuff is crap, and she's quite happy. If you're not pleasing yourself, you haven't pleased anybody important.

JW: And you probably will never feel any satisfaction.

TW: Let's hope not. That's the myth that sustains me.

JW: Getting back to "In the Garden of the North American Martyrs": that was not the first story that you wrote in this collection.

TW: No, by no means. The first published story in there came out in '76. That is the story called "Smokers." Actually, there's another story in here that predates it, called "Face to Face." That was written in '73 or so, though it wasn't actually published until '78.

JW: Do you always have to be sure you've found the right first sentence in order to find the rest of a story?

TW: I simply need a place to begin. Later on, when I revise, I often think of a better first line, especially, of course, if I've decided to change point of view, as I did in this story. Once in a while I'm lucky enough to find the right first sentence in the very beginning. For example, the tone I struck in the first line of "The Poor Are Always with Us" was right and helped me find the rest of the story. I also liked the first sentence I wrote for "The Rich Brother." But that doesn't always happen. I try to be as open to chance as possible when

I'm writing. If I have things too firmly in mind I lose a certain fluidity and ability to be surprised, which is very important to me. In this story I realized I needed to begin with the image of this woman making herself a completely accommodated creature.

JW: What particular passages gave you special trouble? Do you recall any in the story?

TW: Her speech, at the end. I didn't know how far to go with it. To some extent it bursts the bounds of traditional realistic fiction. The voice becomes prophetic. In fact, I think some of those passages are from the Psalms and the Prophets. Jeremiah is the source of a couple of lines. They're all jumbled together in my mind, but they came out, I think, coherently. But she's definitely speaking in a heightened voice there. It isn't a realistic story of the kind, say, in *Dubliners*. And the decision whether to allow that to happen in the story was a tough one to make because it then became a different kind of story—a parable, almost, rather than the kind of story I think of myself as writing.

JW: That ending seems to work very well on a realistic level, though. I guess partly that might be because she's at a podium giving a lecture to an audience.

TW: It lends itself to that, it does. I tried to hold it as close as I could to the possible. I didn't want to lose the story's authority by becoming just clever, or facile.

JW: John Gardner talks about psychic distance, something I've never felt completely confident that I understood. But this story starts from a fairly distant point of view and sort of zooms in quite seamlessly. And it was only on rereading it several times that I could identify the moment when the perspective becomes more intimate. I think this happens with the arrival of Louise's letter. That's where the dialogue begins. I was wondering whether this was something that had given you a lot of trouble—achieving that sort of fluidity.

TW: Sure. It's hard to know when to give up that omniscience. The problem is that if you don't give it up at certain moments, you compromise the story. You get in the way of the character. Your presence in the story is too . . . how can I put it, *consoling*: Well, things can't go wrong because the master of ceremonies is here, right? You've got to fade at certain points. And obviously the problem is knowing just when to do it. Because there certainly is an unapologetically omniscient voice in the beginning, a voice that's different from hers, when we hear things from her point of view. The temptation was to continue to exercise that throughout the story, and here and there I did. I allow myself comments and explanations that are not exactly in her register, in her voice. But my aim was to hand the story over to her.

JW: Did you know much about Louise when you started this version of the story?

TW: By the time I got this far along, in this draft, yes, of course I did. But I had to explore her. And the way I explore my characters is by writing them. I'm not very good at sitting down and thinking a whole story out before I write it. I don't seem to have that gift. I really have to sit down and write the story out, and write my way into the story, and just keep going at it again and again and again, sinking farther and farther into it just by spending more time with it. In that way I get to know the characters. The main character was very, very different in different drafts.

JW: In what ways?

TW: Well, in one draft I had her niece living with her, who'd had to leave home because she was pregnant. So there was an additional onus on Mary and a necessity to work. But that felt cluttered. It was another character to develop, another situation. Once I made the decision to allow the prophetic voice to enter the story, I thought it should have the cleanness of line that a parable has, that it shouldn't have those jagged edges and little tributaries that I'm somehow quite willing and happy to have in a more realistic short story.

JW: There seems to be such a fine line between those slightly tangential moments that add a real texture and verisimilitude, and more unrelated asides that can get you sidetracked. I'm thinking of the moment with the deer, when Mary and Louise are in the car. Aside from its immediate vividness, that moment has clear symbolic resonance. But it's not a moment that would have occurred to everybody to include. You then even emphasize the moment by having Mary say "Deer," which adds the slight irony and humor of the double entendre. Was that something that came to you in an earlier draft or something you added later?

TW: That was something that came to me as I wrote my way into the story. I was imagining myself going along the road, and the sense of the old country asserted itself in the great wilderness that underlies the veneer we live in. That percolated up from a later sense of the story. So that wasn't in an earlier draft, no. I know what you mean. There's a passage in a John Cheever story that I really love, "The Sorrows of Gin," when a man is driving to get his runaway daughter at the railway station, and a flurry of leaves blows across his headlight. Why that breaks my heart, that image, it's hard to say, but it does. And it's not anything you can thematically explain. You could make an argument for it, but really I think it's irreducible. The image works on the nerves more than in the mind. It's a wonderful moment, Cheever at his very best, I think.

JW: In "The Brigadier and the Golf Widow" there's that wonderful line, "Who, after all these centuries, can describe the fineness of an autumn day?"

TW: He tries again and again.

JW: And his descriptions get more and more amazing every time. There's another moment like that at the very end of your story, when Mary realizes she doesn't know what Brébeuf's last words were. And the silence of her audience is beginning to well up, a silence we already know she equates with water and drowning. At that moment she hears someone "whistling in the hallway outside, trilling the notes like a bird, like many birds." That line recalls the beautiful image at the very beginning, at the end of the second paragraph about her thoughts that she kept to herself: "and the words for them grew faint as time went on; without quite disappearing they shrank to remote nervous points, like birds flying away." That relates both to the wilderness theme and also her struggle to reemerge. Was that something that you were aware of right away?

TW: It's an image. Language, especially the language which she speaks at the end, her own language, is freedom, is flight. It's why I use the image of birds there. It's song too.

JW: Was that something that you wrote and then discovered, the connection with the image at the beginning? Or did you have to work that in later?

TW: I'm not exactly sure which came first, whether the image at the end came and then I went back to the beginning and found a way of preparing for it, or the other way. I have a feeling, though, that the image at the beginning was antecedent to the one at the end. That that was a right, natural way to describe someone's language deserting them. Then it was a natural thing to pick it up again at the end.

I wish you could have talked to me when I was writing the final drafts, because then you would know everything about the story. I'd been living with it for four or five months, thinking about it day and night. And I knew literally why every pause was there. I had a reason for it. Now I have to go back and second-guess myself, which is one of the problems with not keeping drafts.

JW: At what point did the ending become clear to you? At what point did you start to get a sense where things might be leading, that there might be this sort of prophetic moment at the end? Did you have a strong sense of direction early on as you were writing it?

TW: That ending became possible through my reading the Parkman book. I wonder if a writer is able to identify the motion in his mind that suddenly delivers up a possibility. I can't do that in retrospect. Because the mind surprises you. I'll bet that Cheever was surprised by the image of those leaves blowing across the headlights of the car when he was writing "The Sorrows of Gin." I'll bet that in the first draft anyway he was taken aback by it. Startled and frightened. I know that when I had the idea of doing what I did in this story, I was surprised by it. Obviously that couldn't have come to me if I hadn't been reading that book, and even had a couple of dreams about it. But beyond saying that, who knows? The mind works even when we're not aware of it working or thinking of it working. Certainly when I'm up here "writing," what I'm really doing much of the time is walking around. I walk a lot. I don't even know what I'm doing half the time up here. But something is happening.

JW: There's a lot of pacing space up here.

TW: Friends of mine come up and say, "Why don't you have a desk in the middle of the room or something like that, or a bed? Why don't you fill this room up?" But what I've always wanted was a place to walk. I just walk back and forth and back and forth.

JW: No window to look out while you're sitting at your desk?

TW: No, absolutely not. That's death for me. I cannot have a window near my desk. I had an acquaintance in Massachusetts who had a bank of windows looking out on the ocean. I don't know how he ever got a day's work done. He didn't actually get a day's work done.

JW: Those moments of surprise that occur when you're writing: are those moments the things that really sustain you?

TW: Yes, they are. That's what I live for. They sustain me even if I don't have very many of them. I live with the expectation that I will have more, the faith that I will have more. What I could predict I will do when I sit down to write is not what I want to end up with. I want to end up with what surprises me along the way, what jumps out at me from the potential of my work and not from what I've already realized about it before I've even started. If I'm simply writing down what I already know, it is of no earthly interest to me. And not only that, everyone else will know it anyway. Simply obvious stuff. I'm not subtle. When I sit down to write, I discover things that I have, for one reason or another, not admitted, not seen, not reflected on sufficiently. And those are the things that I live for in other people's fiction as well as my own.

JW: At one point in this story, you offer this description of Louise: "Enthusiasm for other people's causes did not come easily to Louise, who had a way of sucking in her breath when familiar names were mentioned, as though she knew things that friendship kept her from disclosing." This strikes me as a good example of what we're talking about.

TW: That's an important moment for me in the story because in writing that sentence I came to know something about that character. I didn't start off knowing that about Louise. I discovered it by writing that sentence. You know, language leads you to these discoveries. Until you start practicing the language of the story, start hearing the music of the story, you can't learn what the story has to tell you. That's why it's so important for me to learn from the writing. Writing is not just a process of getting out what I've already thought, what's already in my head. Though it can be for very good writers exactly that. A writer of my acquaintance had a blackboard that ran all around his office, and he would keep detailed notes on the blackboard of everything that was going to happen in the novel he was writing. That worked for him; it wouldn't work for me.

JW: These pivotal moments, these moments of surprise that you talk about happening in your stories: do most of them occur in revision, as opposed to the first draft where you're just trying to get the skeleton down?

TW: Well, it's hard to assign an order to these things, especially now. When I used to work in longhand, it would almost always be in subsequent drafts those things would come to me. Now that I work on a computer like almost everybody else I know, it's hard to say which draft is which because I'm always going back. I don't have stacks of paper. It's an ideal machine for me because all the drafts are killed. The word dies as soon as it becomes obsolete. I don't even have to throw it in the trash can anymore. But yes, revision is a very imaginatively active time for me. I have a hard time letting go of stories because I enjoy revising so much.

JW: Does it seem almost artificial to you to even distinguish between drafts?

TW: At this point it does. I used to have discrete drafts. I had a first and a second and a third and a fourth and a fifth. Now it's impossible to identify different drafts because it's all one, with this new machine we've got.

The truth is, I wouldn't keep drafts anyway. Part of that, I guess, is just wanting to—what would be an explanation? I tend to have effaced a lot of things about my past. I've only recently begun to write about my past. Maybe it's a symptom of that desire to appear in some ideal mode right in the present, as if I'd sprung there, full-blown. I think that has something to do with why I don't keep drafts. If I write something good, I'd like the impression to be that it arrived by magic rather than struggle.

JW: Why does it make me think of the boy in *This Boy's Life* creating his transcripts and letters of recommendation?

TW: Right. He's creating a fictional, ideal boy, isn't he?

JW: At what point did you know that Louise had to be a scholar, a Benedict Arnold scholar?

TW: That was one of those little flashes. I remember writing it. I was getting on toward the end of the story. I had never mentioned what her scholarship was. And I thought that would be perfect. She would have written the book on Benedict Arnold.

JW: I guess this is an example of what my English teachers would have called foreshadowing, but at its best: you sense it's a fact without realizing its full significance. I only noticed it when I was rereading.

TW: Right. You don't know what's going to happen when you first come across it, so it has no meaning then. It's a neutral fact, except that it can color your sense of her a little bit, without your quite knowing it.

JW: A similar moment occurs when Louise says to Mary on the phone "Now don't get your hopes *too* high."

TW: Exactly. It all means something. You just don't know what it means at the time.

JW: In retrospect, the reader can also appreciate the cumulative significance of Mary's physical problems, too—the hearing aid, the lung disorder, and maybe especially the disappearing eyebrows. Have you ever sensed that any of your academic colleagues have been offended by this story?

TW: Oddly enough they seem to like it. None of them seem to think that this applies to them.

JW: They just *know* jerks.

TW: Sure, it's somebody else. It's had the unfortunate effect that I get stuck on a lot of search committees because they think I'll be clean and won't do that kind of thing, which is true. I invented a rather demonic search for the sake of the story. I certainly know that things like that happen, but I've always been impressed with the fairness of the people I work with.

JW: You meet both good people and jerks in any line of work.

TW: You do, absolutely. I just teach in the fall now, and I have been for the last five years. I'm not quite so immersed in the life of the department as I was for the two or three years before. But I've noticed that during tenure cases, even people who have been at odds ideologically with other people in the department don't use that against them when they're up for tenure and promotion. They try to figure out what it is they're really trying to do and call it that way. It's always impressed me, the fundamental fairness of the people here. But I understand that's not true everywhere.

JW: One particular line in the story captures perfectly a kind of pompous fatuousness—during the interview, when Dr. Howells is ruminating on precipitation and says "But it's a *dry* rain."

TW: Well, that's the kind of thing you only hear in interviews, isn't it?

JW: How do names come to you?

TW: I fool around a lot with names. Names are important. It's obvious, I suppose. But often I'll read a story and not be comfortable with it. An unease will come over me, and I won't be able to identify it. And then I'll realize, well, this character has the wrong name.

JW: Is that reading your story or someone else's?

TW: Someone else's. But that happens to me in the beginning of my own stories. I won't be able to write about the character until I get the right name.

JW: And is it just sort of hit or miss?

TW: I keep fooling around with it until I find the name.

JW: Did these names change at all?

TW: Oh yeah. I fooled around with them.

JW: Do you remember what some of the names were for Mary?

TW: I don't remember what the names were, I'm sorry. It's hard to recover all the processes I went through in writing this story.

JW: How come the Marshall Plan?

TW: That was a misstep, I think, because an Arnold Scholar wouldn't have been writing about the Marshall Plan in the first place.

JW: Maybe that's why she didn't do anything with this particular paper—tried something new without success. I like that line, "I can't get enough of the Marshall Plan," because you can't tell for sure whether Dr. Howells is being snide or sincere.

TW: Right. I think that line had a lot to do with it. I think I actually once heard somebody say that, and it went into my bank.

JW: What about the title of the story? Was that from the Parkman book?

TW: No. There's a church up in northern Vermont called the Church of the North American Martyrs. A writer named Roger Weingarten, a poet, had a book of poems called *Ethan Benjamin Bolt* published in the late '70s. And there's a line in there which goes, "Near the garden of the North American Martyrs." I was writing the story at the time and it just lashed out at me, so I asked him if I could use it. There's no way I could quote it as an epigraph because it had nothing to do with what I was writing about. He wasn't writing about any of these things. I asked him if I could use that phrase as the title of the book, and he was pleased to have me do that.

JW: Do you have a hard time with titles?

TW: I have a hard time with titles in that it takes me a while to get them. They're a very important part of the story, so I work pretty hard at getting them. Just as an example, these are all possible titles for a piece I'm working on right now [showing a page-length list]. I'm always writing things down as they come to me. Almost all of these are absolutely terrible. But one of these days I'll write one down and it won't be.

JW: In reading this story as it first appeared in *Antaeus* and then later in the O. Henry anthology, I did notice a few changes. The O. Henry version is exactly the same as the *Antaeus* version, and the changes between this draft and the final one that appeared in your first collection are all relatively minor. Here, for example: "on wet mimeographed paper" becomes "on mimeographed paper which felt wet." Or: "No library and no books to speak of," and in the later version you got rid of the "to speak of."

TW: That was a grotesque emendation, wasn't it? It was no books to speak of . . . if it has no books, how can it possibly be a library, right? It's a comical, grotesque change. Why I changed the other, I don't remember. I think for the sake of accuracy. And also, there's something in the sentence, the sound of the sentence that I like: "on mimeographed paper which felt wet." That sentence duplicates for me the sensation of picking one of those newsletters up—the delayed reaction you have when you pick it up and it feels wet. That's what I wanted to catch in that sentence. Why did I change the other one though?

JW: I wonder if maybe you were thinking that this attributed to Mary an element of superiority or snobbishness that you didn't like?

TW: Could be. It might well have been the reason. It does do that a little.

JW: Because it does sound almost a little like Louise.

TW: Being a little superior about the books in there. No *real* books.

JW: And this suggests that this school, perhaps, is not long for this world.

TW: No, it isn't. They haven't even stocked their library yet.

JW: And then the comma after . . .

TW: I always mess around with commas. After Benedict Arnold is it?

JW: Yes.

TW: I don't know why. I have these fits when I don't like commas at all, and I take them all out of everything. But I don't like comma-ridden prose. Jim Harrison's prose has a lot of velocity and power and he hardly uses commas at all.

JW: This was an interesting one: from "expense of bringing me" to "expense of bringing her." A subtle shift in point of view.

TW: Yeah, I like that better.

JW: Then, a little farther down the page, you changed "as if" to "like."

TW: Technically, of course, this is the more grammatical way but I preferred the colloquial here.

JW: Most of the revisions of the *Antaeus* version are, if not minor, quite subtle. Do you regard these changes mostly as tinkerings?

TW: Yes. Tinkerings.

JW: Here's another change you made: in the early version "sonofab-itch" is run together.

TW: I put it all together? I think that's the way she would have said it. She'd run it together.

JW: And when Mary's waiting for the interview to begin, you just changed the time to twenty minutes from the original half hour.

TW: I'll tell you something else I would change here. This woman would never have written two books. She would have written maybe one book. And that's the way I read it now, when I read it out loud. She never would have gotten another book out.

JW: And you changed "attacks" to "raids."

TW: I'm endlessly fooling with words. Every time I sit down to write, I go through just about everything I've written up to that point. It takes me hours just to get where I can start writing for the day, because I'm fooling around with words all the time. I just reread, with great pleasure, this book of Philip Roth's, *The Ghost Writer*. Zuckerman goes to visit Lonoff, the famous writer. And Lonoff is this old sourpuss who talks about going up to his study and monkeying around with words and taking them out and putting them in and changing around the order and so on. This is this great writer's life. I felt such a sense of dismal recognition.

JW: Reading it ["In the Garden of the North American Martyrs"] again the other day, did you see anything else you'd change now?

TW: Not really. The kind of stories I mostly prefer to read these days are not of this kind, to tell you the truth. It has a lot of symbolic machinery, this story. It has an almost mathematical logic. It leads very purposefully to where it's going. It has a very clear ending, almost a triumphal ending. It's a well-made story. It's written with a great deal of irony. And those are all things that I'm not particularly interested in doing myself right now. I prefer to write a story that doesn't have any obvious symbolic machinery, that is essentially unironic. The voice that tells it might be, but the conception is not. And a story in which the ending is not quite so clean and well pronounced as in this story.

JW: It sounds like you're describing the distinction between this story and, say, "Sanity."

TW: That's a possible example.

JW: How come?

TW: I don't know. It's because I don't have the certainties about things that I think I had then. I have a more tentative feeling about what I know, about what goes on between people. This is a story whose truth is a very abstract truth, it seems to me. It's about power. It's about manipulation. But I pushed the characters to a certain grotesquerie of conception. And now I'm a little more interested, at least for the purposes of my stories, in nuances of relationships between people, and "Sanity" is a good example because that's also a story about power. It's about a girl trying to take the upper hand for her own protection. But the plot is less pronounced.

JW: But in this collection there are stories that have less emphatic endings.

TW: There are stories more of the other kind in this collection.

JW: "Smokers," I think, ends on sort of a more open note.

TW: "Smokers" is more in that line.

JW: Now, did you submit this ["In the Garden," *Antaeus* version]? Did you submit the earlier drafts before you hit on the final one?

TW: No. I knew they weren't right.

JW: Did you submit it any place other than *Antaeus*?

TW: No, I didn't. How did it happen? I sent it there and Dan Halpern called me up about two weeks later. Said how much he loved the story and asked me if I had any others. In fact, I had two other stories that I hadn't even sent out. I sent them to him, and he took those stories too. It was an incredible break for me. I was living in Arizona at the time, and it was a very encouraging thing for me to have that happen. The same as with Michael Curtis publishing that story "Smokers" in the *Atlantic* a couple of years before. In terms of the publication times, it would have been almost four years before, because he published that in '76 and these stories didn't come out until '80. I had a long period where I didn't have anything published at all. But you don't want to be thinking about that. And God knows, you don't ever want to think about how old you are, not for any reason.

JW: So you think it took you a total of four or five months to get that story out?

TW: That's right.

JW: How many drafts would you guess?

TW: Oh boy, that story ate up drafts. Eight or nine drafts for that story before the last *t* was crossed.

JW: How did you decide to place this where you did in the collection?

TW: I was thinking about that the other day because I was looking for it. I couldn't find it. It made me laugh, because I remember I gave a lot of thought to placing these stories in the collection. Each one of them had a great reason for being where it was. Now I couldn't even find it. We think these things are so damn important at the time. And here I am, the author of the collection, and I have no idea where to look for the story. I will go on doing that with my next collection. I will always do it. But the fact of the matter is, when I sit down to read a collection, I skip around, even though I know that the poor son of a bitch who wrote the collection did the same thing I did.

I just got William Trevor's collection *Family Sins* the other day. I skipped around looking for the short ones to read first to see if I liked them, and then I read a couple of the longer ones here and there. I always look for stories whose titles I like. And I tend to read those before stories whose titles seem bland to me, or conventional. So readers are constantly confounding the purposes of writers in organizing their work. A novel is obviously different. Nobody can do that with a novel.

JW: One of my favorites in this collection is "Hunters in the Snow." That's another story that tests some of the sort of traditional conventions.

TW: Does it?

JW: I think it does.

TW: Not formally it doesn't.

JW: No, because it's very well made.

TW: It's a "well-made" story, true.

JW: The whole business about the dog, that's very carefully constructed.

TW: Exactly.

JW: What I mean is that this realistic narrative begins to spiral into the surreal. These guys driving off in the wrong direction with their buddy bleeding to death in the bed of the pickup. I've often wondered if, on one level at least, this story wasn't intended to lampoon the sort of gushy, confessional mentality that's been so prevalent in recent years.

TW: The language they speak is very much that language. That story has been made into a couple of little movies, three of them actually. People keep making it into these half-hour movies. It's very easy to adapt. They take the dialogue directly. And they've all made them with the hope of selling them to PBS, but it's such an ugly little story that they won't show it. I can see why they do it. It's got a good strong narrative line, and the dialogue is funny in a way that the characters who speak it aren't aware of. I like that story. That's one of my favorite stories still.

JW: Does your reading change while you're working?

TW: Yes, it does. When I'm in hot pursuit of my own work, I tend to read history and biography and canonical, classic fiction by inimitable writers like Dickens and Tolstoy. Right now I'm reading Turgenev's *Sportsman's Sketches*.

JW: Inimitable so you won't be tempted?

TW: Absolutely. At these times I try to stay away from contemporary writers. I read them in the lulls, when I'm in a valley between writing periods. I do, in fact, keep up pretty well with contemporary American fiction. But sometimes I need to stand back from it. By reading the older fiction I'm setting myself up in relationship to their standards rather than those of my contemporaries. That's as much of an explanation as I can make for it.

JW: Do you think about that a lot—critical reputation or historical significance—or do you try not to think about it?

TW: No, I don't think about it much. That way lies madness. I can remember thinking, If I ever get a story published—just one—I'll be happy. And I haven't ever lost that sense of excitement at having a story taken somewhere, or even finishing a story that I like a lot. I never, ever thought that I'd be able to have the kind of life that I've been able to have as a writer. It's been an amazing kind of surprise and blessing to me. The rest, as Eliot said, is not our business, it really isn't.

The thing you have to remember, that all of us have to remember who are writers, is that in almost every other way in life, time is our enemy. But time is a writer's friend. Writing happens over time and it gets better over time, with very, very few exceptions. The time that works against you in every other way is working for you in this way. You're seasoning, you're deepening. If you continue to write, and if you ask the best of yourself, and if you're working toward that all the time, it will happen. You don't give up. If you know the sound you want to hear, you'll hit the note eventually.

JW: In one of his interviews, Carver talked about how heartening it is for any struggling writer to look at the early drafts of great writers.

TW: I certainly agree that it is heartening. I enjoy reading the first drafts of other writers. And it's certainly neurotic of me not to want to share mine. I had file cabinets full of things. Not just rough drafts, but stories I had finished that I thought, well, it seems bad to me now but someday it might seem better. When we moved here, I did a real purging. Just emptied it out. It felt great. Carrying out to the garbage can things that I worked months on, years on. A very strange feeling. In what other profession can you do that?

JW: In your introduction to the Chekhov collection you edited [*A Doctor's Visit* (New York: Bantam Books, 1988)], you discuss the sense of proximity and unpredictability in Chekhov. I think of those as being two hallmarks of your work. In "The Missing Person," for example, you never expect when you start the story that it's going to lead—

TW: To the odd places it leads to.

JW: Yes. I wondered whether what you'd written in reference to Chekhov is equally important to you in your own work.

TW: Yes. I was rereading that introduction the other day. And I was amused at myself, as I would have been if someone else had written it, as assigning to Chekhov virtues that really are virtues that I would hope for myself. Do you know what I mean? I'm not saying it's a self-serving introduction so much as one that expresses my own hopes as a story writer. I look at him and maybe what I'm seeing are a lot of my own hopes realized. I guess I'm praising him for the things that I value. And I'm probably not mentioning things that other people would. For example, I don't talk much about his wonderful characterizations, which are of a different kind than interests me. He works a little more from type than I like to. Russian literature abounds in character types. He does that too. In his best stories he particularizes more, like Gurov in "Lady with Pet Dog." Anyway, that is something about his stories that I like—that they are very immediate. Do you like Chekhov's stories?

JW: Yes, but I'm always uncertain about translations. One version is titled "Lady with Pet Dog," another "Lady with Lap Dog." Or take the story "Enemies," which is included in your anthology, *A Doctor's Visit*. I've seen several different translations of that story. Sometimes it's titled "Two Tragedies." The very first paragraph changes dramatically from one translation to another. The first line of one indicates the events are taking place at ten in the morning, and of the others, ten at night. One translator describes the mother giving way to "the first paroxysm of despair," while the next describes her yielding to "the ecstasy of despair." Those kinds of inconsistencies make me nervous, make me wonder how much actual Chekhov I'm getting.

TW: I've read a lot of different translations, too. I think the Constance Garnett translations—they took a beating from Nabokov and from Edmund Wilson and from other people—are the best translations available in English. They might not be the most *accurate*. I understand they're not. But Ronald Hingley, who is accurate, has such a dead ear. Ann Dunnigan has some very, very fine translations, as good as Garnett's. "At Sea" and "In Exile" in *A Doctor's Visit* are both by Ann Dunnigan.

JW: Now you also mention his dissatisfaction with "The Steppe" for being too episodic and loose-knit. And I wonder also if that's something that you're suspicious of in general.

TW: "The Steppe" is not pointed the way his later fiction is. It's like Turgenev in *A Sportsman's Sketches*. You can see very clearly the antecedent of "The Steppe" there, where you've got the young fellow wandering around the province and recording his observations. But you don't have a strong sense of how this is affecting him. What's his stake in what he's reporting here? He's simply the eye; he's the camera of the story. What Chekhov developed so beautifully in his later fiction is the suggestion that the narrator of the story cannot escape the consequences of the story he's telling, that if he does, it's not a story. It's an anecdote, it's a tale, or something else. It's the same with Joyce. In "Araby," for example, the narrator is implicated in his story. The narrator is changed by his story. He realizes his folly as he's standing in the empty gallery. That isn't there in Turgenev, and it's not there in some of the early Chekhov.

JW: In your introduction to another anthology you've edited, *Matters of Life and Death*, you describe the stories that you chose as speaking to us "without flippancy about things that matter." I thought maybe that summed up succinctly your ultimate criterion for a good story.

TW: We all know that some things matter and other things don't matter. And it's bullshit to pretend otherwise. That's what the best fiction really does. It requires that our attention be on matters of importance. Those stories in that anthology are about things that were of urgency to the writers. Not necessarily because they're autobiographical. How could Stanley Elkin's story be autobiographical? But it is clearly a cry about something that is deeply disturbing to him in the makeup of this universe. He wrote a continuation of that particular piece called "The Living End" about a dead man conscious in his grave. It's an amazing, nightmarish work, surreal and at the same time absolutely believable, the way a dream is when you're caught in it. I can only imagine that Elkin is writing about what it's like to be caught in a body that doesn't work anymore. It's a vital spirit, his is. And he's found a way of writing about his situation that isn't autobiographical in the traditional sense but has a spiritually autobiographical truth. You don't have to know that about him to appreciate the work. But I can't help noticing it. I think that's why Poe wrote so much about people being buried alive and walled up in tombs before they're dead, that kind of thing. He had a sense of being different, an outsider in this culture and place, as he was, and ostracized. I think he had a personal sense of being buried alive. And he was writing out of his sense of alienation and being the only living thing in a musty tomb, which was how his society appeared to him. This nightmare feeling gets transmuted into those horrible images in his fiction.

JW: Sometimes it seems such a fine line between flippancy and the kind of vitality that can really make a story breathe. I wonder if you have a hard time walking that line?

TW: I do, at times. When I was a kid, one of the ways I got by was as a cutup, a class clown. Being a wise guy, making people laugh. I can do it. I can make the lines. But fiction isn't a collection of funny lines, or even quotable lines. One of the things about Ray Carver's work, for example, is I can think of very few lines to quote. That tells you something of the power of his work. Everything should be subordinated to the integrity of the story, to its larger, ultimate purposes. And so people like me have to learn to make their sense of humor, such as it is, larger.

Bonnie Lyons and Bill Oliver

Q: What was your motive in writing *This Boy's Life?*

A: I started out jotting things down about my childhood, because I felt them slipping away, and I wanted to have some sort of record. Then I saw patterns emerging. Then I began to hear a voice telling it. Also, I recognized that my childhood made a good story. For years I had seen people perk up when I told them some of the things that happened when I was a kid.

Q: Why did you begin the memoir where you did? You weren't born at ten. Why begin at that point?

A: That was the moment at which my mother and I had coincidental hopes. I was old enough then to share her desire to be fantastically rich, to be on top of the situation. I had enough of a grasp on reality to know that we were not on top of the situation and that life could be better than it was. And so the trip out West that begins the memoir was no longer a matter of her hauling her kid around. It was a joint venture. We both wanted that. We begin this book in transit, in hope, and we end it in transit, in hope. These hopes are going to be disappointed at the end as they were at the beginning, but the fact that hope persisted is what I wanted to leave at the end of the story.

Q: You insist, throughout the memoir, on keeping a clear distinction between the boy and the adult narrator. It's as if you don't see them as different stages of the same person but as completely different people.

A: I don't bring the adult in very often.

Q: He's there, you feel him.

A: Yes, you feel him there.

Q: And while you don't want to make a bridge between the boy and the adult, the reader naturally finds himself wondering, How did the

From "An Interview with Tobias Wolff," conducted by Bonnie Lyons and Bill Oliver, CONTEMPORARY LITERATURE, Vol 31, No 1 (Spring 1990) © 1990. Reprinted with the permission of The University of Wisconsin Press.

confused teenager we're left with at the end, this compulsive liar, become the adult fiction writer? You don't give us much help with that. Why not?

A: Why didn't I make a bridge? Gives too much solace to the reader. The boy doesn't know there's going to be any bridge. The boy lives this life ignorant of what is going to happen to him later—as we all do. The child is alone. The child, as I say in the book, moves out of reach of the man. To the extent that I start giving reasons for how this boy gets transformed into this incredibly wonderful adult who's now telling his story, the minute that bridge exists, and that explanation exists, the boy is no longer alone. He is simply in the process of becoming someone else. I think that would compromise the integrity of his experience, to come in with a comforting adult voice all the time. I don't like that tone in childhood memoirs, generally, letting the kid off the hook with this very adult ironical humor, when things really are quite serious. One of the things I took to heart when I was preparing myself to write the book was Graham Greene's *A Sort of Life*, in which he says that memoirs frequently go bad because writers fail to give due gravity to the things that were grave and serious matters when they were young. I wanted to keep a rigid distinction between the child's perceptions and the adult's. It is a calculated risk because it can seem to be an artificial distinction. After all, there was a bridge of some kind. Was it being coy to withhold it? I would rather run the risk of being coy than of crowding the kid out. You have to make those decisions when you write anything, and you always risk one thing to get another. You have to decide what you want most. I most wanted the reader to have a sense of this kid very much on his own, which he was. My mother was certainly a loving person and would give whatever support she could, but she couldn't always give substantial support because her circumstances didn't allow it. So this boy found himself on his own, and I wanted to give a sense of somebody having to fight his own fight. That meant keeping the adult out. Oh, once in a while, I felt I had to account for the effect of some of these things later on, the way they echo into adult life. But I didn't want to do it very often.

Q: Yes, there are selective leaps into the future. The first one is Vietnam. Was there any calculation about which leaps to make, or in what order?

A: Yes, I wanted the reader to be aware very early on in the book that this boyhood is a progression to a place. That the boyhood obsession with weapons has a terminus somewhere, that it ends in war. There's a logical progression in the kind of life that boys are encouraged to lead and dream of in this country. There's a lot of violence in the book—a lot of male violence. That kind of thing all goes somewhere.

Q: You said about your mother, "I could not, cannot put pen to paper without having her with me." Do you see your mother as a kind of muse?

A: I don't write with my mother in mind as my audience. But every time I form a letter, her presence is infused in that activity, so that the very physical act of writing for me is to some extent a collaboration with her presence. She isn't a muse in the way people usually mean it.

Q: You say in the memoir, "I wanted distinction, and the respectable forms of it seemed to be eluding me. If I couldn't have it as a citizen I would have it as an outlaw." The citizen/outlaw distinction is important throughout the book. Do you think being a writer is a way of accommodating both the citizen and the outlaw?

A: Yes, I do. Exactly. Most of the writers I know consider themselves outlaws and yet lead middle-class lives. There aren't too many Hart Cranes left. And so the impulse to break the rules is in our work. The desire to subvert and to probe and to question and to dig the foundations out from under everybody and to represent fraudulent selves to the world, all that is contained and legitimized in imaginative acts. What is destructive and also self-destructive is transformed. You don't give it up. You just find a way of using it.

Q: For all the humor in the memoir, and the implied optimism— because we know the boy did grow up to be a writer, to have success— there's a sense of futility, a sense that no one can really help another person avoid his or her most self-destructive urges. There's a line in the book: "The human heart is a dark forest."

A: I stole that line. It's from Chekhov. It's in a letter of his. Actually, he says, "The human heart is a slumbering forest." I didn't even know I'd stolen it. But when I was reading his letters I found that line. This was after the book came out, and I thought, well, I must have read this before. But you're right. There is a certain sense of helplessness in the memoir at the way in which people's destinies and natures are going to work themselves out regardless. At the same time, the people I'm writing about do not make themselves available to lessons, to learning much, to being helped much. I have seen people allow themselves to be helped. I didn't. I was not of that sort myself. I seemed to have to learn everything the hard way, to stumble up against every wall before I'd acknowledge that it was there.

Q: One of the things I like about the memoir is that you don't do what childhood memoirs so often do—put most of the blame on the adults. There are some very sympathetically portrayed adults in your book—the nun, the priest, Mr. Howard, Mr. Bolger.

A: Most of the grown-ups I knew, except for Dwight [his stepfather], were very well-meaning.

Q: So we get the sense that, if the boy is not being reached, it's because he's not there to be reached.

A: Doesn't want to be reached. That's right. Secrecy is very important to children. It's one of the only powers they can wield over grown-ups. Your powers are negative when you're a child. Refusing to eat is another power kids have. So, of course, is falsehood. These are ways kids can get even. I never wanted readers to see this kid in the memoir as a victim of the evil adult world. This kid really gets his own back at adults. He's a tough nut. The adults are often his victims.

Q: You talk about your relationship with your best friend, Arthur. You write, "One night he kissed me, or I kissed him, or we kissed each other." I thought, well, that's an interesting formulation. Is it unimportant which of these three possibilities is true?

A: No, it's not unimportant. I wanted not to attribute a quality to the experience it didn't have. I wanted to be very careful about that, because I'm not exactly sure how it happened, and it might have been spontaneous on both our parts. I also wanted the language to reflect that it wasn't a traumatic experience. In fact, a lot of men have told me, on reading that, about similar moments they had with friends—and they went on being friends. Still, it did affect my relationship with Arthur afterwards. I mean, we were both wary. We just didn't know what it meant or how to deal with it. In fact, what did it mean? I don't know what it means *now*. I wanted the language to reflect that, too, by carefully avoiding giving the initiative to either of us. I wanted to show how you are at the mercy of these impulses at that age. Because you're not sure who you are, you're not sure what governs you at any given moment. Things sometimes pass over you like a wind. There's a random quality to many of the experiences of youth.

Q: At one point in the memoir, you talk about defining yourself in opposition to Dwight. In *The Counterlife*, Philip Roth talks about how there is no self except in opposition to others.

A: That's an interesting proposition. I think one of the best things that ever happened to me was that I had this complete creep around me all the time who had no virtues and all the faults. I was going to push against whatever man was around anyway, but what a wonderful thing that the man I had to push against was Dwight.

Q: One reviewer suggested that, in the title of the memoir, you were playing off Philip Roth's *My Life as a Man* or Edmund White's *A Boy's Own Story*. Were you? I thought you were alluding to the magazine *Boy's Life*.

A: Exactly. I meant to suggest an ironic discrepancy between the ideal boyhood portrayed in the magazine and my own experience. I had originally planned to call the book *Boy's Life*, but then I came up with what I thought was the more interesting title.

Q: You said in talking to students earlier today that you try to help beginning writers to find their own voice and the distinctive story they have to tell. Were you implying that each writer has one essential story to tell?

A: No, I was talking about the story they have to tell at that moment. However, I do think that every writer has a kind of "take" on the world that is different from others'. Or has that potential, anyway. The problem is to separate it from the models, the influences, the conventions, the temptations of convention, to try to sieve it out from those things so the writer can begin to recognize what is distinctive in his way of seeing things.

Q: Rereading your work, I wonder if your "take" has to do with imagination and truth and lying.

A: Those questions do keep coming up in my stories. They aren't just philosophical questions to me. They're questions about the conduct of life. They've been very influential in my experience. Imagination was my curse and my blessing when I was young, and I still feel the heavy hand of it.

Q: With the students earlier, you said, "Because I could imagine myself becoming someone else, I could be someone else."

A: That's right. How can you be what you can't imagine being?

Part 2

Q: The curse of it was that it made you very unhappy, frustrated?

A: Yes, frustrated. Because the world doesn't agree with you. The world doesn't share your imaginings of yourself, unless you can pull some kind of an enormous trick on the world and get it to agree, which it will do for only a little while, unless you have the goods to back up that bluff.

Q: Your life and your writing seem to me so directly related to Gatsby. I find it just an overwhelming comparison. Do you see it?

A: Sure, absolutely. I didn't when I was young.

Q: I mean the imagination, changing your name.

A: Self-invention. I think it's very American. We can do that here. Gatsby even invented himself into another class. You can't do that in other countries. Your very speech identifies you. Here you can do that kind of thing.

Q: I wondered if, in writing the memoir, you were like Nick writing about Gatsby.

A: A little bit. A little bit. Yeah, that's a nice image. I like that. That's about right. That's about the way I felt. Nick sees through Gatsby, but he has a real affection for him, too. Then he sees that there was something interesting in what he did. He liked him better than a lot of the people around him, the foul dust that floats in Gatsby's wake.

Q: As long as lying was brought up . . . Most of your characters— many of them, anyway—do tell lies. I realize it's hard to generalize, because they lie for so many different reasons. But what's at the bottom of it? Why is lying so necessary to your characters?

A: The world is not enough, maybe? I'd have to go through every story in which a character tells a lie to try to puzzle that one out. But to lie is to say the thing that is not, so there's obviously an unhappiness with what is, a discontent. Some of the lies are just destructive lies, and at least one of them is a competitive lie. Father Leo ["The Missing Person"] listens to his friend's story, and he feels like he ought to have a story like that to tell. And at the same time, he lies as a way of establishing a common ground with his friend.

Q: James ["The Liar"] is an interesting case. His mother has always complained that he can't carry a tune. But on the bus at the end, he's telling these outrageous lies to the passengers, even making up his own language, and he says, "I *sang* to them in what was surely an ancient and holy tongue" [emphasis added].

A: He's found his voice. He's keeping these stranded people distracted and happy here at the end. He's found something good to do with this craziness of his.

Q: Then there's the boy in the memoir. He's writing out the phony letters of recommendation that will help him get into prep school, and suddenly he sees his true image in this character he's created on paper. As in "The Liar," falsehood helps him discover an inner voice or an inner self. How important is it that these lies are told to strangers?

A: Strangers are more gullible. Also, you're not so accountable to strangers. You're not going to have to live with them. You're free to experiment, so to speak, with a stranger. They're *tabula rasa* as far as you're concerned. It gives you freedom. When I hitchhiked as a kid I used to lay these incredible stories on people, as a way of entertaining them—and myself. I didn't even know what I was going to say. I'd just spin it out. Wing it. I used to lie a lot, but not anymore. That's something I reserve for my fiction now.

Q: I'm often accused of changing stories to make them better.

A: Oh, we all do that. When somebody's telling me a story, and I can feel them hit the rhythm of it, I don't hold them to every nickel and dime. If they say fifty thousand dollars, I don't think fifty thousand dollars, I think a lot of money.

Q: A minute ago, you talked about "winging it." It occurs to me, you've got all these good citizens in your stories, and a fair number of outlaws, too. But there's another kind of character, less common, who is neither the good citizen nor the conscious rule-breaker. This is the character who "wings it." Like James, like Mary ["In the Garden of the North American Martyrs"] when she turns off her hearing aid at the end.

A: Even the outlaws are respecting the rules by being outlaws, allowing themselves to be defined by the social order, if only by opposition. Those who are winging it are really letting go of that connection, of wanting to be defined in some way by the world, either by being inside or outside. So yes, winging it is literally a kind of lifting off, letting go, listening to the voice within and speaking with the magic of that voice rather than the committee around you.

Part 2

Q: Picking up on the phrase "winging it," I noticed, in rereading "In the Garden of the North American Martyrs," all the bird imagery, and I thought, I'll ask him what the students always ask me—did he have all that in mind or not?

A: Yes. I sort of stumble on things as I'm writing the first draft or two, but by the time I've put a story through several revisions I know exactly where every comma has to be. It may be a little bit too overt in this case. I don't know. Because I'm so aware of it, it really sticks out when I read it. There may be impulses in the work that I'm not conscious of, but that kind of stuff I'm very conscious of.

Q: I didn't find it too overt. Including that wonderful bird imagery at the end when she's afraid of sinking and hears someone whistling in the hallway outside, "trilling the notes like a bird, like many birds."

A: And it brings her back. It's a sign of her own voice coming back to her. An image of the words she had lost, like birds flying away.

Q: Do you see your two books of stories simply as collections or do you see each as unified in some way?

A: I think the stories are connected by subject matter and style. The two collections seem to me to be different. I mean, they're obviously by the same person, but each of the collections has a somewhat different character, and that comes from the stories being connected. Next you're going to ask me what connects them, right? It's one of those things I can't unravel backwards.

Q: How about the title of your second collection, *Back in the World*? To take one story and to use it as the title of the collection—as you did with *In the Garden of the North American Martyrs*—is fairly traditional. But to take a phrase from one story [in this instance, "Soldier's Joy"] and to use it as the title of the collection is unusual. By calling it *Back in the World*, did you mean to make the Vietnam background more pervasive?

A: It wasn't just Vietnam. "The world" is what people in religious orders—nuns and priests—call secular life. That's the way Jesus talks about it: The world's yoke is heavy, my yoke is light. So "back in the world" is an expression which has many connotations. I thought it was an expression that caught the spirit of a lot of the stories. I didn't want to use just one story's title this time. When you use the title of one story for the title of a collection, that story really has to carry a lot of weight, because in some way it has to support the claims of all the other stories. I wanted the title to float free. As a matter of fact, I had some pretty good stories that were in the first person that I didn't use in this collection because I wanted a unity of voice and perspective from one story to the next. I wanted you to read it like a novel, with the same kind of narrative presence in each story.

Q: One of my favorite stories in the second collection is "The Missing Person." When I teach that story, there's always a big disagreement among the students about Father Leo and finally about what that story is saying. Some read it as a story about a man with a sincere, deep vocation who is serving a church that does not appreciate his gifts and so wastes them. Others say, no, Leo is a selfish romantic. They don't accept his vocation as genuine in the first place, and they see a positive turn at the end when he says "I'm here" to that neurotic secretary who seeks his protection.

A: That's the way I see it. I see him as a romantic. At the same time, the church is not a benign presence in this story. The story describes how the foundations are rotting, the basement's filled with scummy water, and they're paying crooks to keep it going. I am a Catholic, but that's the way I see the institutional church—I think it's become the cross the believers have to bear. But still, that doesn't give Father Leo an out, because I think his notion of his vocation has been a romantic one. And I think that he has discovered by the end that his vocation is where he is at any given moment and that he has to bring himself completely to that moment. When he says "I'm here," people tend to think of that as a very sad ending. But I always thought of it as a hopeful ending. However, I don't think there's only one right reading. I have to say, too, that I don't think writers own their stories. I don't have the last word on these stories. I think the intention that impels the story for the writer becomes irrelevant after the story is finished, because the story is then an object. It's like a vase or a painting, and it is liable to the interpretations that people bring to it. The writer is not necessarily the best interpreter of the story, because the writer is bound by intention, by what he meant to say. The fact of the matter is, as we all know, some of the most interesting things we say are those things we do not mean to say. And stories contain that matter. I'm often disappointed by the interviews I read with writers. When they start talking about their own work, it seems to me that I have a much richer reading of it than they have, than they seem to have had in mind when they wrote it. So I hesitate to give hard and fast interpretations of my own work. Also, I wrote that story seven or eight years ago, and I had a million things in mind when I wrote it, and I don't remember them all now. I hope they're there to be discovered in the story, but I don't really know. I do know that my sense of the story when I left it was, Leo's been offered another way of seeing his place in the world and of becoming reconciled to it. I don't necessarily mean that he's going to lead this transformed existence afterwards.

Q: Another story I like in that collection is "Desert Breakdown, 1968." One way to describe the movement in the story is that, first, we have this breakup of the family, after they have car trouble in the desert. Mark goes off for the part they need, Crystal [*sic*] loses sight of their little boy, and all of this is very ominous. But then, toward the end, there's a counter movement, back together again. Mark calls his parents for one thing.

A: Out of weakness. Not out of hope.

Q: And then Crystal locates her son and tells off those men who taught him to say "bitch." The reader begins to feel there's this movement back together, however tentative. But then Hope—this predatory woman—appears at the very end holding the two dead rabbits.

A: What a Hope!

Q: It's a very disturbing image you leave us with, one that would seem to contradict whatever positive signs were there.

A: I just don't see this family continuing together. When you look at the way Mark's mind works, and why, you see that his coming back to his wife is, at best, temporary. Perhaps it's a way to satisfy his parents so they'll let him back in the fold and take care of him— because he's not ready to take care of himself in a world which, in this story, is a very predatory world. He's still a baby—as much a baby as his son is. I see this family as a family doomed. But I don't see Crystal as doomed. I find a resourcefulness in her that she's starting to discover. She has to find the means to live in this new landscape that her life has become. As for Mark, all he needs is to have the right chance for escape presented to him. He thinks he will go off with those people in the hearse who pick him up. But what he sees going on among them is so outrageous it shocks him, frightens him off, drives him back to his family. He's ultimately a creature of convention.

Q: I'm sometimes reminded of Flannery O'Connor when I read your fiction. Even some of the story titles are reminiscent of O'Connor—

138

"Worldly Goods," "The Rich Brother," "In the Garden of the North American Martyrs."

A: "The Poor Are Always with Us."

Q: Yes, the very titles suggest a moral, even religious concern. Are you aware of an influence there?

A: Absolutely. I've learned from her stories. They concern moral choice. Choices between good and evil. I think of my own stories as leading up to such a point. The difference is, the choice O'Connor's characters are presented with—or have forced on them—is an irrevocable one, a choice between salvation and damnation. That doesn't happen in such an obvious way in my stories.

Q: In O'Connor's fiction, grace breaks through, usually accompanied by violence. I don't find comparable moments in your stories.

A: I haven't seen too many of those moments myself, so I tend not to write about them. O'Connor's not really a realistic writer. She's a writer of fables. I'm not. I've written a couple, but that's not my mode. Her fiction is made to receive that kind of moment without any sense of dissonance. In my fiction, I think that kind of moment would ring false.

Q: Would you consider "The Rich Brother" one of your fables?

A: That's as close to a fable as I've written. But even there, what compels the rich man to go back for his brother is different from what you'd find in O'Connor. He's going back all right. And I suppose you could say that's an intervention of grace; because he can suddenly imagine his wife standing there and asking him the question God asks Cain: "Where's your brother?" But it's also a natural psychological event in his life. She's going to ask him that question if he goes up to the door without his brother. And he's not going to be able to answer. He's got to go back for him. I guess my sense of what saves people has as much to do with the ordinary responsibilities of family, adulthood, and work as it does these violent eruptions from heaven, which one might look for in vain. I mean, that's the nature of grace. It doesn't come bidden, it comes unbidden. And so I have a different sense of what saves people than O'Connor's. It's grace, but mine takes different forms than hers. She has a somewhat cartoonish idea of fiction. For the deaf, one must shout; for the blind, one must draw large and startling figures. I like her work a lot, though I like it better when she manages to have some affection for her characters, as she does for

139

Parker in "Parker's Back." That's a great story. But sometimes I think the polemicist betrays her humanity. She sets up her characters as weak arguments for which she has a stronger alternative.

Q: You have said that writing is an essentially optimistic act. It assumes that people can be reached, that people can be touched, and even in some cases changed. Do you feel that you write out of one of those impulses? Do you want, for example, to change people?

A: To sit for a moment and realize that other human beings have reality is a change for most of us. Most of us operate on the unacknowledged assumption that we are the only real human beings in the world and the only ones who matter. Stories have the power, I think, to suddenly fill us with the knowledge of other lives and with the importance of those lives to the people who lead them. And, in that way, yes, I write to change people. But I don't mean by changing them that I can bring them around to my point of view.

Q: So you see your work as moral but not prescriptive?

A: I think it's more inquisitive than prescriptive. I don't always have answers to the questions I raise, and I don't feel that I always ought to have answers. The stories of mine I like the least are the ones I can look at now and see I already had all the answers when I was writing them. I think that is a weakness in a story. I love "Master and Man" more than "The Death of Ivan Ilych."

Q: I like "Ivan Ilych" until the light breaks through at the end.

A: That's when the story goes wrong for me, when I see that Tolstoy already had the answer for us.

Q: I was reading your introduction to the collection of contemporary short stories you edited [*Matters of Life and Death*]. In there, you express your boredom with self-conscious experimental fiction.

A: It was overstated, because who's really writing experimental fiction now? I don't see much of it anymore. I'm not hostile to experimental fiction, but there's a kind of self-indulgence that just doesn't interest me.

Q: Even if people aren't writing it all that much, I think there still is, in the academy, a good deal of respect for it.

A: It's fun to teach, because it means something in a comfortable way, and there's a competitive impulse behind its composition that provokes a competitive impulse to disassemble it.

Q: *The Barracks Thief* is your most experimental piece, especially in the handling of tense and point of view. There are shifts from third person to first person and back again, and shifts in tense, too. Why did you choose to tell the story in that way?

A: I don't remember. I tried it all different ways. I spent more time on *The Barracks Thief* than I've spent on any other story. I could, at one time, have given you detailed explanations of why I did the things I did. But, in the end, they were also intuitive choices.

Q: Hubbard talks about how he was taught to picture people doing things, but he can't picture Lewis doing the theft. Philip can, though; in fact, he does picture Lewis doing it.

A: Philip recognizes his connection to Lewis. When the sergeant says a barracks thief is like someone who turns on his own family, Philip feels accused. That's why he feels such complicity with Lewis. Even in the end, he says: Lewis's face floats up to mine like the face in a pool when you're going to drink—it's your own face.

Q: And it's also the face of the Vietnamese he saw, and the face of his brother, too. I thought it was a nice moral balance between Hubbard and Philip: Hubbard can't picture the theft but Philip can. And yet Hubbard's comment to Philip—"You just think what everyone else thinks"—is wonderfully apt. One lacks a kind of imagination, and the other lacks the ability to have an unconventional thought.

A: As for the thief himself, I wanted to give the sense of a person who has no attachment to the past, who has been tremendously hurt by the past but is cut off from his consciousness of it. He lives in the present, almost like an animal. It's his awakening from this animal state that the story is partly about. The reason I wrote that part of the novel in present tense and took the quotation marks off the dialogue was to give it a less detached quality somehow, to make it more vividly immediate and present. So I was shifting point of view and tense in the novel partly as a way of exploring the characters and their different perceptions of time.

Q: The end of the novel is a meditation on time and what time does to us all. Philip had once believed that Lewis's life would be ruined by what happened. Now he realizes that people get over things, for better or worse. He considers how his father seems to have gotten over leaving the family; now he has a new family. I'm also reminded of what the narrator in "Next Door" says—it's terrible what we allow ourselves to get used to. Is time the enemy?

A: No, not at all. It brings problems, but it also brings the answers to them. Things pass. Time acts in different ways in my stories. I don't have a theory of time that you're going to be able to use as a grid to read my fiction. Some writers do. I hear writers talk about time in very systematic ways. I won't do that. It's something I treat in its own way in every story.

Q: The characters in *The Barracks Thief*, like many of your characters, are looking for acceptance. That's what Philip wants in the Army. It's what appeals to him about that night at the ammo dump when he and his two soldier buddies stand up to the local authorities. At the same time, he and the others seem compelled to destroy that very trust they pretend to value more than anything else. Lewis steals, Philip rejects his brother, Philip's father abandons his family.

A: Yes, it's a paradox of our condition that we crave intimacy, and when we have it try to destroy it.

Q: In this same connection, how important is Philip's denial of Lewis in precipitating the thievery?

A: That's a crucial thing, because that's the night Lewis goes off alone, meets the prostitute, and ends up stealing to pay her. After the antiwar people have come to the camp to protest, there's a feeling among the soldiers of unity through opposition. For the first time, Philip feels like one of the boys. Then Lewis comes along and asks him to go to the movies and Philip says no. Philip's with these other guys now, and Lewis isn't cool. Philip doesn't want to risk being uncool with him. It's an important moment in the novel.

Q: Is that one of the original sins in the world according to Wolff— this denial of another?

A: That's right, absolutely.

Q: And that's why Hubbard's line to Philip—"You just think what everyone else thinks"—is such a devastating one. Hubbard instinctively recognizes Philip's need to be one of the group, and that very need is what causes him to betray Lewis.

A: Yes, I think so.

Q: The soldiers in this novel are going to be sent to Vietnam, although we never see them over there. Vietnam is often in the background of your work, but you haven't dealt directly with it yet. You once said you haven't figured out a way to tell the truth about it. What do you see as the particular difficulty?

A: Part of the problem is that the war novel in American literature is one of the most powerful inheritances we have. The writer of a first-rate novel about Vietnam is going to have to invent a novel that will escape the pull of convention, instead of writing a World War II novel and sticking it in Vietnam. The other problem, too, is that the nonfiction about Vietnam has been so good—Michael Herr's *Dispatches*, Philip Caputo's *A Rumor of War*, Ron Kovic's *Born on the Fourth of July*—that I think it's going to take an enormous amount of invention to arrive at something fresh, something that people don't already know, to tell the story in a way that is redolent of the place, that grows from the ground of that particular experience and not from some other.

Q: Do you think Tim O'Brien did that in *Going After Cacciato*?

A: In parts of it he did. I'm particularly admiring of his story "The Things They Carried," which seems to me to be the best piece of fiction about Vietnam. I mean, it's such an unusual approach to telling a story, through the physical weight of the things these soldiers carry. You begin to take on that weight as you read the story. You begin to feel it, one item after another. He knows exactly what he's talking about, the weight of each piece, how it goes on. It's a great story. And that's the kind of thing, that's the fresh eye I'm talking about.

Q: Do you plan to write a novel about Vietnam?

A: The truth is, I don't know what I'm going to write in the future, and I'd rather not talk about it, because I think it's a jinx for writers to yak about their projects. It lets the genie out of the bottle.

Jean W. Ross

CA: You've said you write because you love to tell stories. Did you grow up in a storytelling family?

WOLFF: Yes, I did. Both my father and my mother were great raconteurs, and my brother is also a wonderful storyteller. It's always been the most natural kind of thing for me to do.

CA: When did you start writing the stories down?

WOLFF: I honestly remember writing stories when I was about six years old, and then I always used to write stories in school and write them for my friends when they had assignments. I don't know exactly at what time the idea hardened in me to become a writer, but I certainly never wanted to be anything else.

CA: You've called writing an "essentially optimistic act." Why so?

WOLFF: Because the very act of writing assumes, to begin with, that someone cares to hear what you have to say. It assumes that people share. It assumes that people can be reached, that people can be touched and even in some cases changed. The context of that particular quote is the introduction to a story anthology I edited called *Matters of Life and Death*. I was talking about how so many of the things in our world tend to lead us to despair. It seems to me that the final symptom of despair is silence, and that storytelling is one of the sustaining arts; it's one of the affirming arts. It's one of the most intimate things that people do together. And it assumes community, shared lives with a shared perception of the world. It goes against the grain of cynicism and pessimism. A writer may have a certain pessimism in his outlook, but the very act of being a writer seems to me to be an optimistic act.

CA: What about the short story form appealed to you especially?

WOLFF: I don't know that writers really choose forms; I think forms choose writers. When I started writing short stories, I just felt

From CONTEMPORARY AUTHORS, Vol. 117, by Hal May, editor. Copyright © 1986 by Gale Research Inc. Reprinted by permission of the publisher.

as if I was doing what I ought to be doing. When I write a short story, I feel like I'm somehow cooperating with the story; when I try to work in longer forms, I feel like I'm beating them into existence. I feel a kind of clumsiness that I don't feel when I'm writing short stories. Writing stories feels more natural to me. Maybe it's because it's closer to the act of telling stories, and that's something I've always done.

CA: You dedicated *Matters of Life and Death* to John Cheever. Is he a literary hero?

WOLFF: Yes, he certainly is. I didn't know him, but he was one of my masters, and he's somebody I continue to learn from—not just in terms of his technique and his language, but in his rejection of that easy cynicism that so many writers display as a sign of their sophistication. Cheever's enormous appetite for life is evident in nearly every sentence he wrote.

CA: Are there other writers to whom you feel indebted?

WOLFF: Oh Lord yes. [Ernest] Hemingway, first and last. [Anton] Chekhov. Paul Bowles. Sherwood Anderson. [Guy de] Maupassant. Raymond Carver. Flannery O'Connor. [Albert] Camus. Really, the list has no end so I'd better stop here.

CA: One of my favorite stories of yours is "The Liar." Can you tell me anything of how that story came about?

WOLFF: Well, I was a liar myself when I was a kid. I'm still a liar, really, and I don't mean just in terms of telling stories and being a story writer. I wouldn't ever want to be held to a literal version of the facts when I tell people a story. I don't know that I'm really capable of it. It's not the way I get at things. The other impulse behind that story is my interest in families, and in what happens when someone dies in a family—how the other people in that family go on.

All my stories are in one way or another autobiographical. Sometimes they're autobiographical in the actual events which they describe, sometimes more in their depiction of a particular character. In fact, you could say that all of my characters are reflections of myself, in that I share their wish to count for something and their almost complete confusion as to how this is supposed to be done.

CA: Did *The Barracks Thief* start out as a short story and grow?

WOLFF: It started out as a novel and shrank. *The Barracks Thief* was originally a couple of hundred pages long. What I don't like about most novels that I read is that they seem to me to be padded out with

145

a lot of repetitive detail, just trying to move themselves along into the regulation length of a novel, when they really ought to be about seven or eight pages long—when the heart of the story, if it has any, might really be contained in that space. I tried to follow my own advice here, and when I finished *The Barracks Thief*, I whittled and carved and sculpted that bulk of verbiage that I had written down to its least components, down to the most exact possible statement of the situation, with the hope that the less ornament, the less narrative windbagging I did, the more power would accrue to what was left.

CA: What magazines and journals do you read for fiction?

WOLFF: The *Atlantic*, *TriQuarterly*, *Esquire*, *Antaeus*, *Vanity Fair* occasionally. That's about all I read anymore. I don't have a lot of time. I do try to read the anthologies at the end of the year, *Best American Prize Stories*, *O. Henry Prize Stories*, and *Pushcart Prizes*.

CA: How do you feel about the television and movie adaptations of short stories generally?

WOLFF: They haven't been very good, on the whole, I don't think. The ones I've seen haven't been, anyway. It really does make you aware of the fact that a story is in some ways closer to a poem than it is to a novel—or certainly to a screenplay—because of the language. A story is so short that it must be sustained by some quality in the language, and when you take that away, you're not really left with anything. A novel necessarily has to have a good bit going on in it. A novel almost has to be eventful in a way that short stories don't have to be. They *can* be: take a story like "The Short Happy Life of Francis Macomber" or Flannery O'Conner's wonderful story "Greenleaf." There's a lot of action and event in that. But a story can also succeed without it. Chekhov's "Lady With Pet Dog" has hardly anything *happen* in it that you can actually call an event. It's interior; it's held together by the thoughts and perceptions of the main character, and the rendering of those perceptions and thoughts is all-important to the story; that's where it gets its vitality. But I don't think it would make a good movie. I did think that the adaptation of Flannery O'Connor's "The Displaced Person" was pretty good. That was the best of them all; it really caught the story's vitality. But that's a very eventful story.

CA: For years we heard that the short story was a kind of literary stepsister to the novel in terms of its marketability. Now we're hearing that the short story is coming into a better time. Have you felt hampered by having concentrated on the short story?

WOLFF: I don't really know anything about the marketplace. I've been lucky with my own stories. But there's no question that even the most successful short story collections don't sell much more than a novel of rather mediocre success; I'm sure that's true. People just tend to read more novels than short stories. But I do think that there are more and more readers for the short story writer now than there were ten years ago—really engaged, interested readers.

CA: One of the things that you do so well in your fiction is reveal character in a very few details or words. How do you get to know your characters? Do you spend time with them in some way before the actual writing?

WOLFF: I spend months on each story that I write, and through many, many drafts I discover who my characters are. That is why I rewrite, to try to find ways of getting closer and closer to my characters. That's how it happens. I rarely begin a story knowing a character all the way through. In life, you have to spend a lot of time with people to get to know them, and I have to do that when I write a story. I have to spend a lot of time with my characters, trying things out. I change their names constantly to see which name is truly their name; a name has so much to do with a character. For example, there's a world of difference between calling a character "Billy Lee" and calling a character "Miller." There are certain things that a Billy Lee is that a Miller isn't, and vice versa. When you name someone, that's a holy act. You call some essence into existence by the very name that you then have to bring into the light. I change the names of my characters at different times when I'm writing, and I put them in different situations.

I often find myself dropping the very character I thought would be the *main* character in a story when I first began it, because some other character has come to interest me more than the first character, who might ultimately not have a place in the story at all. Each story proceeds at its own pace and takes its own course.

The one thing that I find it necessary to do that not all writers find it necessary to do is rewrite and rewrite and rewrite. Obviously by the time I come to write the last draft I know where every word is going to go, and every comma. It's in my mind from beginning to end, but there have been lots of surprises along the way that I hope the reader will feel even if I don't feel them when I'm writing that last draft.

CA: Do you write down ideas, bits of dialogue, and the like in a journal or notebook?

WOLFF: I'm always grabbing a napkin at a party and writing something down, or I'll be at dinner and I'll suddenly run out to the kitchen and write something down. My pockets are always stuffed with pieces of paper. I have a pile of different things about two feet high on my desk. Once in a while I take about a week and a half or two weeks off and do nothing but transcribe these ideas in the hope that they'll later come together in some way.

CA: How do you balance teaching and writing?

WOLFF: With difficulty. I find it hard; I won't pretend I don't. But I can tell you I found it a lot harder to balance writing with being a reporter or with being a waiter or with being a busboy or a night watchman. It beats all that.

CA: What kind of writing schedule do you keep?

WOLFF: I try to write a little every day. I try to write in the morning, and I write some in the afternoon if I can. It's hard to do, but I try to keep to it. Always when I'm off I do that—I write five or six hours a day. The rest of the time I do the best I can.

CA: Are you in such a position that you can take semesters off?

WOLFF: Yes, I've been lucky the last few years. This year I had to teach the whole year, but last year I was off all year. Next year I'll be working half time and the year after that I'll be working half time. So I have just now reached a point where I've been lucky enough to get some time off to write. Last year was the first time in seven or eight years that I'd actually taken time off, except what I naturally would get in vacations.

Now, I don't want to bellyache, because I think that for all the disadvantages of being a teacher and a writer, it still is for me absolutely the best combination. I think any writer resents any kind of activity that he's forced to do other than writing, but I still consider myself lucky to be in a profession where I am given a lot of time to write— a lot more than I would be in any other profession—and not only that, but where people care about writing and give you room to breathe if you're a writer; where you're with other people for whom writing is the most important thing. It's good to be in a community of writers. Frankly, the greater world doesn't give a damn whether you write or not, and to be with people who do is a real blessing. Believe me. I went for years without it, and I know a good thing when I have it.

CA: As a teacher of writing, what do you think are the most important things you can do for your students?

WOLFF: I try to make them aware of their strengths as writers, encourage them. I try to make them aware of their weaknesses as writers—not so that they won't try doing the sort of thing that they're not doing well, but so that they'll look harder at what they're doing and learn to overcome their weaknesses. I want them eventually to be able to read their own work with very dispassionate eyes, to be able to divorce themselves from their work—ultimately to become their own best editors; that's what I really want them to learn.

CA: The hardest thing.

WOLFF: It is indeed. It's a kind of achieved schizophrenia, where one moment you're in an ecstasy of creation and the next you've got a machete and you're slashing down your beautiful constructions. It is a hard thing to learn—of course it is—but I think you have to learn it.

CA: Do most of your students come to you with some talent?

WOLFF: I have two kinds of situations. One is that I teach in a writing program. We don't have any quota in our writing program. We can admit as few or as many people as we want. Sometimes we've admitted no more than three. Sometimes we've admitted as many as six or seven. All of those students are talented; we wouldn't admit them if they weren't. And I think their success has borne out our faith in them.

The undergraduates are a different story. I let into my course most of the undergraduates who want to take it. I don't think you can really tell very much about undergraduates—whether they have talent or not. They're too young. They haven't had long enough to look back on their lives, and they haven't been practicing the art of writing long enough to have discovered their own voice and the story that they have to tell and the sound that only they can make. All those things that writers are looking for take time. You know that wonderful line of Chaucer's, "The life so short, the craft so long to learn." That's what it is.

CA: How do your good students begin to get their work published?

WOLFF: They usually begin by sending their work out to literary journals and reviews. As they publish more and more, the editors who read these journals take notice of them and write encouraging letters, in some cases asking to see completed novels or story collections. That's how it begins, at least for the lucky ones.

CA: Do you think you might try a novel again?

WOLFF: Let me put it this way: if I were writing a story and it kept getting longer and longer and I felt as though it were alive, then I would follow it to its conclusion. If that was a novel, then I would have written a novel. But I don't think I would ever sit down and say, "Now I'm going to write a novel."

CA: What's next for you?

WOLFF: Well, I just keep sitting down in front of the typewriter, and what keeps happening to me are stories. If that changes, then whatever chooses me next is what it's going to be.

Part 3

THE CRITICS

Introduction

> To criticize is to appreciate, to appropriate, to take intellectual
> possession, to establish in fine a relation with the criticized
> thing and to make it one's own.
>
> Henry James

Despite the publication of individual stories in prestigious national
magazines and widespread attention to his story collections and memoirs, there is almost no conventional scholarly criticism of Tobias
Wolff's work. Much of this neglect—which this volume hopes to correct—comes quite understandably out of Wolff's status as a contemporary writer of short fiction. Short-story writers are usually given shorter
shrift than novelists, and contemporary writers are a more perplexing
commodity in academia than those already ensconced in a canon. But
Wolff has been widely reviewed in many of the national periodicals by
the important critics of the day. This section of the study of his short
fiction includes a variety of such voices in hopes of creating for the
reader a conversation that displays the craft of criticism while focusing
on the concerns inherent in Wolff's fiction.

Readers will soon notice the differences of opinions expressed in
the reviews. Reviewers of a particular collection will select different
stories to dwell on as loci for their praise and faultfinding. Indeed, the
same story may be the source of admiration for one reviewer and of
concern for another. When *Back in the World* appeared after *In the Garden
of the North American Martyrs*, critics compared the two collections,
reacting more favorably to one than the other. This is as it should be;
no single reviewer can see beyond his or her own perspective—his or
her own educated, informed, but personal and so idiosyncratic vantage
point. This variance is the true energy and soul of criticism.

Among the critics presented here, Brina Caplan believes "Worldly
Goods" to be a flawed story; Richard Orodenker thinks it is emblematic
of the best stories in the first collection. Russell Banks gives interesting
reasons for liking *Back in the World* less than the first collection. Mona
Simpson finds the second book very different in tone from the first.

Michiko Kakutani reacts favorably to both. Richard Eder compares Wolff with other contemporary writers; Jonathan Penner concentrates only on *Back in the World*, examining what he thinks are its strengths and weaknesses.

Taken together these reviews make a fascinating collage of individual points of view, directing themselves to the common focus of Tobias Wolff's short fiction. Honest to themselves and with the author, they create a variety of interpretations. At its best, criticism is always this conglomeration of attitudes, this squabble of informed voices.

In the Garden of the North American Martyrs

Brina Caplan

As steel vaporizes in a beam of laser light, the substance of experience disintegrates when subjected to radical skepticism. Our conceptions of reality could be psychic interventions, the skeptic argues, neither more nor less so than our dreams. However much we protest this argument, we find it difficult to refute. No logical system finally establishes the distinction we make intuitively, at least when awake, between reality and dream. Worse, no formal reasoning proves that our mental reconstructions of the world—our images, symbols, languages—actually tell us about the world instead of, at best, about their own rules of order.

If our experiences and perceptions are simply exercises in self-reference, how much less reflective of reality must be the experiences and perceptions of characters in fiction, who are by definition illusions without existence beyond the printed page. Indeed, deconstructionist critics, viewing fiction in this light, see in it linguistic events rather than meaningful projections of reality and overhear a kind of speech that comments only on itself. The language—not the author—writes the text, they tell us; fiction is the set of changes possible in a self-enclosed system that, like a Rubik's cube, is at once variable and rigidly bound.

Although radical skepticism cannot be formally refuted, it can be opposed. Rather than academic polemicists or philosophers, however, the most convincing defenders of storytelling as an interpretive art are contemporary writers whose careful representation of detail implies that words mirror reality. Against a denial of all truth, they pit individual truths; against the impossibility of general meaning, they set the meaningfulness of small details—apparel, gestures, impulses, the individuated character of human voices. Significant experience emerges, they

"Particular Truth [excerpts]," by Brina Caplan, from *The Nation* 234 (6 February 1982). Reprinted with permission from *The Nation* magazine. © The Nation Company, Inc.

assume, when the storyteller selects from an infinity of disparate and random possible events those that constitute a pattern of living. As the title of Wallace Stevens poem has it, such writers pursue a knowledge of the world by following out "The Course of a Particular." . . .

In realistic fiction, events do not speak for themselves; they require both a shaping grammar that controls incident and explains the convergence of circumstance and personal necessity. Like [David] Plante, Tobias Wolff scrutinizes the disorder of daily living to find significant order; in the best of the stories collected under the title *In the Garden of the North American Martyrs*, he informs us not only of what happened but of why it had to happen as it did.

His characters are various: a prep school freshman; a young mother deserted by her husband; a businessman with a precarious hold on his conscience and his job; an old couple defending property and propriety against obtrusive neighbors; a middle-aged Southerner uncertainly transplanted to a large Northern city. Distant in age, class, and geography, these people have in common lives crowded with the results of previous choices. Amid possessions and routines, they pause before decisions that may fulfill their lives or merely clutter them further.

The heroine of the title story finds herself making a decision of this sort at a time when circumstances have limited her possibilities to the bleak or the ridiculous. A teacher for fifteen years, Mary stabilized her academic career through extreme caution:

> Now and then she wondered whether she had been too careful. The things she said and wrote seemed flat to her, pulpy, as though someone else had squeezed the juice out of them. And once, while talking with a senior professor, Mary saw herself reflected in a window; she was leaning toward him and had her head turned so that her ear was right in front of his moving mouth. The sight disgusted her. Years later, when she had to get a hearing aid, Mary suspected that her deafness was a result of always trying to catch everything everyone said.

Even though bankruptcy closes the college and forces her to accept exile, lecturing to the fog-bound in a dank, obscure corner of Oregon, compliance still seems to Mary the appropriate course. Indeed, remembering her accommodating manner, a former colleague, a woman not known for impulsive generosity, invites her to interview for a job back East at her own urbane and sunny institution.

Not only compared with the dismal conditions of Mary's current job but in itself, the college seems perfect: "It looked so much like a college that movie-makers sometimes used it as a set. *Andy Hardy Goes to College* had been filmed there." Yet, during her visit, Mary detects something amiss. Her host and former colleague, Louise, refuses to discuss job prospects and monopolizes their conversations with complaints about her love life—mentioning only casually and at the last moment that Mary must address a formal assembly of faculty and students. In turn, the department chairman avoids the subject of her qualifications to opine instead about the weather: " 'Of course it snows here, and you have your rain now and then, but it's a *dry* rain.' " Other members of the department do not speak to her at all. The mystery remains unresolved until Mary's tour of the campus confronts her with the power-plant dynamo; there, in the "depths of the service building," before the vast, humming machine, her student-guide explains. "People think the college is really old-fashioned . . . but it isn't. They let girls come here now, and some of the teachers are women. In fact, there's a statute that says they have to interview at least one woman for each opening." No matter how successful her lecture, she is without hope, "brought here to satisfy a rule."

She speaks as scheduled—though not as planned—in the first authentic act of her academic career. Her lecture is spontaneous, visionary, lyric, and simultaneously absurd: like a cog thrown into the works, Mary's pronouncements on justice and love disorder the machinery of expectation. (When distressed faculty members shout from the audience to quiet her, she avoids distraction by turning off her hearing aid.) Her moment of private deliverance is, of course, also a moment of public farce; "In the Garden of the North American Martyrs" does not glorify spontaneity or suggest that moral choice dissolves the conditions that provoke it. Mary's story and the collection of stories that share its title make a claim far less optimistic; there is, Wolff implies, no such thing as meaningless choice. Every decision emerges from a consciousness which it both expresses and modifies. In fact, a hardened core of habits, old compromises, and pragmatic adjustments continues to support a structure that, at its living edges, can reshape or extend itself in surprising ways.

Not every story makes the point convincingly, however. The hazard of realistic fiction lies in its engagement with surfaces, and at times Wolff evokes situations with a skill that verges on facility. "Smokers," for example, offers a too-easy condemnation of adolescent social-climbing, while "Worldly Goods" teases at but does not unravel the complexities of a peculiarly self-isolated Southerner. In both cases, mirroring events has become an end in itself, and the result is sterile flashes of likeness. But when he chooses to, Wolff can do more than find the words for things; at his best, he can use words to test lives against accidental and self-selected conditions. When he concentrates on the interpenetration of mind and circumstance, then his perspective—however trivial the situation or purposefully alien the character—fixes our attention; for there the mirror has become a microscope and, in the words of Wallace Stevens, "Life's nonsense pierces us with strange relation."

Richard Orodenker

In the Garden of the North American Martyrs is Tobias Wolff's stunning first collection of short fiction. Through these gracefully evoked tales, Wolff touches the heart of the human condition and speaks in a voice that is sincere, original, yet familiar—a voice that sounds as if it must last.

His careful, simple prose style is often deceptive. His stories' complex levels of meaning are covered by a delicate veneer. His metaphors reach deep into the imagination. In "Next Door," Wolff moves subtly in and out of the lives of his character. The sounds of domestic intranquillity coming from next door lead the main character to think about other proximities, other geographies, which include the body of his invalid wife. He begins to think about those places that are not on the map, lost cities, "white trees in a land where no one has ever been." Perhaps all of these are really no further away from him than next door.

The characters on whom Wolff focuses manage to gain our sympathies, but slowly, slowly, Wolff reveals them to themselves and then to us. A pair of hunters let their wounded friend bleed and freeze as they expose their own pathetic selves to each other, lose track of themselves, and make a wrong turn on their way to the hospital. An English professor, entering the world of guilt and sorrow, is genuinely touched by a woman, hairless from chemotherapy treatments. He is moved that her life has been somehow saved by a poem (by a McKuenesque poet) that had given her the strength to survive. His experience challenges his own way of thinking, his own habit of passing

From Richard Orodenker, *The North American Review* 267 (June 1982): 60.

judgments on other people, until he must become the one "to sit in the front of the church" and be watched by others. Wolff's characters, like the nameless narrator of "Smokers," are "those who knew that something was wrong but didn't know what it was."

The author does not moralize, though his concerns are usually moral in nature. His characters are Everymen, like Davis in the brilliant story, "Worldly Goods." Davis, victimized in a harmless automobile accident, must deal with a claims adjuster, a modern version of Knowledge, who gives Davis the kind of advice he will need to get by in the world, that is, to screw before he himself is screwed. Davis stands on moral principle, but that is not enough. A friend tells him, "Nothing is good enough for you." Davis cannot see beyond the surface issues; he will drive his life the way he resolves to drive his maimed automobile "the way it was until it fell apart." And, ironically, his car is stolen from him, the way all our worldly goods are, in time, taken from us. In "Passengers," this theme is reprised once again: if a person must change his ways, what if he "wasn't sure just what was wrong with his ways?" We may admire the heroine's ability to see through her pathetic lover in "Face to Face," but what she sees never really goes beyond the heart of pity. We know that she is coming face to face with herself, deciding, as her lover has, "always to be alone." But does she know this? It is a process, writes Wolff, that might "take forever." For characters who can never "imagine things coming together," conversely, they must see things "always falling apart." How difficultly or belatedly they will come to know (as [Wharton] does in "Poaching") if ever they have "been offered an olive branch and were not far from home."

So "Mend your lives. . . . Turn from power to love," the feeble history teacher of the title story advises us. And Wolff responds poetically: how do we do so in a world where our own hands seem to be things we are holding for someone else? To protect us is the insulating power of lies. As Wolff demonstrates in "The Liar," lies, like fictions, sometimes bring people closer to the truths—in this case, that people do have something in common with each other in their relishing of lies *and* in their loathing of lies—"a shared fear."

Many of the stories of *In the Garden of the North American Martyrs* end on an introspective note. The narratives filter down to a moment alone with a character, who may be sitting alone in a closet, smoking a joint or lying on a blanket, dreaming up at the stars or lecturing passionately but with her hearing aid turned off. There they reflect and, maybe, learn. To us, they are specks on a large photograph that, when enlarged, reveals expressions on faces that are troubling, fearful, human.

Anatole Broyard

It seems to me that a curious thing happens when an author gives another author a complimentary statement to print on the dust jacket of his book. He begins by trying to say what he thinks, but then he becomes aware of how he sounds—and in adjusting the sound of his statement to his notion of how he himself wants to appear, he often alters it in mysterious ways, so that what we get in the end is the author giving us an example of his style in an indirect relation to someone else's.

Even so, I believe that Tobias Wolff deserves, at least approximately, the flattering things that Raymond Carver and Leonard Michaels say about him. In several of the 12 stories that make up *In the Garden of the North American Martyrs*, he tries to do something difficult, subtle and technically ambitious.

In one case, at the end of a story called "Next Door," he imposes a tangential fantasy of one of the characters on the central problem of the story, to which it has no apparent relation. Yet the ambiguity of each part of the story is such that they seem to modify each other, as if by accident.

The device reminds me of a psychological experiment I heard about. A psychoanalyst who had a neurotic patient in therapy imposed on him under hypnosis a second, synthetic neurosis that was not directly related to the first. When he solved the second neurosis—which was possible because he knew its causes—the first neurosis was also cured. The analyst who performed the experiment subsequently decided that it was dangerous to tamper with human personality in this way and thus never repeated it.

Short stories may be dangerous too, in the ways that they tamper with our personalities, but we always have the option of not reading them. Or, if we do read them, we may find ourselves cured, at least temporarily, of one or another of our anxieties.

Mr. Wolff, who is young, works with subtle dislocations, the kind of dislocations that change us without our realizing it. A 75-year-old man celebrates his 50th wedding anniversary with his 78-year-old wife by taking a cruise. But the rampant sexual activity of other people on the cruise disturbs his long-established serenity, and when he is asked to make a speech to the passengers about the secret of long-lived happiness, he surprises himself in what he says.

In the title story of the collection, a young woman who teaches in a college deliberately subdues her imagination in the conviction that tenure is given to whose who hold on in a steadfast manner. When she discovers that she is mistaken and that she has been invited to give a talk only to satisfy a statutory requirement, she invents for the occasion a sadistic tribe of Indians whom she describes in an orgy of anthropological vengeance.

A priggish perfectionist professor who is so mistrustful of flair or glamour that he is irritated by the glitter of minerals in the pavement of a street, finds himself thrown by pity into the company of a nurse who writes sentimental poetry. Sitting in her living room, where red cushions are arranged on the floor around a fat candle, he listens to her poetry and is amazed to find himself beginning to like it. He was attracted to the nurse by her thick, blond hair, which turns out to be a wig, and when she takes off the wig to reveal a bald head, he simply cannot find it in himself to look at her critically. Suddenly he is released from the tyranny of literature into the chaos of ordinary emotions.

A divorced woman who is politely and distantly courted by the cousin of a friend agrees to go away for a weekend with him, only to discover that there are peculiarities that are essentially beyond communication, differences of personal rhythms that are inaudible to the people trapped in them. A story about a liar suggests that lying can be a kind of prayer, or a bad poem, or an inhibition of love. It can also be, as Mr. Wolff says, an example of speaking in tongues.

Some of the stories that make up *In the Garden of the North American Martyrs* are not very ambitious, and these are not very good. Mr. Wolff is at his best when he is taking wild chances, as any self-respecting young author should be.

Back in the World

Russell Banks

One comes to Tobias Wolff's *Back in the World* with dangerously raised expectations, for his two previous books, *In the Garden of the North American Martyrs* (a volume of short stories) and *The Barracks Thief* (a single long story), were exceptionally fine works of a fully mature writer. This collection of stories is mostly concerned with the inner lives of middle-class loners in the Sun Belt. They are lapsed materialists in a material world trying to ignite a spiritual flame despite being cut off from all traditional sources of the spirit—family, church, art, even politics. Most of Mr. Wolff's characters are motivated by unenlightened self-interest. They may be yuppies, but they are trapped and manipulated by the system, and that makes them sympathetic. Mr. Wolff views their entrapment as something to be both feared and pitied and their attempts at escape—through fantasy, drugs, exercise, electronic toys, and casual sex—as dignified. These microchippers, real-estate speculators, compulsively exercising cocaine addicts, and frantic adulterers are victims, not exotic objects of derision, and consequently one reads the stories with an open heart.

Even so, it must be said that this book is a considerable falling off for Mr. Wolff. *Back in the World* does not measure up to *The Barracks Thief* and *In the Garden of the North American Martyrs*. Whereas the earlier stories used digression to build a dialectic, to make something *happen*, these seem instead to meander into narrative cul-de-sacs. And whereas stories like *The Barracks Thief* and "Hunters in the Snow" or "The Liar" used exposition to create atmosphere and a sense of crisis, the more recent stories often seem gabby and self-indulgently reluctant to get on with the telling, as in the opening pages of "The Missing Person," about a priest who, without any obvious skills, is drifting downward from one minor post to another until he finds his calling, as it were, raising funds for a small convent.

"The monsignor took Father Leo out to dinner at a seafood house and explained the situation to him. The suggestion of the committee was actually a directive, he said. The monsignor had no choice in the matter. But he had been calling around and had found an open position, if Father Leo was interested. Mother Vincent at Star of the Sea needed a new chaplain. Their last chaplain had married one of the nuns. It so happened, the monsignor said, looking into his wine, swirling it gently, that he had done several favors for Mother Vincent in his days at the chancery. In short, if Father Leo wanted the position he could have it. The monsignor lit a cigarette and looked out the window, over the water. Gulls were diving for scraps."

In *Back in the World* there's too much of this kind of writing, suetlike prose studded with an occasional image (like the gulls "diving for scraps"), inserted for literary flavor rather than for any dramatic purpose and serving only to make the obvious more obvious. There are frequent flashy but cheap effects here that make one withdraw from a story, puzzled and detached, exactly when one should be suspending disbelief and entering the author's fictional world. Information-packed sentences in an opening paragraph, which should inform and seduce the reader, often violate their apparent intent by opting for unexpected irrelevancies, as in this early sentence from "Coming Attractions": "He'd been leaving early for almost a month now and at first Jean thought he was committing adultery against his wife, until she saw him on the ice one Saturday afternoon while she was out shoplifting with her girlfriend Kathy." Unfortunately, the story's got nothing to do with shoplifting or Kathy.

Two stories, "Leviathan" and "The Rich Brother," are as fine as anything Mr. Wolff has written. "Leviathan" lets us enter the lives of Mitch and Bliss and Ted and Helen, who have reached their 30's but haven't noticed it yet. They're trim, tanned, affluent, smart and sexy, but, like the rest of us, they're mortal—aging clay. They do everything they can to avoid facing that fact, life's main fact, and the thing they most like to do is cocaine. The story, very funny and very sad, is a description of an all-night 30th birthday party for Helen, with only her husband, Ted, and her best friends, Bliss and Mitch. It is about Helen; she is the one who is able to glimpse what all four of them, stubbornly, desperately, have avoided seeing. "They watched over Helen's shoulders as Helen bent down to sift the gleaming crystal. First she chopped it with a razor. Then she began to spread it out. Mitch and Bliss smiled up at her from the mirror, and Helen smiled back between them. Their faces were rosy with candlelight. They were the faces of three well-wishers, carolers, looking in at Helen through a window filling up with snow."

"The Rich Brother" is more complex. It is a retelling of the prodigal son parable, told from the point of view of the good son, who makes lots of money in real estate and then has to spend it taking care of his younger brother, an incompetent, gullible seeker after transcendence who keeps sliding helplessly from cult to commune to cult, calling his brother to rescue, house, and feed him until he finds another group to join. The story is a small classic about family life in America, what's left of it.

These two stories, along with brilliant moments scattered throughout the others, keep *Back in the World* from disappointing altogether. If anything, one awaits Mr. Wolff's next book with all the more eagerness.

Mona Simpson

People in Tobias Wolff's stories often ask each other questions like "What's the worst thing you've ever done?" They say these things while driving cars, while on watch at United States military installations, and during parties. They say, "You are about to hear my absolute bottom-line confession. The worst story ever told." Less often, it's "Why don't you tell us something good you did? The thing you're most proud of." From the publication of Wolff's first collection of short stories, *In the Garden of the North American Martyrs* in 1981, Wolff has shown an interest in the very worst things people do to each other. He also notes more charitable deeds. He has a supple ability to find moral dimensions in ordinary American life. Fortunately, he is also a master of humor.

At least three stories in the first collection seem among the most memorable stories of the last 20 years. Perhaps the best story is "An Episode in the Life of Professor Brooke." The story follows a grown-up goody-goody who, when asked to recount his worst deed, panics and thinks back to small crimes committed when he was 13. Through the humor of bumbling, priggish Professor Brooke, Wolff leads the reader into more serious, charged territory. The inner lives of prigs, righteous citizens, quiet well-behaved neighbors, provide a springboard for Wolff. The upright ones watch from their windows—unwillingly

Reprinted by permission of *The New Republic*. © 1985 The New Republic, Inc.

becoming entangled with their more passionate and dangerous neighbors.

Wolff's second book, *The Barracks Thief*, appeared quietly in 1984 and received belated attention this year, winning the PEN/Faulkner award. In the 101-page novella about three young paratroopers waiting to be shipped to Vietnam, Wolff once again deftly stages a small-scale moral drama. A mysterious series of thefts occur within their company, involving each of the three boys: thief, victim, bystander. Our narrator, neither the thief nor the victim, at first feels guilt, as if he may have somehow committed the crime without knowing it. When the thief is caught, the protagonist swells with the idea of revenge, though years later he confesses that he is uneasy with his ostensibly firm moral convictions. "I didn't set out to be what I am," he says at the book's close. "I'm a conscientious man, maybe even what you'd call a good man—I hope so. But I'm also a careful man, addicted to comfort, with an eye for the safe course." Again, the story is told by the good man, neither the victim nor the perpetrator—ironically, the only one of the three who ultimately goes to Vietnam.

Wolff's new book, *Back in the World* (a phrase soldiers in Vietnam used for their civilian future), contains ten stories in a more somber mode. A plainer, more subdued quality of language is immediately apparent. Consider the new stories' opening lines: "Jean was alone in the theater." "There was a park at the bottom of the hill." "There were two brothers, Pete and Donald." Compare these to first lines from *In the Garden of the North American Martyrs*: "My mother read everything except books." "Professor Brooke had no real quarrel with anyone in his department, but there was a Yeats scholar named Riley whom he could not bring himself to like." "I woke up afraid." Where each opening from the earlier collection introduces a quirky, fallible, human voice, the beginnings in *Back in the World* feel omniscient, universal, with biblical resonance. In these new stories, Wolff works with the same thematic concerns, the same passion for moral questions, but his fictional canvas is sparer and simpler. He has, for the most part, abandoned the domestic, the familiar righteous citizen, and all his incumbent irony. He has chosen more dramatic, emblematic characters.

In the first collection, we were deposited inside normal American bedrooms and kitchens, doctors' offices, familiar academic conventions. We watched the violence and adultery of next-door neighbors. There are fewer witnesses, fewer citizen's arrests in this book. We've become the criminals ourselves. Central characters include a teenage shoplifter,

a failed and corrupted priest vacationing in Las Vegas, a 21-year-old
Silicon Valley Porsche-owning computer wizard, a wealthy real estate
broker and loser brother he fetches home from yet another religious
commune. Although the new stories are less funny and familiar than
Wolff's earlier work, they achieve a new kind of power. They are
stripped-down moral fables.

In "Say Yes" a wife asks her husband, "Let's say I am black and
unattached and we meet and fall in love. . . . Will you marry me?"
He answers, "If you were black you wouldn't be you." Later, the wife
locks herself in the bathroom. She tells her husband to turn off the
light. She wants the room dark before she will come to bed with him.

> He sat up but he couldn't see a thing. . . . His heart pounded the
> way it had on their first night together, the way it did when he woke
> at a noise in the darkness and waited to hear it again—the noise of
> someone moving through the house, a stranger.

In "Soldier's Joy" a young private asks an older enlisted man, "What
was your best time?" "Vietnam," he answers.

Some readers may prefer Wolff's earlier terrain, richer in physical
detail, and singularly funny. One might prefer the earlier works' gradual
elevation of domestic comedy toward a heightened moral plateau, a
slow build in the manner of Preston Sturges's great film *Sullivan's
Travels*. With an artist as serious and honest as Tobias Wolff, the stories
beg comparison only with each other.

Michiko Kakutani

"We used to talk about how when we got back in the world we were
going to do this and we were going to do that," says a character in one
of Tobias Wolff's fine, angular stories. "Back in the world we were
going to have it made. But ever since then it's been nothing but
confusion." Though this happens to be a Vietnam veteran talking about
the disillusion he experienced on returning home after the war, he
might well be speaking for any one of Mr. Wolff's disaffected heroes.
Frustrated, lonely and divorced from their youthful expectations, these
people all drift through the present, trying to get by day to day, by
telling assorted stories and lies. For them, as for Mr. Wolff, lying—in

166

this case, fiction-making—represents a way of imposing a narrative order on their lives, as well as a means of connecting with others and with their receding dreams. Hooper, the hero of "Soldier's Joy," considers making up a story about himself, so as to help comfort a distraught soldier in his command. And in "The Missing Person" a shabby priest concocts an outrageous tale about killing a man—just in order to have something to share with his new friend, a fast-talking con man with lots of tall tales about his past. Father Leo, writes Mr. Wolff, "believed about half of what he heard. That was fine with him. He didn't mind having his leg pulled. He thought it was the sort of thing men did in lumber camps and on ships—sitting around, swapping lies."

Jean, the 15-year-old shoplifter in "Coming Attractions," lies to ward off boredom, to ward off fear and to protect her delicate father from distress, whereas Mark, the unemployed singer in "Desert Breakdown, 1968," cherishes an elaborate fantasy in which he becomes a star, goes on stage to take a bow and then delivers a phony childhood reminiscence, designed to humiliate his anxious parents.

Other characters in *Back in the World* simply tell stories—both "real" ones and made-up ones to reconcile their wished-for identities with the dull reality of their daily lives, or to convey something about themselves by indirection: "Our Story Begins" features a shaggy-dog anecdote that functions as a prelude to a marital break-up, and "Leviathan" a self-dramatizing tale of heroism that fails to achieve its desired affect.

As this volume of stories, along with a previous collection (*In the Garden of the North American Martyrs*) and a prize-winning novella (*The Barracks Thief*) abundantly demonstrate, Mr. Wolff is a masterful story-teller, a natural raconteur, who is willing to take all sorts of technical risks. Sometimes those risks don't completely pay off: "The Rich Brother," a kind of contemporary parable about Abel and Cain, set down in colloquial but slightly formalized prose, never quite manages to sketch in the moral ambiguities suggested by its action; "Our Story Begins"—which uses the frame device of a story within another story—leaves the reader all too aware of the narrative machinery at work.

If such efforts fail to trace a perfect emotional arc, however, they are not without their pleasures; even the weakest stories in *Back in the World* are enlivened by gleaming moments that display Mr. Wolff's quick eye, his gift for meticulous observation. The sound of magazine pages being turned with the quick snap of anger; the glitter of a sparkly ceiling in a cheap Las Vegas hotel; the swollen look that too-white, too-new sneakers give to a young girl's feet—such details take on an understated metaphorical power in these stories. Mr. Wolff shows he is as fluent in evoking mood through naturalistic descriptions of the mundane—"The woman had all the shades pulled down. It was like evening inside: dim, peaceful, cool. Krystal could make out the shapes of things but not their colors"—as he is in creating a Sam Shepard-esque sense of menace through the manipulation of bizarre images: a hearse, filled with partygoing kids, speeding through the desert; an old bicycle lying at the bottom of a chilly swimming pool.

In the end, though, what really makes the finest of these stories so compelling is the author's sympathy for his characters, his clear-eyed but generous sense of their weaknesses, their frustrations and disappointments. Most of the people in *Back in the World* are losers or lapsed dreamers, weary people who have passively allowed circumstance and blind chance to dictate the shape of their lives: in "The Poor Are Always With Us," a [character] throws away two cars—and his financial security—on a silly bet; in "Desert Breakdown" an aspiring singer desultorily contemplates abandoning his pregnant wife and child at a local gas station. Aimless about their future, oblivious to the consequences of their past actions, these people all inhabit that precarious emotional terrain where discouragement threatens to turn into despair and a sense of permanent dislocation. Some have had a taste of success, a glimpse of that place where fantasy begins to merge with fact, but that only makes their current loss of control all the more distressing. As one character observes to a friend: "Dave was centerfold material for a while there, but nowadays things just keep messing up on him. It's like the well went dry."

There is not a lot of hope for these people, but Mr. Wolff suggests the promise of some kind of redemption in their fumbling efforts to connect with one another, and even in their sad attempts to shore up their dignity with their pipe dreams and clumsy fictions. This is what enables these characters to go on, and it is also what invests these stories with the burnished glow of compassion.

Jonathan Penner

Tobias Wolff knows a lot. He knows about men and women and children, and about America in its variety. His people are kids, soldiers, wives, successful in business or failed in art. They're devotees of love, of drugs, of technology. Wolff's taste for experience seems, as a major writer's should seem, promiscuous. All 10 of these stories are told in the third person. This narrative mode permits an exterior view of even the central figure, which seems to be why Wolff employs it. He's disinclined to tell stories from the inside out, to present a world through the thoughts and feelings of a viewpoint character.

Instead, Wolff tries to create windows on the soul through speech and action. In pure form, that is the way of drama. In fiction it tends to be awkward, artificial, inefficient, and extraordinarily difficult.

Yet at his best Wolff turns the handicap into an added grace, making his method appear easy or even inevitable. The central character of "Coming Attractions," 15-year-old Jean, works in a movie theater. After closing up for the night, she's waiting alone for her boss to come and drive her home. We see inside her scarcely at all. But the pathos of her life, and the heroism with which she meets it, emerge through phone calls that we hear her make, followed by a series of inspired events.

This story, like several others collected here, combines a traditional emphasis on character with a contemporary looseness of plot. There's no clear forward march, no resolution, no comes-to-realize. Helpless to change her circumstances, Jean wages war within them. She is an existential heroine, who continues to act, no matter how ineffectively or irrelevantly, and thus to be. At the end, though nothing has changed in her, something has in us.

"The Poor Are Always with Us," another grand story, takes place among computer engineers in Silicon Valley. The milieu is authentic: protagonist and antagonist meet when they bring their Porsches in for servicing. The audacious plot turns on a wager, the consequences of which change several lives. Here again, the inner world is illuminated through word and deed.

Other stories, less lustrous, shine in places and parts. "The Missing Person" follows the trajectory of Father Leo, who longed to be a missionary in Alaska, as he sinks through level below level of a demeaning career. He's spiritual advisor to a gaggle of hip nuns—one a disc jockey—who call him "Padre" or just "Pod." Equally memorable is Krystal, the heroine of "Desert Breakdown, 1968," who loves the word "never" because it reminds her of Beethoven shaking his fist at the heavens.

Still, many of these stories do not seem adequately lit. Collectively, they show the limits of what exterior signs can tell us of people's brains and viscera. Only a partial humanity percolates through action and speech. Not even a writer as good as Wolff can eschew *he thought* and *he felt* forever.

The distress that his method creates is seen first of all in dialogue. Speech in fiction, in order to be efficient for the author's purposes, needs to be inefficient for the characters'. Wolff's dialogue falls easily into addresses, so eloquently explanatory that they look less like speech than like writing.

One sometimes feels, eerily, that the characters are aware of the reader's need for information. At times the ostensible viewpoint character becomes little more than a conveniently placed eye and ear, used by the author to let us eavesdrop on a story-within-the-story.

In "Our Story Begins," a busboy walking home from work stops at a coffeehouse. There he overhears a story told by one patron to another—a story that continues for nine pages. Afterward, completing a kind of narrative sandwich, the busboy continues his walk home. He has (so far as Wolff lets us know) no response whatever to the overheard story. Any connection between it and his own story is obscure.

"Leviathan," a close to generic story of four friends gathering for cocaine and confessions, lies at the nadir of this collection. The anecdotes are boring, the action thin. Yet even here, Wolff does so much well that his gifts are continually evident.

Those gifts are lavish. His ear is sharp for every kind of speech. He can be very funny. He can be lyrical. His people display consistency and irrelevance—that odd blend of the mechanical and the random that we embrace as free will. His decorative surfaces turn out to be weight-bearing. His details, innocently planted, germinate. *Back in the World* is a striking and an exciting collection by a writer unusually fine.

Richard Eder

The land of disquiet explored by a segment of American fiction is prosperous, druggy and largely devoted to games. A lot of work gets done, or it couldn't be paid for. But you don't see the work; it isn't really part of life except as an off-stage drain on the spirits.

The games that the inhabitants consider their real life are played in a state of crowded anxiousness. They offer an illusion of companionship, but they are essentially solitary. Everyone brings his or her own board; the other players can be painlessly evicted and sent away.

Tobias Wolff, like other masters of the territory such as Ann Beattie and Frederick Barthelme, writes of the pain inside the painlessness. In the depleted atmosphere, every scream is silent. Each of Wolff's stories is an amplifier picking up the sound that cannot get through.

Like an ophthalmological surgeon with huge hands, Wolff presents the paradox of a big energy applied to microscopic artisanry. The stories in *Back in the World* fairly prance with a natural storyteller's repressed high spirits. The best of them are feverish and dramatic; there is a hint that the protagonist is getting ready to bust out of the stillness, that a week or two after the story ends, pity and terror and, who knows, even laughter will replace disquiet. Perhaps Wolff himself will move on.

Meanwhile, he writes with a lavish display of skill. His achievement is not any special originality of situation, character or point of view, but an impressive elaboration of models we already know. It can verge upon gilding the lily.

Certainly the first story in the collection, "Coming Attractions," is a compelling variation on the theme of the lonely adolescent. [Jean] works nights in a movie theater, cleaning up after the last show. She wanders about the empty house, picking up remnants of human habitation: a dropped sweater, a half-chewed ham-bone. Watch that hambone, it is enticingly excessive and out of place.

Because everything else fits almost too well. Waiting for her boss to give her a ride home, [Jean] calls her father, three thousand miles away, and gets her stepmother who doesn't want to wake him, especially if it's about a problem. "He's more of a good news person," she says cheerfully. [Jean] calls home, but her mother is out on a date and there's only her little brother, watching television, and as lonely as she is. She looks up a stranger in the phone book and chats with him for a while. The world isn't home to [Jean]; she can't break through. So when she gets back, past midnight, and sees a bicycle at the bottom of the condo swimming pool, she dives in and pulls it out, almost drowning. When trapped in a maze, hurl yourself at its walls.

Salinger's adolescents have passed this way; Wolff's [Jean] has her own desolation, more brilliance in some ways, less interior grace. Similarly, in a story about a saintly, incompetent priest whom the world regularly dumps upon, we get more than a hint of the hapless but alluring Guy Crouchback in Evelyn Waugh's war trilogy.

171

Father Leo, who dreams of being a missionary, drifts haplessly through the Catholic parishes of his city. He ends up as chaplain at a convent whose members are in a frenzy of theological modernization. Leo can find no lambs to save; nobody wants to be a lamb any more. One of the nuns married his predecessor; others have left or taken jobs in town. One is a disc jockey.

Wolff writes with delightful irony about Father Leo's unexpectedly successful team-work with an extroverted fund-raiser who treats him to expensive lunches and ultimately absconds. Leo remains an innocent; finally finding his lamb in a forlorn middle-aged woman who is looking for love but settles for charity.

If Wolff handles the notion of a Divine Fool descending in a manner reminiscent of Waugh, he lacks the former's chilly faith that this is just what is supposed to happen to Divine Fools. Treated with such chill, Crouchback emerged with a comical radiance; lacking it, Father Leo gets a sentimental softening.

On the other hand, Wolff's story about the duel between an aging boy-wonder of the electronics business, and a young and rigid technocrat, has a wildness that mounts steadily out of a casual encounter. The duel is a mad series of wagers. The older man keeps betting his automobiles and losing; the younger man wins while never managing to understand the agony of someone who once won all his bets, and never will again.

The notion of the crazed wager is not new; Roald Dahl did something of the kind in his tale of a rich man who bet his fortune against other people's fingers. But Wolff makes something more than a tale out of it. It is a parable, in a way, but sufficiently unpredictable to avoid a parable's sleekness.

Another story that emerges from disquiet into a kind of grand ominousness has a jobless young man driving his pregnant wife and child across the Western desert. When the car breaks down, the disaster manages to turn his apparent strength into childish weakness, and her apparent dependence into a magnificent adaptability. The story is less perfect, in some ways, than some of the others; yet it holds a promise of Wolff's continued growth, from surprise parties to real surprise.

Chronology

1945 Tobias Jonathan Ansell Wolff born 19 June to Rosemary Loftus and Arthur Saunders "Duke" Wolff in Birmingham, Alabama.

1949 Parents separate. Tobias lives with his mother in the western United States; brother, Geoffrey, remains with Duke Wolff on the East Coast.

1961 Begins prep school at The Hill School in Pottstown, Pennsylvania. Leaves the school in 1963.

1964–1968 Trains as a Green Beret. Conversant in Vietnamese, Wolff serves a tour of duty in Vietnam that coincides with the Tet Offensive of January 1968. Concludes his service as a first lieutenant.

1972 Receives a B.A. from Oxford University, England, in English language and literature.

1975 Receives an M.A. from Oxford in English language and literature. *Ugly Rumours*, a novel, published in England by Allen and Unwin. Marries Catherine Dolores Spohn. Works as a reporter for the *Washington Post*. Becomes a Wallace Stegner Fellow in creative writing at Stanford University; meets and becomes lifelong friend of Raymond Carver.

1976 Publishes his first short story, "Smokers," in the *Atlantic Monthly*.

1978 Receives an M.A. from Stanford University in English. Hired at Goddard College in Plainfield, Vermont, to teach fiction writing. Awarded a National Endowment for the Arts Fellowship in creative writing.

1979 Teaches at Arizona State in Tempe. Son, Michael, born. Awarded Mary Roberts Rhinehart Award and fellowship in creative writing by the Arizona Council on the Arts and Humanities.

1980   Begins teaching at Syracuse University in New York. Son, Patrick, born.

1981   *In the Garden of the North American Martyrs* published by Ecco Press. Title story included in *Prize Stories, 1981: The O. Henry Awards.*

1982   *In the Garden of the North American Martyrs* receives the St. Lawrence Award for fiction and is published in England in 1982 as *Hunters in the Snow* by Jonathan Cape. Awarded a Guggenheim Fellowship for fiction. Serves as editor for *Matters of Life and Death: New American Short Stories,* published by Wampeter Press. "Next Door" included in *Prize Stories, 1982: The O. Henry Awards.*

1984   *The Barracks Thief,* a novella, published by Ecco Press, as is *The Barracks Thief and Other Stories,* which includes six stories from *In the Garden of the North American Martyrs.*

1985   *Back in the World* published by Houghton Mifflin. Awarded the PEN/Faulkner Award for fiction for *The Barracks Thief.* "Sister" selected for *Prize Stories, 1985: The O. Henry Awards.* Receives a National Endowment for the Arts Fellowship in creative writing.

1986   *Back in the World* published in England by Jonathan Cape. "The Rich Brother" selected for *Best American Short Stories.* "Leviathan" included in *Pushcart Prize, XI.*

1987   "The Other Miller" included in *Best American Short Stories. The Barracks Thief* (novella) published by Jonathan Cape.

1988   *The Stories of Tobias Wolff* published in England by Picador, Pan, in association with Jonathan Cape (includes *In the Garden of the North American Martyrs, The Barracks Thief,* and *Back in the World*). "Smorgasbord" chosen for *Best American Short Stories.* Editor of *A Doctor's Visit: Short Stories by Anton Chekhov,* published by Bantam.

1989   *This Boy's Life: A Memoir,* published by Atlantic Monthly Press. Receives the Rea Award for the short story "Our Story Begins." Daughter, Mary Elizabeth, born.

1990   Awarded a Whiting Foundation Writer's Award and the *Los Angeles Times* Book Award for *This Boy's Life.*

1991   Receives the Ambassador Book Award of the English Speaking Union.

1992   "Firelight" selected for *Best American Short Stories*. Editor of *American Fiction*.

1993   "The Life of the Body" included in *Pushcart Prize, XVII*. Editor of *Ploughshares: Stories* and of *The Picador Book of Contemporary American Stories*.

1994   *In Pharaoh's Army: Memories of the Lost War*, published by Alfred A. Knopf. Finalist for the National Book Award. Receives the *Esquire*-Volvo-Waterstone's Award for nonfiction, England; the Lila Wallace–*Readers' Digest* Foundation Award; and the Lyndhurst Foundation Award. Editor of *Best American Short Stories* and *The Vintage Book of Contemporary American Short Stories*.

1995   Prepares third short story collection, tentatively titled *No Place Like Home*, for publication in fall 1996.

Selected Bibliography

Primary Works

Collections

Back in the World. Boston: Houghton Mifflin, 1985. Published in London by Jonathan Cape. Includes "Coming Attractions," "The Missing Person," "Say Yes," "The Poor Are Always with Us," "Sister," "Soldier's Joy," "Desert Breakdown, 1968," "Our Story Begins," "Leviathan," "The Rich Brother."

The Barracks Thief and Other Stories. New York: Ecco Press, 1984. Includes *The Barracks Thief*, "Hunters in the Snow," "Smokers," "Wingfield," "In the Garden of the North American Martyrs," "Poaching," "The Liar."

In the Garden of the North American Martyrs. New York: Ecco Press, 1981. (Also published as *Hunters in the Snow.* London: Jonathan Cape, 1982.) Includes "Next Door," "Hunters in the Snow," "An Episode in the Life of Professor Brooke," "Smokers," "Face to Face," "Passengers," "Maiden Voyage," "Worldly Goods," "Wingfield," "In the Garden of the North American Martyrs," "Poaching," "The Liar."

The Stories of Tobias Wolff. London: Picador, 1988. Includes *In the Garden of the North American Martyrs*, *Back in the World*, *The Barracks Thief*.

Uncollected Stories

"Firelight." *Story* 39, no. 4 (Autumn 1991): 27–36.

"Lady's Dream." *Harper's*, December 1992, 75–78.

"The Life of the Body." *Triquarterly* 83 (1991–92): 51–64.

"Memorial." *Granta* 44 (Summer 1993): 173–87.

"Migraine." *Antaeus* 64–65 (1990): 338–45.

"Mortals." *The Sound of Writing*, National Public Radio, Fall 1991.

"No Tracks in the Snow." *New York Times Magazine*, 20 December 1992, 19ff.

"The Other Miller." *Atlantic*, June 1986, 56–61; *Alaska Quarterly Review* 9, nos. 1 and 2 (Fall and Winter 1990): 30–42.

"Sanity." *Atlantic*, December 1990, 110–14.

"Smorgasbord." *Esquire*, Summer 1987, 236ff.

Stories in Anthologies

"Champagne." [Excerpt from *This Boy's Life*.] In *A Literary Christmas*, edited by Lilly Golden, 21–28. New York: Atlantic Monthly Press, 1992.

"Desert Breakdown, 1968." In *The Editors' Choice: New American Stories, Volume 1*, edited by George E. Murphy, Jr., 286–314. Boston: Bantam/Wampeter, 1985.

"Firelight." In *The Best American Short Stories*, edited by Robert Stone and Katrina Kenison, 348–59. Boston: Houghton Mifflin, 1992.

"Hunters in the Snow." In *A Reader of New Fiction*, edited by Robert Fromberg and R. Best, 163–82. Peoria, Ill.: I-74 Press, 1981. In *The Art of the Tale: An International Anthology of Short Stories, 1945–1984*, edited by Daniel Halpern, 774–85. New York: Viking, 1986.

"In the Garden of the North American Martyrs." In *Prize Stories, 1981: The O. Henry Awards*, edited by William Abrahams, 105–16. Garden City, N.Y.: Doubleday, 1981. In *Winter's Tales 26*, edited by A. D. Maclean, 165–76. New York: St. Martin's, 1980.

"Leviathan." In *The Pushcart Prize, XI*, edited by Bill Henderson, 201–11. Wainscott, N.Y.: Pushcart Press, 1986.

"The Liar." In *Buying Time: An Anthology Celebrating 20 Years of the Literature Program of the National Endowment for the Arts*, edited by Scott Walker, 291–309. St. Paul, Minn.: Graywolf, 1985. In *American Short Story Masterpieces*, edited by Raymond Carver and T. Jenks, 421–35. New York: Delacorte, 1987. In *The Substance of Things Hoped For: Short Fiction by Modern Catholic Authors*, edited by John B. Breslin, S.J., 41–57. Garden City, N.Y.: Doubleday, 1987. In *American Stories: Fiction from Atlantic Monthly*, edited by C. Michael Curtis, 108–23. San Francisco: Chronicle Books, 1990. "The Life of the Body." In *The Pushcart Prize, XVIII*, edited by Bill Henderson, 416–30. Wainscott, N.Y.: Pushcart Press, 1993.

"Mortals." In *Listening to Ourselves: More Stories from "The Sound of Writing,"* edited by Alan Cheuse and Caroline Marshall, 267–76. New York: Doubleday, 1994.

"Next Door." In *Prize Stories, 1982: The O. Henry Awards*, edited by William Abrahams, 254–59. Garden City, N.Y.: Doubleday, 1982. In *The Random Review*, edited by Gary Fisketjon and Jonathan Galassi, 277–82. New York: Random House, 1982.

"The Other Miller." In *The Best American Short Stories, 1987*, edited by Ann Beattie and Shannon Ravenel, 233–46. Boston: Houghton Mifflin, 1987. In *Contemporary West Coast Stories*, edited by C. Michael Curtis, 29–41. Old Saybrook, Conn.: Globe Pequot Press, 1993.

"Our Story Begins." In *The American Short Story: Short Stories from the Rea Award*, edited by Michael M. Rea, 143–56. Hopewell, N.J.: Ecco Press, 1993.

Selected Bibliography

"Passengers." In *The Literary Dog: Great Contemporary Dog Stories*, edited by Jeanne Schinto, 132–44. New York: Atlantic Monthly Press, 1990.

"The Rich Brother." In *The Best American Short Stories*, edited by Raymond Carver and Shannon Ravenel, 289–306. Boston: Houghton Mifflin, 1986. In *American Families: 28 Short Stories*, edited by Barbara H. Solomon, 314–32. New York: New American Library, 1989. In *American Voices: Best Short Fiction by Contemporary Authors*, edited by Sally Arteseros, 64–82. New York: Hyperion, 1992.

"Sanity." In *Graywolf Annual Eight: The New Family*, edited by Scott Walker, 323–33. St. Paul, Minn.: Graywolf, 1991.

"Say Yes." In *Sudden Fiction: American Short-Short Stories*, edited by Robert Shapard and James Thomas, 74–78. Salt Lake City: Peregrine Smith, 1986. In *Wives and Husbands: 20 Short Stories about Marriage*, edited by Michael Nagler and William Swanson, 275–81. New York: New American Library, 1989.

"Sister." In *Prize Stories, 1985: The O. Henry Awards*, edited by William Abrahams, 199–205. Garden City, N.Y.: Doubleday, 1985.

"Smorgasbord." In *The Best American Short Stories*, edited by Mark Helprin and Shannon Ravenel, 250–64. Boston: Houghton Mifflin, 1988. In *New American Short Stories 2: The Writers Select Their Own Favorites*, edited by Gloria Norris, 73–89. New York: New American Library, 1989.

"Soldier's Joy." In *Soldiers and Civilians: Americans at War and at Home*, edited by Tom Jenks, 26–43. New York: Bantam, 1986. In *The Esquire Fiction Reader, Volume II*, edited by Rust Hills and Tom Jenks, 138–54. Green Harbor, Mass.: Wampeter Press, 1986.

Novel

Ugly Rumours. London: Allen and Unwin, 1975.

Novella

The Barracks Thief. New York: Ecco Press, 1984.

Memoirs

In Pharaoh's Army: Memories of the Lost War. New York: Alfred A. Knopf, 1994.
This Boy's Life: A Memoir. New York: Atlantic Monthly Press, 1989.

Articles and Introductions

Best American Short Stories, 1994. Edited and with an introduction by Tobias Wolff. Boston: Houghton Mifflin, 1994, xiii–xviii.

Broken Vessels by André Dubus. Introduction by Tobias Wolff. Boston: David R. Godine, 1991, xi–xix.

A Doctor's Visit: Short Stories by Anton Chekhov. Edited and with an introduction by Tobias Wolff. New York: Bantam, 1988, vii–xvi.

"Long Found Friends." *Life*, September 1990, 95.

Matters of Life and Death: New American Stories. Edited and with an introduction by Tobias Wolff. Green Harbor, Mass.: Wampeter Press, 1983, ix–xi.

The Picador Book of Contemporary American Stories. Edited and with an introduction by Tobias Wolff. London: Picador, 1993, vii–xii.

"Ray Carver Had His Cake and Ate It Too." *Esquire*, September 1989, 240ff.

The Vintage Book of Contemporary American Short Stories. Edited and with an introduction by Tobias Wolff. New York: Random House, 1994, xi–xvi.

Secondary Works

Interviews

Burke, Michael D. *FM Five* (San Francisco) 3 (Winter 1986): 10–11.

Lyons, Bonnie, and Bill Oliver. "An Interview with Tobias Wolff." *Contemporary Literature* 31, no. 1 (Spring 1990): 1–16.

Ross, Jean W. "CA [*Contemporary Authors*] Interview." In *Contemporary Authors, Volume 117*, 496–98. Detroit: Gale Research, 1986.

"The Stories Our Memory Tells Us: An Interview with Tobias Wolff." *Alaska Quarterly Review* 9, nos. 1 and 2 (Fall and Winter, 1990): 7–13.

Woodruff, Jay. "Interview with Tobias Wolff." In *A Piece of Work: Five Writers Discuss Their Revisions*, 22–40. Iowa City: Iowa University Press, 1993.

Articles in Periodicals

Allen, Bruce. "American Short Fiction Today." *New England Review* 4 (Spring 1982): 478–88.

———. "Nam Book Year's Best." Review of *The Barracks Thief. Christian Science Monitor*, 7 June 1985, B7.

America. Review of *In the Garden of the North American Martyrs. America*, 8 September 1984, 108–9.

American Book Review. Review of *In the Garden of the North American Martyrs. American Book Review* 5 (January 1983): 22.

Bailey, Peter J. " 'Why Not Tell The Truth?': The Autobiographies of Three Fiction Writers." *Critique: Studies in Contemporary Fiction* 32, no. 4 (Summer 1991): 211–23.

Banks, Russell. "Aging Clay and the Prodigal Son." Review of *Back in the World. New York Times Book Review*, 20 October 1985, 9.

Selected Bibliography

————. "When We Talk about Ray Carver." *Atlantic*, August 1991, 99–103.
Bannon, Barbara A. Review of *In the Garden of the North American Martyrs*. *Publishers Weekly*, 28 August 1981, 390.
Book List. Review of *Back in the World*. *Book List*, 1 October 1985, 193.
Books and Bookmen. Review of *Back in the World*. *Books and Bookmen*, February 1986, 22.
Boruch, Marianne. "Folktales." Review of *The Barracks Thief and Other Stories*. *New England Review and Bread Loaf Quarterly* 9 (Autumn 1986): 98–110.
Brien, Alan. "Pop-up Images." Review of *Hunters in the Snow*. *New Statesman* (London), 12 August 1983, 27.
Broyard, Anatole. "Books of the Times." Review of *In the Garden of the North American Martyrs*. *New York Times*, 25 November 1981, C21:1.
Caplan, Brina. "Particular Truths." Review of *In the Garden of the North American Martyrs*. *Nation*, 6 February 1982, 152–55.
Choice. Review of *In the Garden of the North American Martyrs*. *Choice*, January 1982, 630.
Clute, John. "Reports from the Regions." Review of *The Stories of Tobias Wolff*. *Times Literary Supplement* (London), 13 May 1988, 532–33.
Cornwall, John. "Wolff at the Door." *Sunday Times Magazine* (London), 12 September 1993, 28–33.
Cox, Shelley. Review of *Back in the World*. *Library Journal*, 15 October 1985, 104.
DePietro, Thomas. "Minimalists, Moralists, and Manhattanites." *Hudson Review* 39 (Autumn 1986): 487–94.
Desmond, John F. "Catholicism in Contemporary American Fiction." *America*, 14 May 1994, 7–11.
Dolan, James C. Review of *In the Garden of the North American Martyrs*. *Best Sellers*, November 1981, 293.
Dyer, Geoff. "Tanglewood Tales." Review of *Back in the World*. *New Statesman* (London), 24 January 1986, 28.
Eder, Richard. Review of *Back in the World*. *Los Angeles Times Book Review*, 17 November 1985, 3.
Esquire. Review of *Back in the World*. *Esquire*, October 1985, 230.
Flower, Dean. Review of *In the Garden of the North American Martyrs*. *Hudson Review* 35 (Summer 1982): 274–89.
Garrett, George. "American Short Fiction and the Literary Marketplace." *Sewanee Review* 91 (Winter 1983): 112–20.
Gilbert, Matthew. Review of *Back in the World*. *Boston Review* 10 (December 1985): 27.
Givens, Ron. Review of *The Barracks Thief and Other Stories*. *Newsweek*, 7 April 1986, 82.
Glasser, Perry. "Reading in Love." *North American Review*, December 1985, 75ff.

Graham-Dixon, Andrew. "The Desert and the Ivory Tower." Review of *Back in the World*. *Times Sunday Magazine* (London), 12 January 1986, 82C.

Greenwell, Bill. "Goose Corn." Review of *Hunters in the Snow*. *New Statesman* (London), 23 July 1982, 23.

Hill, Douglas. "Delectables from All over for Connoisseurs of Short Fiction." Review of *The Barracks Thief and Other Stories*. *Globe and Mail* (Toronto), 8 February 1986.

Kakutani, Michiko. "Books of the Times." Review of *Back in the World*. *New York Times*, 2 October 1985, 27.

Kaufmann, James. "Giving Voice to Man's Unspeakable Thoughts." Review of *Back in the World*. *USA Today*, 11 October 1985, 4D.

————. Review of *In the Garden of the North American Martyrs*. *Los Angeles Times Book Review*, 3 January 1982, 8.

Kirkus Reviews. Review of *Back in the World*. *Kirkus Reviews*, 15 August 1985, 824.

————. Review of *In the Garden of the North American Martyrs*. *Kirkus Reviews*, 15 August 1981, 1036.

Krist, Gary. Review of *In the Garden of the North American Martyrs*. *Chicago Review* 33 (Summer 1983): 78–80.

Library Journal. Review of *In the Garden of the North American Martyrs*. *Library Journal*, 1 October 1981, 1946–47.

Listener. Review of *The Stories of Tobias Wolff*. *Listener*, 14 April 1988, 32.

Montrose, David. "Waiting for the Future." Review of *Back in the World*. *Times Literary Supplement* (London), 24 January 1986, 82.

Motion, Andrew. "Dragging Out a Life Sentence." Review of *Hunters in the Snow*. *Observer* (London), 25 July 1982, 30.

New York Times Book Review. Review of *Back in the World*. *New York Times Book Review*, 5 October 1986, 58.

————. Review of *The Barracks Thief*. *New York Times Book Review* 90, 2 June 1985, 42.

————. Review of *The Barracks Thief and Other Stories*. *New York Times Book Review*, 2 March 1986, 34.

————. Review of *In the Garden of the North American Martyrs*. *New York Times Book Review*, 17 October 1982, 45.

Observer. Review of *The Barracks Thief*. *Observer* (London), 12 July 1987, 23.

Orodenker, Richard. "The Art of the Story: 1*." *North American Review* 267 (June 1982): 58–61.

Penner, Jonathan. "Tobias Wolff and the Taste for Experience." Review of *Back in the World*. *Washington Post Book World*, 3 November 1985, 5.

Pritchett, V. S. Review of *Back in the World*. *New Yorker*, 25 November 1985, 163.

Prose, Francine. "The Brothers Wolff." *New York Times Magazine*, 5 February 1989, 22ff.

Selected Bibliography

Publishers Weekly. Review of *Back in the World*. *Publishers Weekly*, 5 September 1986, 100.

Rothstein, Mervyn. "Wolff Returns to Vietnam in Fiction." *New York Times*, 28 October 1985, C14.

Saari, Jon. Review of *Back in the World*. *Antioch Review* 44 (Winter 1986): 118–19.

San Francisco Review of Books. Review of *The Barracks Thief*. *San Francisco Review of Books* 10 (Summer 1985): 16.

Schreiber, Le Anne. "Controlled Fiction and Reckless Endings." Review of *In the Garden of the North American Martyrs*. *New York Times Book Review*, 15 November 1981, 11ff.

Sheppard, R. Z. "Spirits of '76." Review of *Back in the World*. *Time*, 2 December 1985, 97–98.

Simpson, Mona. "The Morality of Everyday Life." Review of *Back in the World*. *New Republic*, 9 December 1985, 37–38.

Skow, John. "Memory, Too, Is an Actor." *Time*, 19 April 1993, 62–63.

Spice, Nicholas. "Worlds Apart." Review of *Back in the World*. *London Review of Books*, 6 March 1986, 17.

Steinberg, Sybil. Review of *Back in the World*. *Publishers Weekly*, 30 August 1985, 414.

Sutcliffe, Thomas. "Things Falling Apart." Review of *Hunters in the Snow*. *Times Literary Supplement* (London), 30 July 1982, 812.

Taylor, Linda. "Disarmingly Armed." Review of *The Barracks Thief*. *Times Literary Supplement* (London), 6 November 1987, 1227.

Village Voice Literary Supplement. Review of *In the Garden of the North American Martyrs*. *Village Voice*, October 1981, 3.

Virginia Quarterly Review. Review of *In the Garden of the North American Martyrs*. *Virginia Quarterly Review* 58 (Spring 1982): 54.

White, Curtis. Review of *In the Garden of the North American Martyrs*. *American Book Review* 5 (January 1983): 22–23.

Wolff, Geoffrey. "Advice My Brother Never Took." *New York Times Book Review*, 20 August 1989, 1ff.

Index

183

The Author

James Hannah is associate professor of English at Texas A & M University. He is the author of two short-story collections, *Desperate Measures* and *Sign Languages*, and was in 1988 the recipient of a National Endowment for the Arts Fellowship for fiction. He lives with his wife, Cecelia, and his two daughters, Elizabeth and Sarah, in College Station, Texas.

The Editor

Gordon Weaver earned his Ph.D. in English and creative writing at the University of Denver and is a professor of English at Oklahoma State University. He is the author of several novels, including *Count a Lonely Cadence*, *Give Him a Stone*, *Circling Byzantium*, and most recently *The Eight Corners of the World*. His short stories are collected in *The Entombed Man of Thule*, *Such Waltzing Was Not Easy*, *Getting Serious*, *Morality Play*, and *A World Quite Round*. Recognition of his fiction includes the St. Lawrence Award for Fiction (1973), two National Endowment for the Arts fellowships (1974 and 1989), and the O. Henry First Prize (1979). He edited *The American Short Story, 1945–1980: A Critical History* and is currently editor of the *Cimarron Review*. Married and the father of three daughters, he lives in Stillwater, Oklahoma.

DATE DUE

PRINTED IN U.S.A.